THE GREEK CRISIS IN THE MEDIA

Media reporting on the Greek crisis has been often biased and has deepened the rift between Greece and the outside world. George Tzogopoulos offers a sober and courageous analysis of both the Greek crisis and the international media reporting on Greece.
Hansjörg Brey, Southeast Europe Association, Munich, Germany

George Tzogopoulos provides an insightful commentary on what has arguably become the gravest economic crisis to afflict an European Union member state. He does so from the vantage point of being an academic who became a prolific media commentator helping non-Greek journalists to interpret what has been going on inside the country over the last few traumatic years. What Tzogopoulos offers in this books is a comprehensive guide as to how the news media at home and abroad have both portrayed and contributed to the development of this particular story. In doing so he captures the still great uncertainty as to how the political economies of both Greece and the wider EU will recover from what has been the greatest challenge to the integrationist project since its inception after the Second World War.
Dominic Wring, Loughborough University, UK

In these times of crisis, Europe is in desperate need for mutual recognition between its peoples. Instead, old stereotypes and new accusations have surfaced again in its political landscape. Nowhere is this pattern more acute than in the case of the Greek crisis and its perception by outsiders. This book provides a fascinating first account of this story while providing a critical assessment of the claims made in the media. The research is absolutely thorough and the analysis spot on. A must for anyone interested in the fate of the EU and the impact of the financial crisis on its citizen's collective imagination.
Kalypso Nicolaidis, University of Oxford, UK

George Tzogopoulos' book is first account to analyse the role of journalists in a crisis threatening the integrity of the eurozone. As an instructive interlocutor for many foreign journalists during these critical years, the author is ideally placed to analyse how the stories coming from Greece were framed for outside audiences.
Damian Mac Con Uladh, Correspondent for *The Irish Times*, Greece

To my parents, Nikos and Eirini

The Greek Crisis in the Media
Stereotyping in the International Press

GEORGE TZOGOPOULOS
*The Hellenic Foundation for European
and Foreign Policy, Athens, Greece*

ASHGATE

© George Tzogopoulos 2013

All rights reserved. No part of this publication may be reproduced, stored in a retrieval system or transmitted in any form or by any means, electronic, mechanical, photocopying, recording or otherwise without the prior permission of the publisher.

George Tzogopoulos has asserted his right under the Copyright, Designs and Patents Act, 1988, to be identified as the author of this work.

Published by
Ashgate Publishing Limited
Wey Court East
Union Road
Farnham
Surrey, GU9 7PT
England

Ashgate Publishing Company
110 Cherry Street
Suite 3-1
Burlington, VT 05401-3818
USA

www.ashgate.com

British Library Cataloguing in Publication Data
Tzogopoulos, George.
The Greek crisis in the media : stereotyping in the international press.
  1. Financial crises–Greece–History–21st century–Press coverage–Europe. 2. Financial crises–Greece–History–21st century–Press coverage–United States. 3. Journalism–Objectivity–Europe. 4. Journalism–Objectivity–United States. 5. Greece–Foreign public opinion, European. 6. Greece–Foreign public opinion, American. 7. Stereotypes (Social psychology) in mass media.
  I. Title
  070.4'493309495-dc23

The Library of Congress has cataloged the printed edition as follows:
Tzogopoulos, George.
The Greek crisis in the media : stereotyping in the international press /
By George Tzogopoulos.
   pages cm
   Includes bibliographical references and index.
   ISBN 978-1-4094-4871-6 (hardback) – ISBN 978-1-4094-4872-3 (ebook) – ISBN 978-1-4094-7401-2 (epub) 1. Financial crises–Greece–History–21st century. 2. Global Financial Crisis, 2008-2009–Press coverage–Europe. 3. Global Financial Crisis, 2008-2009–Press coverage–United States. 4. Stereotypes (Social psychology)–In mass media. 5. Greece–Economic conditions–21st century–Press coverage. 6. Greece–Foreign public opinion, American. 7. Greece–Foreign public opinion, European. I. Title.
   HB3807.5.T96 2013
   070.4'493309495076–dc23

2012043593

ISBN 9781409448716 (hbk)
ISBN 9781409448723 (ebk – PDF)
ISBN 9781409474012 (ePUB – PDF)

Printed and bound in Great Britain
by MPG PRINTGROUP

Contents

List of Figures		*vii*
List of Tables		*ix*
List of Abbreviations		*xi*
Acknowledgements		*xiii*
1	At the Epicentre of Attention	1
2	Ignoring Future Generations	15
3	Between Scylla and Charybdis	37
4	A New Trend in Journalism	63
5	Poleconomics in Unreliability	75
6	How is It to Live in Greece?	107
7	Greece as a Special Case: But Ideal for Journalists!	131
8	Post Scriptum	157
Appendix		*167*
Sources Accessed		*169*
Index		*203*

List of Figures

2.1	Historical evolution of the Greek debt (data based on Eurostat and the EC)	17
2.2	General government deficit as GDP percentage from 2004 until 2008 for the PIIGS (Eurostat data)	20
2.3	General government deficit as GDP percentage for 2009, 2010 and 2011 for the PIIGS (Eurostat data)	26
2.4	Gross replacement rates for PIIGS (OECD data for 2008)	30
2.5	Total tax to GDP ratio including social security contributions in PIIGS for 2009 (EC data)	31
2.6	Size of shadow economy in the PIIGS as GDP percentage (OECD data, 2008–2012)	32
2.7	Expenditure on health and pharmaceuticals as GDP percentage (OECD data for 2007)	32
2.8	Debt of PIIGS in 2009, 2010 and 2011 as GDP percentage (Eurostat data)	34
2.9	Balance of the current account as GDP percentage for the PIIGS in 2009, 2010 and 2011 (Eurostat data)	34
3.1	10-year spreads of Greek Government Bonds from October 2009 until August 2010 (Bloomberg Data)	42
3.2	10-year spreads of Greek Government Bonds from November 2010 until October 2011	45
3.3	IFOP poll results on the first Greek bailout. The question asked is: should France/the UK/Germany/Spain/Italy provide Greece with financial aid in the interests of European solidarity?	59
3.4	IFOP poll results after Greek national elections of June 2012. The question asked is: Wish to exclude Greece from the eurozone in the event of default of payment?	61
4.1	Volume of articles from 2005 until 2009 and from 2010 until 2011	65
4.2	Volume of articles on Greece in 2010 and 2011	66
4.3	Articles published by political opinion-forming newspapers per country	66
4.4	Volume of articles on Greece, Ireland and Portugal published by each title for both 2010 until 2011 (in total)	70

4.5	Volume of articles on Greece, Ireland and Portugal published by all titles for 2010 and 2011 together (British newspapers excluded)	71
4.6	Volume of articles on Greece, Italy and Spain published by the economic newspapers for 2010 and 2011 together	72

List of Tables

2.1	Greek deficit and debt as GDP percentage before and after revision for 2000, 2001, 2002 and 2003	19
2.2	Public announcements on the Greek budget deficit from September until October 2009	25
2.3	Ranking of the PIIGS according to the Global Competitiveness Report (2008–2012)	27
2.4	Corruption Perception Index of the PIIGS according to the Transparency International (2008–2012). In this case 0 means that a country is perceived as highly corrupt and 10 means that a country is perceived as very clean	28
4.1	British newspapers	64
4.2	French newspapers	64
4.3	German newspapers	64
4.4	Italian newspapers	64
4.5	US newspapers	65
7.1	Inconsistency between words and deeds in Greek politics (2010–12)	135
7.2	Recent and characteristic examples of nepotism in Greek politics for New Democracy and PASOK	139

List of Abbreviations

ADEDY	Civil Servants' Confederation
AEI	American Enterprise Institute and IIF – Institute of International Finance
CDS	Credit Default Swaps
DTCC	Depository Trust & Clearing Corporation
EC	European Commission
ECB	European Central Bank
ECFR	European Council on Foreign Relations
EEC	European Economic Community
EFSF	European Financial Stability Facility
ESM	European Stability Mechanism
EP	European Parliament
EU	European Union
GENOP DEI	General Federation of Working staff in the Public Electricity Company
GSEE	General Confederation of Greek Workers
IMF	International Monetary Fund
ISDA	International Securities and Derivatives Association
KKE	Communist Party Greece
LAOS	Popular Orthodox Rally
MTFSP	Medium Term Fiscal Strategy Plan
ND	New Democracy
OMT	Outright Monetary Transactions
OSCE	Organisation for Security and Co-operation in Europe
PAME	Pan-workers Struggle Front
PASOK	Pan-Hellenic Socialist Movement

PIIGS	Portugal, Ireland, Italy, Greece and Spain
PSI	Private Sector Involvement
SYRIZA	Radical Coalition of the Left

Acknowledgements

I was privileged to write this book, experiencing the Greek drama as both a journalist and a commentator in the media. When the crisis broke out in October 2009, I was a columnist for the historical Greek daily *Apogevmatini* (evening newspaper), writing every day on its last page. I remember I was shocked when I realised how important the problem was and what kind of austerity measures would be required. I also recall I was afraid to tell the truth to my readers as I didn't want to terrify them. When I dared to argue for the first time that the public sector had to be reduced and salaries and pensions to be diminished, I received various phone calls and emails from people complaining and expressing their anger. This period, however, didn't last long. My newspaper – one of the first victims of the Greek crisis – closed down due to economic problems and its personnel remained unemployed. I had to look for another job.

One month after the Greek Government signed the first Memorandum of Understanding with its creditors in May 2010, I was lucky to find a job with Greece's most prestigious think-tank as a postdoctoral fellow. This is the Hellenic Foundation for European and Foreign Policy (ELIAMEP). A significant part of my duties has been to respond to the media requests looking for commentators on politics and international relations. I could never imagine that in a period of approximately 24 months I would need to discuss the Greek crisis for TV and radio programmes as well as for print and electronic newspapers all over the world, not only in Europe and the USA but also in Australia, Brazil, Canada, China, Iran, Japan and Mexico. A unique experience, especially in a time of crisis, and one I also share by narrating the Greek drama.

Starting to write this book I was in a serious dilemma. My country, Greece, was suffering from an unprecedented crisis. Thus, I felt initially the inner need to support it, especially seeing it being sometimes attacked if not vilified in the international arena. On the other hand, however, I feared that emotionalism would lead nowhere. I thought, by contrast, it could be an excellent opportunity to say the truth and admit it. This truth had been hidden by the majority of Greek politicians who were governing like there would be no tomorrow and who finally led the country to the brink of collapse. I was not prepared to follow their paradigm. This was my decision: to look at the Greek crisis from a realistic and cold perspective, accept fair international criticism but also comment on inaccuracies and discuss presuppositions for a policy of change.

I am aware that the current crisis is not Hellenic per se, but affects other countries of the eurozone as well. Portugal, Ireland, Italy and Spain have started to experience the pain. Nonetheless, I do believe that it is finally the right time for Greece to acknowledge its unforgiveable mistakes and reform from within. Whatever the EU suggests or decides in enforcing European economic governance and paving the way for a political union, the Greek crisis is principally a domestic problem. This is my main argument. The Hellenic Republic, and obviously its politicians, should stop blaming others, mainly Germany, but instead it needs to work hard – thus benefiting from the current European supervision – in order to modernise the economy, reconstruct the state, beat corruption, tackle tax evasion, punish illegal oligarchies and implement reforms. The main responsibility for the current drama certainly lies within the country itself and its incompetent political personnel and bankers who badly served and misrepresented national interests.

This book would have been a non-starter without the help and support of various people. I want to thank them all – whether they agree or not with my approach – starting with the journalists and scholars who were prepared to talk to me, not only formally but also informally on various occasions. A list with their full names is included. Scholars such as Professors Theodoros Couloumbis, Loukas Tsoukalis and Yannis Stournaras – currently Greek Finance Minister – as well as Dr Thanos Dokos and Dr Dimitri Sotiropoulos were additionally keen on discussing in detail various aspects of the book with me. Moreover, I am grateful to the Bodossaki Foundation which generously sponsored my research at ELIAMEP from September 2010 onwards. The enthusiasm of Mr Rob Sorsby, Ashgate Senior Commissioning Editor, has also played a catalytic role in the publication of the book. Above all – and as always – I want to thank my father, mother, Theano-Damiana and my friends who are now paying a heavy price for a crisis they are not responsible for.

Chapter 1
At the Epicentre of Attention

'Fuel smuggling is a critical problem: not only because it is estimated to cost €1billion per year but also because it takes place in a period of fiscal difficulty which sees legitimate taxpayers paying a heavy, almost exhausting price'.[1] Although this is only an excerpt from a political speech in the Hellenic Parliament, the phrase of former Prime Minister Lucas Papademos is highly symbolic because it sketches out different but interconnected dimensions of the Greek crisis. In particular, it demonstrates that political elites lack the appropriate will or are unable to eradicate the illegal activities of oligarchies such as fuel smugglers and thus improve the fiscal position of the country.[2] It, additionally, connotes that a feeling of injustice prevails in the society deriving from the perception of the majority of ordinary citizens that the burden of the problem has not been distributed in a fair way. More significantly, it outlines the unique character of the Greek crisis which is full of bizarre and distinctive elements, shocking European leaders and making foreign journalists particularly curious in analysing domestic developments in the country.

International media had not extensively dealt with Greece until the last quarter of 2009. Exceptions certainly exist. The Olympic Games organised in Athens in August 2004, the Helios plane crash in August 2005,[3] the terrorist attack on the US Embassy in January 2007,[4] the violent demonstrations of December 2008 at Syntagma Square[5] and the opening of the new Acropolis Museum in June 2009[6] attracted the attention of foreign journalists. Duration of media coverage, however,

---

1   Speech by prime minister of Greece, Lucas Papademos, in the Hellenic Parliament, 2012 [13 January] Available at: http://www.primeminister.gov.gr/2012/01/13/7352 [accessed September 2012].

2   Until autumn 2012 the price of heating oil was approximately 40 per cent lower than that of diesel due to a different tax level. Although the quality of oil was the same, this differentiation – aimed at securing lower prices for heating in the country – has led to an increase of illegal fuel trade. Unable to beat this, the new coalition government led by Mr Antonis Samaras decided after its election on 17 June 2012 to balance prices and level the tax of heating oil to balance that of diesel.

3   On 15 August 2005 a Cypriot airline carrying 115 passengers and 6 crew members plowed into a hill north of Athens. All people on board were killed.

4   On 12 January 2007 a rocket fired from street level hit the US Embassy in Athens. No casualties were reported and little damage was caused with the exception of the US eagle emblem. A terrorist group known as Revolutionary Struggle took responsibility.

5   On 6 December 2008 Greek police fatally shot a teenage boy. This incident led to various protests and demonstrations in Athens by anarchists and student groups, causing serious material damage and clashes with the police.

6   In June 2009 the new Acropolis Museum – with a direct view on the Parthenon – replaced the old one, a small building which was being constructed from 1865 until 1874.

was limited and did not exceed a few days or weeks. At the same time, general interest – with the exception of the Olympic Games – remained relatively small. As a whole, coverage of developments in Greece was mainly an affair for foreign correspondents and could be rather considered as a routine work.

This trend, however, has been reversed since the national elections of 4 October 2009. The victory of the socialist party (PASOK) signalled a change in Greek politics after five and a half years, prior to which the conservative party (New Democracy, ND) had been in power. More crucially, it marked the beginning of an unknown adventure for the country on economic, political and social levels. Being unable to access international markets at reasonable interest rates, the newly elected government was confronted with the spectre of bankruptcy. It had no alternative but to make decisions and apply tough measures, almost unthinkable for decades. These included spending cuts in salaries and pensions, tax rises, various reforms – as for example the liberalisation of the so-called closed professions – and privatisation of public land and enterprises. Within this context, the main challenge of the ruling party was to lead the chorus away from pathologies such as bureaucracy, clientelism, corruption and lack of transparency.

The problematic status of the Greek economy has caused dramatic consequences on a national level. In the country, numerous citizens have seriously suffered from the impact of the austerity policy and recession and experienced the adverse consequences of unemployment and poverty. At the same time, the problem has not been limited within the boundaries of the state itself. In particular, the Hellenic Republic – a eurozone member state – can be considered a catalyst for economic development in other countries of the common currency area as well as for European economic governance: although the country only represents approximately 2.5 per cent of the eurozone economy, a potential metastasis of its crisis explains the amount of attention paid to it by political elites, bankers and academics worldwide.

Greece has indeed been a test case of how the EU could better deal with the debt crisis.[7] The Maastricht Treaty had not provided for exceptional crisis and the eurosystem had been ill-equipped to tackle a crisis like the one that exploded at the beginning of 2010.[8] Europe's response – in co-operation with the International Monetary Fund (IMF) – started with a crucial bailout package worth €110 billion, agreed in May 2010. Greece has not been the only eurozone country at risk and therefore a European Financial Stability Mechanism (EFSF) was set up on 9 May 2010 as an instrument to support member states in difficulty. This new special vehicle was worth up to €750 billion. Ireland and Portugal were forced to ask for the activation of the bailout mechanism in November 2010 and March 2011, respectively, removing

---

Minister of Culture at the inauguration of the new museum was Mr Antonis Samaras, current prime minister of Greece.

7 L. Tsoukalis. 2011. The JCMS Annual Review Lecture: The Shattering of Illusions – And What Next, *Journal of Common Market Studies* (49) Annual Review, 26.

8 K. Featherstone. 2011. The Greek Sovereign Debt Crisis and the EMU: A Failing State in a Skewed Regime, *Journal of Common Market Studies* 49 (2), 201.

from Athens the stigma of the only eurochain being under tutelage of the EU and the IMF. In June 2012 it was the turn of Spain to seek a €100 billion bailout to rescue its banking system. In the meantime, the EU continued its efforts to better respond to the ongoing crisis by establishing the European Stability Mechanism (ESM).[9] If this permanent mechanism is ratified by member states, it will replace the contemporary EFSF in mid-2013, thus improving Europe's lending capacity.

The European umbrella of the debt problem is unquestionable. The necessity for a collective response by Brussels is not doubted either. Nonetheless, the Hellenic Republic is arguably a 'special case' within the eurosystem, being the highest priority for European policymakers even after the bailout of May 2010. Failing to meet it fiscal targets, paralysed by high recession and confronted with domestic public anger, questions on the sustainability of its debt multiplied in the first months of 2011. To prevent a chaotic Greek default, the EU decided on a second rescue package worth €109 billion on 21 July. For the first time in eurozone history, the private sector was involved, implying a loss in the net value of sovereign bonds of the country. On the basis of this agreement, Greece was given a new opportunity to fulfil its obligations, show remarkable progress in implementing reforms and restore market confidence. In the following months the decision of 21 July was replaced by two new ones on 26–27 October 2011 and 13 February 2012 respectively. The dictated haircut for private bondholders finally amounted to 53.5 per cent of the face value of bonds, while the new bailout was worth €135 billion. The problem, however, was far from being solved and discussions did not stop with this orderly debt-restructuring. In the summer of 2012 the participation of the official sector in the haircut started to receive attention.[10] At that time, the inclusion of the European Central Bank (ECB) in the haircut could not be eliminated as a possibility.

Journeying back to developments from October 2009 until the autumn of 2012, it becomes evident that they were unprecedented. Greece can possibly be regarded as the most important battleground of an economic war, which has been fought not only within the eurozone but also the global financial system. In May 2010, for instance, finance ministers from Canada, Korea, France, the United Kingdom and the USA – as past, current and future chairs of the G20 – expressed their particular interest in the Greek crisis by taking a positive position on the new economic adjustment programme the government of the country would follow. Their joint statement asserted:

> We welcome the strong economic programme Greece is putting in place with the financial assistance of the Member States of the eurozone and the IMF. This programme merits the support of the international community. In addition to the

---

9 The European Stability Mechanism. 2011. *ECB Monthly Bulletin*, July, 71–84. Available at: http://www.ecb.int/pub/pdf/other/art2_mb201107en_pp71-84en.pdf [accessed September 2012].

10 J. Strupczewski. 2012. Spain discusses state bailout; ECB seen writing off Greek debt [27 July]. Available at: http://www.reuters.com/article/2012/07/27/us-eurozone-spain-idUSBRE86Q0JS20120727 [accessed Augsut 2012].

financial assistance being provided by eurozone members, we pledge support for the IMF's exceptional financing for Greece on an expeditious basis. Determined and consistent implementation of the program by Greece, combined with this exceptional assistance from the member states of the eurozone and IMF, will help restore financial stability in Greece and promote market confidence.[11]

The USA and China are among the world economic superpowers which have urged the EU to provide an efficient solution to the Greek crisis. The US President Barack Obama, for example, said after a meeting with German Chancellor Angela Merkel in June 2011 that 'America's economic growth depends on a sensible resolution of this issue' and that it 'would be disastrous for [it] to see an uncontrolled spiral and default in Europe'.[12] For his part, the Governor of the People's Bank of China, Zhou Xiaochuan, welcomed the European agreement of 21 July 2011, repeating Beijing's long-standing view that 'a prosperous and stable Europe is of indispensable significance to stability and development in the world'.[13]

The world financial crisis is far from over and the Greek problem has been interwoven into it. The years to come will be crucial. The Hellenic Republic will have to pass through a painful phase of major changes which are not popular. This stage will possibly last a decade in the view of German Finance Minister, Wolfgang Schäuble.[14] As far as the difficulty of the process is concerned, former Prime Minister George Papandreou mentioned in September 2011 at the Federation of German Industry that 'a superhuman effort is being made to meet stringent targets' and Greek citizens are making 'enormous sacrifices to support the country'.[15] In spite of this difficulty, former French President Nicolas Sarkozy saw it as a 'moral

---

11 Joint Statement on Greece by Finance Ministers of Korea, Canada, the United States, the United Kingdom and France 2010 [3 May]. Available at: http://www.treasury.gov/press-center/press-releases/Pages/tg684.aspx, [accessed September 2011].

12 Remarks by President Obama and Chancellor Merkel in a Joint Press Conference 2011 [7 June]. Available at: http://www.whitehouse.gov/the-press-office/2011/06/07/remarks-president-obama-and-chancellor-merkel-joint-press-conference [accessed September 2011]. Three months later, on 16 September 2011 – as the Greek crisis was continuing to unfold – the US Secretary of Treasury, Timothy Geithner, attended an ECOFIN session in Wroclaw in order to closely monitor economic developments at the EU level.

13 PBC website. 2011. Governor Zhou Xiaochuan Welcomes the Outcome of the July 21 Summit of Euro Area and EU Institutions 2011 [23 July]. Available at: http://www.pbc.gov.cn/publish/english/955/2011/20110723203707630902329/20110723203707630902329_.html [accessed September 2011].

14 Interview of Dr Wolfgang Schäuble with *Wirtschaftwoche* 2011 [24 September]. Available at: http://www.wolfgang-schaeuble.de/index.php?id=37&textid=1476&page=1 [accessed September 2011].

15 Speech by Prime Minister Papandreou at BDI 2011. Looking ahead: Europe's development and solidarity [27 September]. Available at: http://www.primeminister.gov.gr/english/2011/09/27/bdi-day-of-german-industry-looking-ahead-europes-development-and-solidarity-prime-ministers-speech-in-berlin/ [accessed September 2011].

obligation' of the family of Europe to express its solidarity by helping Greece.¹⁶ Similarly, his successor, President François Hollande, expressed his conviction that the country would remain in the Euro after a meeting with its new Prime Minister, Antonis Samaras, in August 2012.¹⁷

The effectiveness of policies adopted as a remedy for the Greek problem will be assessed by future historians. However, journalists have been the first to have the opportunity to closely monitor and cover developments. Their work has been both significant and challenging. On the one hand, journalists have been obliged to report and analyse news in a time of particular uncertainty while financial markets were operating faster than politicians, but, on the other, they have been privileged in dealing with the most important economic crisis for the West by exploring the crucial Hellenic parameter and its implications for the euro and the global financial system. In so doing, journalists working for international media have had to understand modern Greek culture in order to familiarise themselves with the domestic pathogenies which could more easily explain the philosophy of politicians and the mentality of citizens in the country.

For the Hellenic Government, the financial crisis has constituted a challenge not only at economic, political and social levels, but also at the communication level. In order to respond to the increased requests of foreign journalists and make its positions internationally known, it needed to adopt a new, efficient strategy. The main objective was to achieve a constant and co-ordinated presence of the Greek political elite in various TV and radio programmes and in the pages of newspapers, either by granting interviews or by publishing articles. Former Finance Minister George Papaconstantinou, for example, gave approximately 400 interviews to international media from the beginning of October 2009 until the end of 2010.¹⁸ Further to this, Greek authorities have continuously attempted to facilitate the work of foreign journalists by offering them background information. The official website of the Ministry of Finance has been upgraded to give access to useful material translated into English. Provisional statements of the budget execution, press releases, newsletters and general government data are now regularly uploaded.¹⁹

Dealing with international media has been certainly a priority for the Greek Government since October 2009. Nevertheless, its assessment on the quality of

---

16 Declaration of French President Nicolas Sarkozy after his meeting with Greek Prime Minister George Papandreou 2011 [30 September]. Available at: http://www.elysee.fr/president/les-actualites/declarations/2011/declaration-du-president-de-la-republique-a.12130.html [accessed October 2011].

17 Déclaration du Président de la République à l'issue de l'entretien avec Monsieur Antonis Samaras, Premier Ministre de la République Hellenique 2012 [25 August]. Available at: http://www.elysee.fr/president/lesactualites/declarations/2012/declaration-du-president-de-la-republique-a.13801.html?search=SAMARAS&xtmc=samaras&xcr=1 [accessed September 2012].

18 G. Tzogopoulos interview with Ms Filio Lanara, Head of the Press Office at the Ministry of Finance under Minister George Papaconstantinou, 17 January 2011.

19 Ibid.

coverage has been rather negative. Speaking at a conference in November 2010, the then Prime Minister Papandreou made extensive references to the role of foreign journalists within the framework of the Hellenic crisis and negatively commented on their stance. In particular, he said:

> We have been playing out the worst financial crisis in our modern history, and doing so under the glare of international media. [...] First, let me thank you all, all media, for making Greek citizens experts in finance overnight. Everybody in Greece from 7 to 97 knows what spreads and credit default swaps are. These have become household terms, even in the remotest of villages. The international media has also been instrumental in highlighting many of the underlying problems that precipitated the Greek economic crisis, but I would say how these are also linked with wider problems on our globe, concerning the financial system and global governance.
>
> However, on the other hand, there has also been a degree of media speculation, if you like, which has exacerbated the fiscal problems that do exist and did exist, making them often even harder to solve. What we found out over the last few months is that there is also a mob psychology in the markets. They can get very excited and create bubbles, or very fearful to risk and stampede. And this is what we saw, but we also saw that this speculative psychology can be exacerbated by speculation in the media.²⁰

The former Greek prime minister went further than simply criticising foreign journalists for their work: he also asserted that a significant part of the problem was the speculation by international media in their coverage of the crisis. A similar point has also been made in the official report of the Hellenic Association of Press Attachés on foreign publications for the Greek economy in the years 2009 and 2010.²¹ This report maintained that European media played an important role and in several cases even influenced developments 'either by anticipating the collapse of the Greek state and its exit from the eurozone or by publishing inaccurate information'.²²

Coverage of the crisis by German media triggered intense reaction in Greece, especially in the first quarter of 2010. Former Speaker of the Hellenic Parliament

---

20 Speech by Prime Minister Papandreou at Newexchange Conference 2010 [11 November]. Available at: http://www.primeminister.gov.gr/english/2010/11/11/newsxchange-2010-conference-prime-ministers-speech/[accessed September 2011].

21 The Association of Press Attachés was founded in 1981 and has 205 members. It belongs to the Hellenic Secretariat General of Information & Communication and the Secretariat General of Mass Media. Its secretaries and communication council work in various press offices of the Hellenic Republic worldwide.

22 Report of the Association of Press Attachés 2010 [November]. Available at: http://icp-forum.gr/wp/wp-content/uploads//2010/11/EUROPEAN-MEDIA_GREECE_A.doc [accessed October 2011].

Philippos Petsalnikos, for instance, expressed his frustration by inviting the then German Ambassador in Greece at that time, Wolfgang Schultheiss, to discuss his country's press reports.²³ Moreover, Mr Petsalnikos sent a letter to *Stern* magazine, defending Greek people and arguing that they only needed solidarity and support from the German side.²⁴ At the same time, the Vice-President of the Greek Government, Theodoros Pangalos, could barely contain his anger regarding Berlin's stance: he recalled World War II and commented that several villages in Greece were trying to be recompensed following German occupation. Referring to Germany, he said in an interview he granted: 'They took away the Greek gold that was in the Bank of Greece, they took away Greek money, and they never gave it back […] they shouldn't complain too much about stealing and not being very specific about economic deals'.²⁵

Using Greek authorities' comments as a source of information, it is questionable whether foreign journalists have witnessed developments in the country in an accurate way. Is the coverage of the Hellenic crisis unfair indeed? Or, is it mainly the inefficiency of Greek policymakers and their impact on the eurozone and the world economy which have attracted the attention of international media? This book attempts to elaborate on these questions by offering an analysis of the way Greece was portrayed in the first three years of the crisis. Its main objective is to explore how journalists gradually turned their attention towards a small country like the Hellenic Republic, producing various stereotypes by concentrating on its economic and social problems and outlining aspects of the everyday life of people. It also aims to offer insights into the particular interests of elite nations and their economic motivations as they penetrated the media discourse. Furthermore, the book will attempt to discuss whether foreign journalists exaggerated in their coverage by overemphasising the problems of the country and assess, thus, their stance. Finally, it will discuss whether they followed a similar stance in relation to other problematic countries of the eurozone, namely Portugal, Ireland, Italy and Spain.

From Theory into Practice

There is lively academic discussion on the role of journalists and their relation to politics. Theoretically, the media can be considered 'watchdogs' in Western liberal

---

23 Press release on the meeting of the Speaker of the Hellenic Parliament with the German Ambassador 2010 [25 February]. Available at: http://www.petsalnikos.gr/frontend/article.php?aid=377&cid=69 [accessed September 2011].

24 *Stern* website. 2010. Wir erwarten nicht, dass die Deutsche uns retten [3 March]. Available at: http://www.stern.de/politik/ausland/griechenlands-parlamentspraesident-wir-erwarten-nicht-dass-die-deutschen-uns-retten-1547803.html [accessed September 2011].

25 Interview of Theodoros Pangalos with *BBC* journalist Malcolm Brabant 2010 [25 February]. Available at: http://www.pangalos.gr/portal/?p=647 [accessed September 2011].

democracies should the ideal norms of professional journalism be followed.[26] Nevertheless, the plethora of information and the lack of space or time certainly require a selection procedure, which makes the objectivity concept seem a utopia. As Michael Schudson puts it, this notion appears 'anomalous'.[27] Noting that the concept of objectivity is rather limited, the media have to be regarded as instruments which possibly construct the reality.

Communication scholars have developed several models of political economy in order to analyse the operation of media organisations. Peter Golding and Graham Murdoch, for example, acknowledge the structural relations between owners and journalists and concentrate on the interplay between economic organisations and cultural, political and social life.[28] In parallel to them, John McManus links news production to economic interests of enterprises owning media firms,[29] while Edward Herman and Noam Chomsky argue that the media serve dominant political elites.[30] In the final account, various factors can explain the selection procedure in reporting the news by journalists. These include state censorship, high entry costs to establish new media enterprises, political partnerships, advertising influence, rise in public relations and news routines.[31]

The theoretical framework is of increased significance as it certainly provides the basis for an understanding of the way media organisations operate and journalists work. This becomes even more important in the case of the coverage of the Greek crisis because the whole theme mainly revolves around a critical economic issue and a possible default of a eurozone country. Nevertheless, what remains problematic is providing the evidence and proof that particular media have had specific financial interests at stake which have been dependent on the course of the Greek economy. This said, claims that speculation or rogue-trading have marked their coverage of the Hellenic crisis can be reported, but cannot be confirmed.

Along with political economy models, there are two parameters which also contribute to the understanding of the Greek crisis by international media. The first is that the problem of the Hellenic economy is not imaginary, but an existing and serious one. Therefore, a possible negative tinge in the coverage cannot but be expected. The second parameter is related to the reaction of foreign journalists, who were not familiar with modern Greek culture when they approached

---

26 J. Curran. 2005. 'Mediations of Democracy', in *Mass Media and Society*, edited by J. Curran and M. Gurevitch, London: Arnold, 122–3.

27 M.Schudson. 1999. Discovering the News: A Social History of American Newspapers, in *News: A Reader*, edited by T. Howard, Oxford – New York: Oxford University Press, 295.

28 P. Golding and G.Murdock. 1991. Culture, Communications, and Political Economy, in *Mass Media and Society*, edited by J. Curran and M. Gurevitch, London and New York – Melbourne – Auckland: Arnold.

29 J. McManus. 1999. Market Driven Journalism: Let the Citizens Beware, in *News: A Reader*, edited by T. Howard, Oxford – New York: Oxford University Press, 295.

30 E. Herman and N. Chomsky. 1988. *Manufacturing Consent: The Political Economy of the Mass Media*, New York: Pantheon.

31 J. Curran. 2002. *Media and Power*, London and New York: Routledge, 148–51.

developments in the country: although Greek journalists are used in covering events such as violent demonstrations and continuous strikes on a frequent basis, this is not the case for their colleagues working in international media, who – as distant observers – are maybe surprised if not shocked.

Exploring the Coverage

An important issue for the book was the selection of appropriate sources which were used. For its purpose, access to international press was considered ideal because it facilitated the attempt for a systematic analysis of the coverage at various stages by allowing better insight into potential shifts. The specific newspapers which were chosen were divided into different groups in order to achieve a broader understanding of the Greek crisis by foreign journalists working in various media organisations in several countries. The first consisted of three leading economic newspapers: the American *Wall Street Journal*, the British *Financial Times* and the German *Handelsblatt*. The second of eight opinion-forming newspapers from Britain, France, Germany, Italy and the USA, covering both the conservative and the liberal political spectrum were *The Times* and *The Guardian*, *Le Figaro* and *Le Monde*, *Frankfurter Allgemeine Zeitung* and *Süddeutsche Zeitung Il Corriere della Sera* and *La Repubblica*, *The Washington Post* and *The New York Times*. The third group consisted of two tabloids: *The Sun* (UK) and the German *Bild*.

The archives of the abovementioned newspapers were accessed via electronic resource engines and the Lexis-Nexis database. The search was refined according to the lemma 'Greece', translated into 'Grèce', 'Griechenland' and 'Grecia'. Furthermore, material collected derived from both the print and the electronic content of newspapers. This said, no categorisation was made according to the specific position of articles within print media because no information was provided regarding electronic stories in the archives or of the printed material either. As far as the translation from French, German and Italian to English was concerned, this was based on the author's knowledge of the languages. My Greek nationality is possibly considered as the common denominator.

For the analysis of the data, both quantitative and qualitative methods were used.[32] The quantitative part demonstrated the volume of articles published containing the lemma 'Greece'. It also showed differences in the attention paid to the country by the media at various chronological points in the period from October 2009 until December 2011. Furthermore, the qualitative analysis went into more depth by exploring themes, which were also published in the first months of 2012. This was based on the logic of framing.[33] Framing is considered as the 'second-

---

32 For a discussion on the usage of quantitative and qualitative methods see for example: A. Bryman. 2004. *Social Research Methods*, Oxford: Oxford University Press.

33 R. Entman. 1993. Framing: Toward Clarification of a Fractured Paradigm, *Journal of Communication* 43(4).

level' of agenda-setting[34] and essentially involves selection and salience. To frame, in other words, is to select some aspects of a perceived reality and make them more salient in a communicating text, 'in such a way as to promote a particular problem definition, causal interpretation, moral evaluation, and/or treatment recommendation for the item described'.[35] This method was of special importance for the book as offered insights into the main issues foreign journalists concentrated on when discussing the crisis and hence constructing their image of Greece.

The qualitative content analysis – as opposed to the quantitative one – could hardly focus on a plethora of articles. As a more time-consuming research method, it needed to concentrate on smaller cases.[36] Here, an issue of sampling was raised. Noting that representativeness is not applicable in qualitative analysis, the sample of the articles containing the lemma 'Greece' was selected purposively. The main criterion was that of typicality. On these grounds, a flavour of the wider population of news and comment items on the Hellenic crisis was sought to be given. In this case, subjectivity was almost inevitable but this deficiency could not be avoided if the qualitative nature of articles was to be explored.

The results of the quantitative and qualitative content analysis were complemented by an additional research technique: interviewing. In particular, a set of in-depth interviews with journalists, bankers and policymakers familiar with the Greek crisis was conducted. In so doing, the book will attempt to elaborate on a broader analysis of the crisis itself as well as of the international media modus operandi by offering various explanations for the coverage.[37] A table with the interviewees, the date and the way of contact is included. As there was a crucial ethics issue, however, no references were made to specific journalists in the text, with the exception of the former Head of the Press Office at the Ministry of Finance under Minister George Papaconstantinou, Ms Filio Lanara, who has given me her permission. Last but not least, I write this book being regularly used as a source of information in international media.[38] Quotes from my interviews have appeared not only in some of

---

34 The 'first level' of agenda-setting refers to the capability of the media to set the order of importance of particular issues and was pioneered by Maxwell McCombs. As he puts it: 'agenda-setting is a theory about the transfer of salience from the mass media's pictures of the world to the pictures in our heads'. See: M. McCombs. 2004. *Setting the Agenda: The Mass Media and Public Opinion*, Cambridge: Polity Press, 68.

35 R. Entman. 1993, 52.

36 M. Patton. 1990. *Qualitative Evaluation and Research Methods*, Sage: Newbury Park – London – New Delhi, 169.

37 The main selection criteria for the interviewees have been their role within the Greek crisis as well as their availability. Most of the interviews have been contacted face-to-face in Athens.

38 From November 2010 onwards I have been regularly interviewed by *Associated Press*, *Reuters* and *Al Jazeera*. Also in the following media organisations, per country alphabetically: *ABC*, *Australian Financial Review*, *Sydney Morning Herald* (Australia), *Österreichischer Rundfunk* and *oe.24.at* (Austria), *Exame* (Brazil) *European Voice*, *L' Echo* and *Le Soir* (Belgium), *BBC*, *Bloomberg*, *CNBC*, *The Independent* and *The Times* (Britain), *Capital Daily*

the newspapers accessed but also in additional titles and news programmes. I have thus practically experienced how foreign journalists see the Greek crisis and what kind of questions they tend to ask. In other words, I have closely monitored their work, not only interviewing them for the purpose of the research but also being their interviewee while reporting or commenting on Greece for their media organisations. I consider this experience catalytic in writing this book.

Mapping the Book

The book starts with an overview of the Greek crisis from a historical perspective, 'At the Epicentre of Attention'. Chapter 2, 'Ignoring Future Generations', highlights the irresponsible decisions made by various Greek politicians from 1981 until 2009, and elaborates on the concept of clientelism which marked the policy of both the conservative and the socialist party. Using relevant histograms, the chapter demonstrates how the public debt exploded during this period, wounding the national dignity of the country. It additionally focuses on the role of the EU and its weakness in assessing the reliability of statistics provided by the Hellenic Government, especially after the 2004 economy census, as well as on the stance of markets which were continuously lending money at low interest rates. Perhaps, however, the most important part of the chapter is the comparison of Greece's performance in the eurozone with that of other problematic countries, specifically Portugal, Ireland, Italy and Spain, before the outbreak of the crisis. Data collected for all the states and presented in relevant bar chart graphs clearly demonstrate which state was the weakest link in the common currency area.

The Greek drama in the years 2009–2011 is analysed in Chapter 3, 'Between Scylla and Charybdis'. Here, the contrast between pre-election promises and hard realities are portrayed after the socialist party came to power in October 2009. The chapter concentrates on the pressure put on the Hellenic Government by markets

---

(Bulgaria), *CBS radio* (Canada), *Diario Financiero* (Chile), *CCTV, CNTV, China Business News, China Daily* and *Global Times* (China), *Globus* and *Nova TV* (Croatia), *Berlingske, Danish National TV, Danish Radio, National News Agency* and *Politiken* (Denmark), *France 24, Le Monde, Radio France, Radio France International, L'Express* and *Le Figaro* (France), *Dnevnik, Utriski Vesnik* and *Kanal 5* (FYROM), *Bild, Frankfurter Allgemeine Zeitung, RTL, Tagespiegel* and *ZDF* (Germany), *de Volkskrant* and *www.nu.nl* (Holland), *Népszabadság* (Hungary), *Southeastern European Times* (inter-Balkan agency), *IRINN TV* (Iran), *Irish Times* and *RTÉ* (Ireland), *ADN Kronos, Il Corriere della Sera, Il Fatto Quotidiano, Lettera43* and *Rai Radio* (Italy), *Kyodo News, Sankei Shimbun* and *TBS* News (Japan), *Lithuanian Public Radio* (Lithuania), *Milenio Semanal* (Mexico), *Gazeta Wyborcza, Polish radio, POLSAT, Rzeczpospolita* (Poland), *Dagsavisen* (Norway), *TVI* and *Sabado* (Portugal), *New Times, Russia Today* and *Voice of Russia* (Russia), *Cadena SER, El Pais, Diari ARA, La Razon, La Vanguardia* (Spain), *Sverige Radio* (Sweden), *La Liberté, Neue Zürcher Zeitung, Italian radio, Radio Suisse Romande* and *Schweizer Fernsehen* (Switzerland), *Anadolou* and *TRT* (Turkey), *Ukranian Investment Magazine* (Ukraine), *US Today* and *Washington Times* (USA).

which led the EU to provide financial assistance – in co-operation with the IMF – in May 2010, July and November 2011 and February 2012. In so doing, it deals with austerity measures taken and their impact on Greek citizens and explains the reasons for the country's inability to meet its targets and efficiently respond to the needs of the economic adjustment programme. The book acknowledges the European dimension of the debt crisis but mainly focuses on whether the problem of the Hellenic Republic has been principally its own responsibility.

The next section of the book is devoted to coverage of the Hellenic crisis itself by the international media. Chapter 4, 'A New Trend in Journalism', presents the data of the quantitative analysis. The volume of articles containing the lemma 'Greece' are shown and comparisons are drawn according to the nationality as well as the ideology of newspapers. Further to this, coverage of the Hellenic crisis by the media is divided into different phases on the basis of the increased or decreased interest shown by foreign journalists at particular junctures. A significant objective of Chapter 4 is also to place coverage of the Greek crisis into a wider context and compare the media attention paid to the Hellenic Republic to that of Portugal, Ireland, Italy and Spain.

The qualitative nature of the articles is then examined in the following two chapters. Chapter 5, 'Poleconomics in Unreliability', assesses how the international newspapers covered the financial problems of the country and which themes they extensively concentrated on in their news and comment stories. It investigates the perceived roots of the Greek crisis, emphasising the efficiency and credibility of national politicians. Particular attention is also paid to the media debate, whether and how the Hellenic Republic had to be saved by Europe in the period before the first bailout package. Parallel to this, economic policies and remedies – often ironic ones –suggested for Greece by international newspapers is explored. The analysis is mainly synthesised around the options of default versus successful management of the crisis. It additionally elaborates on the prospect of Greece's exit from the eurozone as a potential remedy for the survival of the common currency.

Continuing in this vein, Chapter 6, 'How is It to Live in Greece?' explores articles qualitatively. In this case, however, the focus is on the social and everyday dimension of the crisis. Specifically, the chapter explores how international media portrayed problems such as corruption, bureaucracy, impunity, public administration inefficiency, the lack of consensus among political elites and the reaction from trade unions. It also deals with the coverage of continuous demonstrations and strikes and concentrates on stereotypes produced in the media discourse concerning the lives of ordinary citizens. An attempt to discuss whether the coverage included positive stories such as the successful course of Hellenic shipping is also incorporated.

Evaluating coverage of the Hellenic crisis by the media is embarked upon in Chapter 7, 'Greece as a Special Case: but Ideal for Journalists!' In particular, it elaborates on the reasons why the Hellenic Republic differs from other PIIGS, attracting thus the interest of foreign journalists to a larger extent. Here, the quality and accuracy of coverage is assessed and an answer to the question as to whether international media should be criticised – as the Greek Government believes

– is given. The chapter explains their stance vis-à-vis Greece and downplays conspiracy theories behind its economic crisis, showing that there is no evidence that credit default swaps (CDS) are responsible for the rising borrowing costs. Moreover, it refers to the critical issue of sources accessed by foreign journalists in their coverage and comments on the efficiency of the communication strategy of the Hellenic Government. It concludes by assessing whether analysis of coverage of the Greek crisis by the international media can offer new thoughts and ideas for the literature of political communication.

Finally, the post-scriptum does not have the form of a typical conclusion summarising findings. By contrast, it attempts to go further. Its main objectives are to explain the continuation of media interest in Greece, to focus on the period of political instability between the twin elections of 6 May and 17 June 2012 and their aftermath, to discuss the role of journalists in the new era of economic war and to explore whether they have learned lessons from the first years of the coverage. The post-scriptum also goes beyond the proposals of foreign journalists as to how Greece can get out of the crisis, suggesting what I consider as a panacea for an end to the current drama: a democratic revolution led by gifted and sincere young Greek people, inspiring a wind of change in the Hellenic society.

Chapter 2
Ignoring Future Generations

The term default is not a new one in the modern history of the Hellenic Republic. Nor was it used for the first time after October 2009 when the country became the hub of the European debt crisis. In 1893, Prime Minister Harilaos Trikoupis was forced to declare bankruptcy after an International Financial Commission had been established to supervise the repayments of the external debts of the country.[1] Approximately 40 years later, in 1932, Eleftherios Venizelos, the then prime minister, also declared a state bankruptcy within the framework of the Great Depression and being under the burden of interest payments on foreign loans to integrate refugees from the Minor Asia Catastrophe into Greek society.[2] Kenneth Rogoff and Carmen Reinhart go even further in their account. They argue that 'until well after World War II, Greece found itself virtually in continual default'.[3]

In the period after the end of World War II the Hellenic Republic did not enjoy political stability. It suffered from a Civil War from 1945 until 1949 and from a military junta from 1967 until 1974. Nevertheless, its Western orientation and its subsequent co-operation with the USA in the struggle against the Soviet Union guaranteed its economic survival. The Truman Doctrine and Marshall Plan of 1947 mirrored Washington's will to boost its strategic partnership with its allies in South Eastern Europe and contain Moscow's expansionist aspirations. This Cold War parameter benefited Greece and – in spite of political fluidity – protected it from falling into communism. After the consolidation of democracy in 1974, the road to economic prosperity was finally open to the country and its citizens. But – as we will see – this opportunity turned into a nightmare a few decades later due to maladministration and overspending.

On the Road to Default

The turning point in Greece's political course after the junta collapse was its adhesion to the European Economic Community (EEC) in 1981. This important achievement can be principally attributed to the personal diplomacy and policy of Constantinos Karamanlis, prime minister of Greece and leader of the conservative

---

1 R. Clogg. 2002. *A Concise History of Greece*. Cambridge: Cambridge University Press, 69.
2 Ibid., 107.
3 C. Reinhart, C. and K. Rogoff. 2009. *This Time is Different: Eight Centuries of Financial Folly*. Princeton: Princeton University Press, xx.

New Democracy (ND) from 1974 until 1981. His critical contribution to the European orientation of the country is also acknowledged by his political opponents. Administrations which followed, however, had a rather poor if not catastrophic performance. Its impact is largely felt by people experiencing the current economic crisis and pain of austerity measures, unemployment and poverty.

Two parties and five figures had the responsibility of governing Greece from 1981 until 2009.[4] Along with the conservative ND, the other political party was the socialist PASOK. Andreas Papandreou (PASOK) was prime minister of Greece for a period of 11 years in total. He remained in power from 1981 until 1989 and from 1993 until 1996. Constantinos Mitsotakis (ND) became prime minister from 1990 until 1993 and Costas Simitis (PASOK) from 1996 until 2004. Costas Karamanlis, nephew of Constantinos Karamanlis, governed the Hellenic Republic from 2004 until 2009.

There is a common element in all Greek administrations from 1981 onwards which can explain the current drama: statism. In particular, a state-driven policy pattern was marking economic policy for decades.[5] The state was exercising 'disproportionate influence over the economy, through extensive regulation, protectionist measures, transfers and subsidies' Featherstone and Papadimitriou, 2008: 51.[6] The general idea that its role could be a panacea was prevailing. Subsequently, populism was continuously rising in Greek politics and economics. As a result, any government seeking to be economical in its administration would almost immediately face strong reaction from opposition parties which were investing in costly promises in order to attract voters. On that basis, consensus was largely absent from the political arena.

Along with statism, overspending interwoven into corruption marked the policy of all governments from 1981 until 2009. In particular, Greek politicians who were seeking re-election constructed over the years a system of clientelism. Offering different types of political favours – mainly appointments in the public sector – they managed to collect numerous votes from citizens who were also finding this 'silent accord' convenient. In other words, politicians were often buying people's votes by selling their ability to hire or provide similar services such as job promotions. As Loukas Tsoukalis puts it, 'Greek politics is clientele politics par excellence'.[7] For their part, citizens were considering political acquaintances as a

---

4 In 1990 a unity government under Xenophon Zolotas and Tzanis Tzanetakis was also formed for a period of a few months because after two rounds of national election no government could be created.

5 G. Pagoulatos. 2003. *Greece's New Political Economy: State, Finance and Growth from Postwar to EMU*. Basingstoke and New York. Palgrave Macmillan, 47.

6 K. Featherstone and D. Papadimitriou. 2008. *The Limits of Europeanization: Reform Capacity and Policy Conflict in Greece*. New York: Palgrave Macmillan, 51.

7 L. Tsoukalis. 2012. Greece in the Euroarea: Odd Man out, or precursor of things to come?, in *Resolving the European Debt Crisis*, edited by W. Cline and G. Wolff. Peterson Institute for International Economics, Special Report, 21, 23.

necessary pre-requisite in their career and life. Without these acquaintances, their personal efforts to follow the path of meritocracy could be often futile.

The policy of overspending interwoven into corruption was also related to important public contracts regarding construction works and other services, as for example in the health sector. Following the logic of overpricing, public funds were largely distributed. One of the most important examples is relevant to the organisation of the Athens Olympic Games in 2004. Although the initial estimation for the cost of the Games was to be less than €8 billion, the final amount allegedly exceeded €13 billion: the Olympic Complex in Athens cost €399,000,000 when it was theoretically supposed to cost €3,100,000, according to the candidate file.[8]

The explosion of public debt over the years was the logical consequence. Figure 2.1 demonstrates its evolution as a GDP percentage in comparison with that of the euroarea.

The public debt of Greece was increased from approximately 20 per cent as a GDP percentage at the beginning of 1980s to 129.4 per cent in 2009. The creation of a giant public sector in Greece with numerous useless state-owned enterprises was an additional, negative development. According to an analysis of OECD for 2007, the country had 'one of the highest disparities between the number of public servants as percentage of the workforce and their compensation as percentage of total compensation'.[9] At the same time, the Greek public sector has become particularly known for its remarkable inefficiency. Its productivity was never measured, its personnel could rarely – if ever – be punished for ill-serving public interests and the quality of its services never assessed. Small groups theoretically protecting social rights of civil servants – trade unions – were blocking reforms and opposing modernisation.

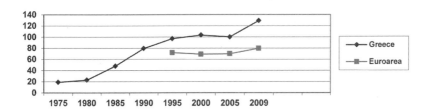

Figure 2.1   Historical evolution of the Greek debt (data based on Eurostat and the EC)

---

8   Ministry of Defence website. Cost of Olympic Games 2011 [28 June]. Available at: http://www.mod.gr/el/enimerosi/konovouleytiki-drastiriotita/erwtiseis/4528-kostos-olympakon-agwnwn.html [accessed November 2011].

9   Greece at a Glance: Policies for a Sustainable Recovery. Available at: http://www.oecd.org/dataoecd/6/39/44785912.pdf.

Overall, money borrowed by the state was spent on productive investments at a disappointing level. From 2000 until 2009, productive investments represented only 22.6 per cent of its GDP. By contrast, consumption amounted to 88.8 per cent.[10] Parallel to this, European funds were arguably distributed in an efficient way. The country along with Ireland, Portugal and Spain were identified as the main beneficiaries of the Structural and Cohesion Funds.[11] Nonetheless, maladministration was a critical factor in the Greek case. In one of the most striking examples, Professor Heraclis Polemarchakis wondered how a Greek city, Larissa, the capital of the agricultural region of Thessaly, topped the list worldwide for the per capita ownership of Porsche Cayenne. Professor Polemarchakis analysed the Greek reality in 2009 and argued:

> The proliferation of Cayennes is a curiosity, given that farming is not a flourishing sector in Greece, where agricultural output generates a mere 3.2 percent of GNP in 2009 (down from 6.65 per cent in 2000) and transfers and subsidies from the European Commission provide roughly half of the nation's agricultural income.[12]

The 'surreal situation' in Larissa offers an apt metaphor for the inability of Greece to benefit from European funds. The incapacity of its government to improve the use of loans from the European Investment Bank and private investors to co-finance already EU-funded projects was another aspect of the problem.[13]

Financial Magic and the Euro

An additional critical juncture on the road to default was Greece's adhesion to the eurozone in 2001. This was the result of Prime Minister Costas Simitis' theoretical commitment to political and economic modernisation. At that time, the participation of the country in the common currency area was perceived an excellent success which would guarantee a better economic future. Indeed, for many years the Hellenic Republic was easily borrowing from markets which were

---

10 C. Meghir, D. Vayanos and N. Vettas. 2010. *The Economic crisis in Greece: A Time for Reform and Opportunity*. [5 August]. Available at: http://greekeconomistsforreform.com/wp-content/uploads/Reform.pdf [accessed July 2011], 5.

11 L. Tsoukalis. 2005. *What Kind of Europe*. Oxford and New York: Oxford University Press, 55.

12 H. Polemarchakis. 2011. Credit and crocodile hearts. Available at: http://www2.warwick.ac.uk/fac/soc/economics/research/centres/eri/bulletin/special_edition_final_revised.pdf, Bulletin of the Economics Research Institute – The University of Warwick [accessed February 2012].

13 B. Marzinotto. 2011. A European fund for economic revival in crisis countries [February]. Available at: http://www.bruegel.org/fileadmin/bruegel_files/Publications/Policy_Contributions/2011/PC_A_European_fund_for_economic_revival_in_crisis_countries_BM.pdf [accessed February 2012].

confident that a euroarea country would never face a bankruptcy threat. Maybe the most significant failure of markets in the new century!

Three years later, however, the reliability of Greek statistics came to the forefront. In particular, the issue was first publicly discussed when a census was organised by the then newly elected government of New Democracy in 2004. Its Minister of Finance, George Alogoskoufis, decided to frustrate his political opponents by challenging information they had provided during the PASOK administration and launching a thorough fiscal audit. As a result, Eurostat expressed a reservation on the quality of the Greek figures in March of that year and in September the Greek general government deficit and debt data were significantly revised for the whole reporting period 2000–03.[14] The data were once again reconsidered in the following years.

Table 2.1 Greek deficit and debt as GDP percentage before and after revision for 2000, 2001, 2002 and 2003

	2000	2001	2002	2003
Deficit before revision	2%	1.4%	1.4%	1.7%
Deficit after September '04 revision	4.1%	3.7%	3.7%	4.6%
Final Deficit Estimation	3.7%	4,5%	4.8%	5.6%

The decision of Mr Alogoskoufis – mainly driven by political motivations – was unsuccessful and opportunistic. The revision of Greek figures for 2000, 2001, 2002 and 2003 also implied that the Hellenic Republic had lacked the appropriate credibility and seriousness to join the common currency. *Vanity Fair* magazine commented correctly:

> In 2001, Greece entered the European Monetary Union, swapped the drachma for the euro and acquired for its debt an implicit European (read German) guarantee. Greeks could now borrow long-term funds at roughly the same rate as Germans – not 18 per cent but 5 per cent. To remain in the eurozone, they weren't meant, in theory, to maintain budget deficits below 3 per cent; in practice all they had to do was cook the books to show that they were hitting the targets.[15]

---

14   European Commission. 2010. Report on Greek government deficit and debt statistics [8 January]. Available at: http://eur-lex.europa.eu/LexUriServ/LexUriServ.do?uri=SPLIT_COM:2010:0001(01):FIN:EN:PDF [accessed April 2011].

15   M. Lewis. 2010. Beware of Greeks bearing bonds [1 October]. Available at: http://www.vanityfair.com/business/features/2010/10/greeks-bearing-bonds-201010 [accessed April 2011].

The unreliability of statistics was also analysed by a Greek former member of the International Monetary Fund. In particular, in an interview for the *BBC* in February 2012, Ms Miranda Xafa explained that Greece had not been ready to join the euro in 1999 when the decision was initially made. She also referred to head of the national statistics agency and asserted: 'We used to call him the magician, because he could make everything disappear. He made inflation disappear. And then he made the deficit disappear'.[16] Ironically, the governor of the Bank of Greece at the time the country entered the euro was Mr Lucas Papademos, the technocrat economist who was appointed prime minister in November 2011 in order to save it from chaotic bankruptcy!

Whether the Hellenic Republic deserved to be part of the eurosystem at the dawn of the new millennium will remain a debatable issue. What matters, however, is the result. As a member of the eurozone, the country enjoyed a fake prosperity for almost a decade. Instead of reforming its economy within the eurosystem and committing to economic convergence, the Simitis and Karamanlis administrations governed like there would be no tomorrow in the country. They preferred the policy of over-borrowing, ignored future generations, transferred responsibilities to their successors and deceived public opinion. In one of the most cynical lies during his term, former Prime Minister Costas Karamanlis was assuring Greek citizens that the national economy 'had been already fortified against the crisis'.[17] Numbers, however, presented in Figure 2.2 show a rather different trend.

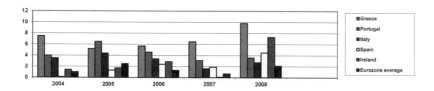

Figure 2.2 **General government deficit as GDP percentage from 2004 until 2008 for the PIIGS (Eurostat data)**

The data demonstrated above confirms that the course of the Greek deficit from 2004 until 2008 remained uncontrolled due to maladministration by the Karamanlis government. They also demonstrate that the country was in a worse position

---

16 A. Little. 2012. How magic made Greek debt disappear before it joined the euro. *BBC* website [3 February]. Available at: http://www.bbc.co.uk/news/world-europe-16834815 [accessed February 2012].

17 See for example excerpts from the speech of Costas Karamanlis at the Athens Chamber of Commerce & Industry. 2008 [8 July]. Available at: http://www.axiaplus.gr/Default.aspx?id=42431&nt=108&lang=1 [accessed April 2011].

compared to other problematic countries of eurosystem. The only exception is in the year 2005 when the deficit of Portugal exceeded that of the Hellenic Republic.

From Fake Prosperity to Hard Realities

The collapse of Lehman Brothers in September 2008 was the first earthquake shaking the world financial system. Although the crisis had initially revolved around private institutions and their exposure to subprime loans as well as to other risky investment programmes, it started to include sovereign states soon. The euroarea did not manage to escape from being infected by the American problem. Within this context, the Hellenic Republic became the next victim while its bonds acquired an almost equal value to that of toxic financial products.

The danger for an expansion of the American crisis was crystal clear in the aftermath of Lehman Brothers' bankruptcy. But were Greek politicians aware? Judging from the quality of public debate in the country the answer is negative. While the government of Mr Karamanlis was proud of its supposed reforms, the main opposition party of Mr Papandreou was asserting that the global financial crisis had only been an excuse for the poor economic performance of the country and the reduction of state revenues.[18] Nevertheless, it seems that both Mr Karamanlis and Mr Papandreou had been aware of the real problem but were holding back the truth from the public for political reasons. In other words, they were both participating in a theatrical play at the expense of Greek citizens. Former German Minister of Finance Peer Steinbrück explains in his account that Mr Papandreou had visited him towards the end of January 2009 and had no illusions as to the economic and financial conditions of his country and for the immediate challenges if he was elected. He also observed that the future prime minister was aware he would need to 'remove from fire hot chestnuts left by the conservative government of Mr Karamanlis'.[19]

The result of the 7 June 2009 European Parliament (EP) election in Greece signalled that the government party, centre-right ND, had not been on the right track. The main centre-left opposition party, PASOK, was voted for by 36.65 per cent of supporters while ND by 32.29 per cent.[20] Surveys conducted in June 2009 also suggested that Greek public opinion showed dissatisfaction with their conditions of life. According to a poll organised by Public Issue and published on 21 June in *Kathimerini* newspaper, 79 per cent of the Greek people believed the

---

18 Speech by George Papandreou in the Hellenic Parliament 2009. [17 June]. Available at: http://www.papandreou.gr/papandreou/content/Document.aspx?d=6&rd=77 39474&f=1359&rf=1307755822&m=12343&rm=12724796&l=2 [accessed April 2011].

19 P. Steinbrück. 2010. *Unter dem Strich*. Hamburg: Hoffman und Kampe, 121, 122.

20 European Parliament (EP) website 2009. Results of the 2009 European Elections, Greece. Available at: http://www.europarl.europa.eu/parliament/archive/elections2009/en/greece_en_txt.html [accessed July 2011].

country was heading in the wrong direction, with economy and unemployment their highest concerns.[21] Hit by various scandals and national disasters and being unable to deliver its pre-election promises, the ruling party was continuously disappointing its public.[22] ND also had to tackle significant internal problems. Having 151 seats in the Hellenic Parliament – as the lowest majority required – its unity had to be tested almost every day.

The months which followed the June 2009 EP election would be crucial for the political future of the country. National elections in Greece were not due before 2011. The four-year mandate of ND would normally end in September of that year. However, PASOK had said it would force them by March 2010 on the occasion of the parliamentary election of the president of the Hellenic Republic. The Greek Constitution declares that in the case where no presidential candidate is elected, the parliament is dissolved and elections are called.[23] On that basis, PASOK announced it would withhold support for the re-election of President Mr Karolos Papoulias – whom it would otherwise have favoured – in order to urge an early election and possibly accelerate its return to power. In an interview with the weekly *Real News* newspaper, on 2 August 2009, its leader George Papandreou explained the position of his party regarding Mr Papoulias and argued that Greece had been in a total deadlock, seeking a new beginning and a policy change.[24]

The opportunistic stance of the opposition party would possibly keep Greece in a prolonged pre-election period until March 2010. Within the framework of this political instability it was questionable whether the government party could stay in power for four years. At the beginning of September 2009, Prime Minister Karamanlis put an end to this dilemma by announcing a snap election. In particular, on 2 September, Karamanlis said he needed a fresh mandate in order to deal with the economic crisis. 'The consequences of the economic crisis are visible, we have two difficult, crucial

---

21 Public Issue website 2009. Varometro, Iounios 2009 (Barometer, June 2009). Available at: http://www.publicissue.gr/1185/varometro-june-2009/ [accessed August 2011].

22 Members of ND, for example, have been arguably involved in the Vatopedi Monastery scandal. Specifically, it was alleged they were approving the transfer of valuable state property to the monastery in exchange for real estate of a much lower value. Moreover, in August 2007, wildfires had been out of control in various Peloponnese cities, destroying various cities and villages and killing approximately 60 people. Similar fires also destroyed parts of Greece in August 2009.

23 The voting procedure can be based on three different rounds. To be elected, a presidential candidate has to gather 200 out of 300 votes in the first round or an equal amount of votes in the second one. If a third round is required, the presidential candidate needs to secure 180. In the case no president is elected, elections are called and the voting procedure is continued by a new parliament. In this stage the presidential candidate needs 180 votes in the first round, 151 in the second one or a plurality in a possible third round.

24 PASOK website 2009. [2 August]. Synenteyksh Giwrgou Papandreou sthn efhmerida *Real News* (Interview of George Papandreou with *Real News*. Available at: http://www.pasok.gr/portal/resource/contentObject/id/79fea74d-1cdc-48bc-9879-3b1cdc25ad82 [accessed July 2011].

years ahead of us', he said.[25] This statement of Mr Karamanlis marked the beginning of a new era in Greek politics which a few months later led to unprecedented developments not only for the modern history of the country but also of that of the EU.

The economy was the main issue in the pre-election campaign. Both the prime minister and the main opposition leader explained their strategies at the International Fair of Thessaloniki on 5 and 12 September 2009 respectively.[26] Costas Karamanlis warned the Greek people for the first time that a policy based on austerity measures would be the only remedy for the country amid the financial crisis. He – inter alia – proposed to freeze public hiring and wages as well as to impose cuts in public spending. However, his credibility was rather limited after a period of five and a half years in office during which the performance of ND had been disappointing. A GPO company poll conducted after Karamanlis' speech in Thessaloniki suggested that 57.4 per cent of the Greek people assessed his economic plan as negative despite 50.8 per cent believing he had been sincere.[27]

George Papandreou, for his part, endeavoured to persuade public opinion that – if elected – he would be able to find sufficient resources and relaunch the economy of the country. His political rhetoric connoted his will to return to power by delivering various promises, the implementation of which was doubtful. In particular, explaining his party's economic programme at the International Fair of Thessaloniki on 12 September 2009, the leader of PASOK concentrated on a possible €3 billion stimulus package on a platform of taxing the rich and helping the poor. Further to this, he promised to pay increases above the rate of inflation, a grant relief to businesses and households and hiring of unemployed persons.[28] Mr Papandreou's phrase 'there is plenty of money' was the key message of his pre-election campaign and the one which would contradict his economic policy from the end of 2009 onwards.

The result of the 4th October election was overwhelming for PASOK, which gathered 43.92 per cent of the vote: the conservative party suffered the largest defeat in its history – until the next one in May 2012 – and secured only 33.48 per cent.[29] This result led the outgoing prime minister to resign on the night of the election and

---

25   D. Kyriakidou. 2009. Greek PM calls snap election, blames economic crisis [2 September]. Available at: http://www.reuters.com/article/2009/09/02/us-greece-election-idUSTRE5815ZZ20090902 [accessed July 2011].

26   There is a tradition which links the International Fair of Thessaloniki to Greek politics. Every September, Greek party leaders give a speech mainly focusing on their economic strategy.

27   GPO survey on political developments 2009. [7 September]. Available at: http://www.eklogika.gr/uploads/files/Dimoskopiseis/MEGA-GPO.pdf [accessed August 2011].

28   PASOK's website. 2009. Omilia Giwrgou Papandreou sthn 74h Diethnh Ekthesh Thessalonikis (Speech of George Papandreou in the 74th International Exhibition of Thessaloniki). Available: http://www.pasok.gr/portal/resource/contentObject/id/88010eb4-9503-4dd7-8301-ed9bab0d1fdd [accessed August 2011].

29   Ministry of the Interior Website 2009. Ethnikes Ekloges 2009 (2009 National Elections). Available at: http://ekloges-prev.singularlogic.eu/v2009/pages/index.html [accessed August 2011].

ND to an intra-party election for its leadership which was finally won by Mr Antonis Samaras, the current premier of the country.[30] Although the developments within ND were important for Greek politics, what was of much higher significance was the economic policy the new government had to follow: its mission was particularly hard, noting that its pre-election campaign rhetoric had almost ignored the need for austerity measures. The newly elected Prime Minister George Papandreou was optimistic he would be able to apply his economic plan and 'kick off' the Greek economy. Nevertheless, no one could at that time predict what would follow.

Playing with Numbers

After a decade of fast growth but fake prosperity, the weakness of the Greek economy was made evident in October 2009. By 24th October, the new government was supposed to present to Brussels its fiscal consolidation programme. In so doing, its first priority was to provide a correct estimate of the budget deficit for 2009, announcing that earlier fiscal data had been misreported.[31] In September and October 2009, Greek politicians and bankers, however, seemed to play with numbers when discussing the Greek budget deficit of the year.[32] The tradition of falsifying figures and data was well preserved!

Table 2.2 shows that in a period of approximately five weeks, eight different numbers had been announced, ranging from 6 per cent to 12.5 per cent.[33] Figures and institutions who participated in the announcement of the estimates include former Ministers of Finance Ioannis Papathanassiou and George Papaconstantinou, Governor of the Bank of Greece Georgios Provopoulos and the Greek Statistics Agency.

---

30 The two main contesters for the leadership of ND were Mr Antonis Samaras, former Culture Minister, and Ms Dora Bakoyannis, former Foreign Minister. It was the first time in ND's history that its leader was elected by voters of the party and not its Congress. On 29 November 2009, Mr Samaras won 50.06 per cent of the vote, Ms. Bakoyannis 39.72 per cent and Mr. Psomiades 10.22 per cent (ND website. 2010. Hi Historia mas (Our History). Available at: http://www.nd.gr/our-history;jsessionid=C070071834C87A178FEA 43781463075F [accessed August 2011].

31 M. Matsaganis and Ch. Leventi. 2011. The distributional impact of the crisis, in *The Greek Crisis in Focus: Austerity, Recession and Paths to Recovery: Special Issue*, edited by V. Monastiriotis, Available at: http://www2.lse.ac.uk/europeanInstitute/research/hellenicObservatory/pdf/GreeSE/GreeSE%20Special%20Issue.pdf, [accessed July 2011], 5–6.

32 As we shall see, one of the most important aspects of the Greek crisis is related to the so-called credibility deficit of the country and this is not related to the government which is in power.

33 G. Tzogopoulos. 2009. To Elleimma: Poion na pistepsoume (The Greek deficit: Whom can we trust?), *Apogevmatini ths Kyriakhs*, 25 October.

Table 2.2　Public announcements on the Greek budget deficit from September until October 2009

Date	Public announcements
17 September 2009	Talking to *Bloomberg*, Mr Papathanassiou says that the 2009 budget deficit is an estimated 6 per cent of GDP
24 September 2009	According to a report of www.in.gr website, which is based on sources from the Bank of Greece, the deficit for 2009 is estimated to range between 7 per cent and 8 per cent of GDP
29 September 2009	Mr Papathanassiou says that if necessary measures are not taken, the deficit will be 8 per cent of the GDP by the end of 2009
30 September 2009	The Greek Statistics Agency informs Eurostat that the Greek deficit to range from 6 per cent to 6.5 per cent
6 October 2009	Mr Provopoulos estimates from Istanbul that the Greek deficit will be 10 per cent of GDP in the end of the year
8 October 2009	After a meeting with Mr Papandreou, Mr Provopoulos expresses his optimism that the deficit will not be over 10 per cent
9 October 2009	After a meeting with Mr Papaconstantinou, Mr Provopoulos says that the deficit will be 12 per cent and possibly over 12 per cent for 2009
21 October 2009	Mr Papaconstantinou argues that the deficit will be 12.5 per cent of GDP

The Governor of the Bank of Greece, Georgios Provopoulos, gave a TV interview in May 2010 in which he explained the reason for the publicly announced miscalculated data. Mr Provopoulos argued he had informed Greek political leadership 'on time' but the final estimation of the 2009 budget deficit depended on measures which would be taken by the newly elected government. In the same TV interview he also suggested that the Bank of Greece had outlined the problem from October 2008.[34] Indeed, as its 2009 Annual Report maintains, there was 'an urgent need for a credible medium-term plan that will include bold out necessary reforms, with fiscal consolidation being the top priority'.[35] In spite of this important report, however, the Governor of the Bank of Greece did not avoid publicly announcing different estimates of the Greek budget deficit in October 2009 and actively participating in the play with numbers at expense of his compatriots.

What is striking is that even the last estimate of Mr Papaconstantinou, who calculated the 2009 budget deficit 12.5 per cent of GDP, proved to be wrong in the short term. On 5 November 2009, the Greek Government assessed this percentage to be increased by 0.2 per cent. In April 2010, however, an additional

---

34　*Kathimerini* website. 2010. Provopoulos: Eixame enhmerwssei thn politikh hgesia/We had informed political leadership [4 May]. Available at: http://news.kathimerini.gr/%20%3Chttp://news.kathimerini.gr/4dcgi/_w_articles_politics_1_04/05/2010_399715 [accessed August 2011].

35　Bank of Greece Annual Report 2008 [April]. Available at: http://www.bankofgreece.gr/BogEkdoseis/Annrep2008.pdf[accessed August 2011], 17.

significant revision took place. According to the EU statistic agency figures, the deficit would stand at 13.6 per cent.[36] In its news release, Eurostat also expressed a reservation on the quality of the data reported by Greece 'due to uncertainties on the surplus of social security funds for 2009, on the classification on some public entities and on the recording of off-market swaps'. On 15 November 2010, the Greek budget deficit was once again revised and reached 15.6 per cent of GDP in 2009.[37] This was the last calculation. Finally putting the Greek deficit into a wider context, it was the largest one compared to other PIIGS, with the exception of Ireland.

The crisis in Ireland is mainly related to its banking system. This parameter explains the increase of the Irish deficit to particularly high numbers – from 14.3 per cent to 31.3 per cent of GDP – in only one year, from 2009 to 2010.

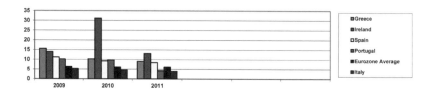

Figure 2.3   **General government deficit as GDP percentage for 2009, 2010 and 2011 for the PIIGS (Eurostat data)**

Prelude to a Crisis

International messages that the Greek economy was problematic started to become widespread in 2009. The performance of the country in various international surveys and assessments was dramatic and much worse compared to Ireland, Italy, Portugal and Spain. Various reports reflected the existing and unquestionable problem. According to the Global Competitiveness Report of the *World Economic Forum* of 2009–10, Greece was ranked in 71st position among 133, while one year later it was relegated to the 83rd position among 139 states.[38] Factors negatively influencing business were considered to be inefficient government bureaucracy, corruption, restrictive labour regulations, policy instability and tax regulations.[39]

---

36   Eurostat newsrelease. 2010. [22 April]. Available at: http://epp.eurostat.ec.europa.eu/cache/ITY_PUBLIC/2-22042010-BP/EN/2-22042010-BP-EN.PDF [accessed August 2011).

37   Eurostat information note on Greek fiscal data 2010. [15 November]. Available at: http://epp.eurostat.ec.europa.eu/portal/page/portal/government_finance_statistics/documents/Report_EDP%20GR%20-%20final.pdf, 15 November [accessed August 2011].

38   Global Competitiveness Report 2010–2011. Available at: http://www3.weforum.org/docs/WEF_GlobalCompetitivenessReport_2010-11.pdf [accessed August 2011].

39   Ibid.

Table 2.3 presents the performance of Greece in comparison to other PIIGS from 2008 until 2012, and shows that its score was remarkably lower in five consecutive reports.

Table 2.3   Ranking of the PIIGS according to the Global Competitiveness Report (2008–2012)

	2008–09	2009–10	2010–11	2011–12	2012–13
Ireland	22nd place	25th place	29th place	29th place	27th place
Spain	29th place	33rd place	42nd place	36th place	36th place
Portugal	43rd place	43rd place	46th place	45th place	49th place
Italy	49th place	48th place	48th place	43rd place	42th place
Greece	67th place	71st place	83rd place	90th place	96th place

In parallel to the lack of competitiveness, according to various official surveys, the position of Greece concerning corruption was particularly disappointing. In November 2009, *Transparency International* placed Greece in the 71st position along with Bulgaria, FYROM and Romania.[40] This was the poorest performance within the EU, while the score of Greece was reduced from 4.7 in 2008 to 3.8 in 2009. In the highlights of the survey it is outlined that Greece:

> Is a particularly concerning case. The 2009 score reflects insufficient levels of anti-corruption enforcement, lengthy delays in the judicial process and a string of corporate corruption scandals which point to systemic weaknesses. Greece's poor score shows that joining the EU does not automatically translate into a reduction in corruption. Immediate and sustained efforts are required to ensure the country lives up to acceptable levels of transparency and accountability.[41]

The data announced by the same organisation in 2010 was even worse for Greece, placing it in the 78th and last position among the EU countries.[42] Table 2.4 puts Greek performance into a wider context and highlights once again that it differs

---

40   International Transparency Corruption Perception's Index 2009 [November]. Available at: http://www.transparency.org/policy_research/surveys_indices/cpi/2009/cpi_2009_table [accessed August 2011].

41   Ibid.

42   International Transparency Corruption Perception's Index 2010. Available at: http://www.transparency.org/policy_research/surveys_indices/cpi/2010/results [accessed August 2011].

from other problematic PIIGS of the common currency area, receiving the lowest scores in the Corruption Perception Index.

Table 2.4   Corruption Perception Index of the PIIGS according to the Transparency International (2008–2012). In this case 0 means that a country is perceived as highly corrupt and 10 means that a country is perceived as very clean

	2008	2009	2010	2011	2012
Ireland	7.7	8.0	8.0	7.5	6.9
Spain	6.5	6.1	6.1	6.2	6.5
Portugal	6.1	5.8	6.0	6.1	6.3
Italy	4.8	4.3	3.9	3.9	4.2
Greece	4.7	3.8	3.5	3.4	3.6

Taking the international performance of Greece and the initial revision of the 2009 budget deficit from 6 per cent to 12.7 per cent of GDP, into account, a wind of scepticism was created in the EU and the markets: as a whole, investors became nervous that Greece would not be able to pay its creditors back – as finally happened in the next few months – and were demanding higher interest rates for buying its bonds.

The three major credit rating agencies, namely Fitch, Moody's and Standard & Poor's, decided to downgrade Greek bonds. Specifically, on 7 December, *Standard & Poor's* put the country's A- sovereign rating on negative watch and the next day *Fitch*, which had cut Greece to A- when the government revealed the higher deficit, cut Greek debt to BBB+ with a negative outlook. On 16 December, *Standard & Poor's* cut Greece's rating by one notch to BBB+ from A-, saying austerity steps announced by Prime Minister Papandreou were unlikely to produce a sustainable reduction in the public debt burden. Furthermore, on 22 December, *Moody's* cut Greek debt to A2 from A1 and became the third rating agency to downgrade Greece.[43] Moreover, in January 2010, *Moody's* explained that the Greek along with the Portuguese economies may face a 'slow death' as they would have to dedicate a high proportion of wealth to paying off debt.[44] In the first months of 2010, investors' uncertainty was also mirrored in quarterly surveys conducted by *Bloomberg*. In January of this year,

---

43   Timeline: Greece's economic crisis 2010 [11 March]. Available at: http://www.reuters.com/article/2010/03/11/us-eurozone-greece-economy-timeline-idUSTRE62A1KY20100311 [accessed August 2011].

44   M. Brown. 2010. Moody's: Greece, Portugal risk slow death [13 January]. Available at: http://online.wsj.com/article/SB10001424052748704362004575000800814712706.html [accessed July 2011].

60 per cent assessed Greek bonds as highly risky as the Argentinian ones.[45] Greece's painful game with default had already started.

Greek Chaos

The Greek state entered the crisis period having had a tendency to spend more than it produced, incapable of putting its economics in order and in a desperate need to change its growth model.[46] Problems had deteriorated as a result of political failures during past decades, and now resembled a modern Lernaean Hydra. The control of government spending was not adequate and the dramatic rise of public expenditure by about 9 per cent of GDP between 2006 and 2009 was the main cause of the widening fiscal deficit.[47] When PASOK came to power it was almost unable to calculate how many civil servants were employed and paid by the state! Therefore, a census was conducted aimed at assessing their specific number. The official report published in July 2010 maintained 768,009 people were working in the public sector.[48]

The amount of the average pension needed to be paid in Greece was a subsequent issue of concern. According to OECD, public pension entitlements in the country were among the most generous.[49] Pension expenditures at 11.9 per cent of GDP were among the highest. In comparison to other PIIGS, only Italy's percentage was higher (14.1 per cent), while those of Ireland (3.6 per cent), Spain (8 per cent) and Portugal (10.8 per cent) were lower.[50] Furthermore, Figure 2.4 represents the gross replacement rate[51] for the five problematic EU countries, demonstrating that the Hellenic Republic is a particularly high earner.

---

45   M. Dorning and C. Dodge. 2010. China losing to US among investments of choice [21 January]. Available at: http://www.bloomberg.com/apps/news?pid=newsarchive&sid=asETTCYSxjfA [accessed July 2011].

46   G. Tzogopoulos interview with Professor Gikas Hardouvelis. 2009. *Apogevmatini*, 6 December, 20. Gikas Hardouvelis is Professor in the Department of Banking & Financial Management at the University of Piraeus, Greece, and Chief Economist and Head of Economic Research of the Eurobank EFG Group. Under the Papademos government he was his special advisor on economic affairs.

47   OECD Report. 2010.

48   Census Report Results 2010 [30 July]. Available at: http://apografi.gov.gr/2010/07/379 [accessed August 2011].

49   OECD Report 2010.

50   Pensions at a Glance: Retirement-Income Systems in OECD and G20 countries 2011. Available at: http://www.dgaep.gov.pt/upload//RIareas/Pensions_at_a_glance_2011.pdf [accessed February 2012].

51   The gross replacement rate shows the level of pensions in retirement relative to earnings when working.

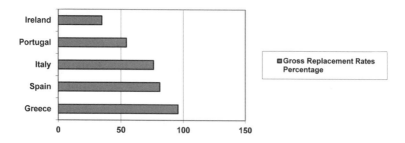

Figure 2.4   Gross replacement rates for PIIGS (OECD data for 2008)

Although the official retirement age in Greece was 65 years, early retirement was widespread and the average age of labour market exit was 62.4 for men and 60.9 for women.[52] At the same time, the OECD 2009 report discusses the early retirement problem in Greece and asserts:

> The comparatively lax conditions to qualify for a minimum pension tend to increase incentives for early retirement. Despite their low level, minimum pensions are relatively generous in relation to the contributions paid by their beneficiaries, which creates perverse incentives for certain workers to retire early without an actual reduction in benefits.[53]

Incentives provided for workers to access early retirement schemes often included bizarre cases. For instance, pensions were given by the Greek state to daughters of military officers and various civil servants if they were not married.

Furthermore, the operation of state-owned enterprises was also painful for the Greek economy, contributing to primary deficits. The National Railway and Athens Public Transportation Company constitute examples of loss-making public enterprises. According to a list of legal entities owing the Greek state, published by the Ministry of Finance in September 2011, the first owes more than €1 billion and the second more than €150 million in total.[54] As former President of the National Bank of Greece, Vassilios Rapanos explains the 'increase in public spending is related to public sector's expansion, the productivity of which is much lower compared to the one of the private sector'.[55] Indeed, maladministration was mainly to blame for years and conditions had not improved in 2009. The annual report of

---

52   Ibid., 5.

53   Ibid., 5.

54   Finance Ministry list 2011 [8 September]. Available at: http://www.gsis.gr/debtors/kerdoskopika-np.html, 8 September [accessed September 2011].

55   V. Rapanos 2009. Megethos kai evros drastiriotiton tou dhmosiou tomea/Size and Activities Breadth of the Public Sector [November]. Available at: http://www.iobe.gr/media/delttyp/keimerg1.pdf [accessed August 2011], 65.

the Public Administration watchdog for this year confirmed the lack of appropriate management and the inefficiency of state controls and inspections.[56] There is a variety of state departments which fail to provide quality services to Greek citizens. The aforementioned report mainly focuses on the ones dealing with environment, urban planning, transportation and public works. It also explains that local government organisations failed to apply court decisions or did so after long delays.[57]

Relatively limited revenues from taxes were another problem in Greece. The country's total tax to GDP ratio including social security contributions amounted to 30.3 per cent in 2009 while the EU average was 35.8 per cent. Figure 2.5 demonstrates that the Hellenic Republic was placed fourth in the list of PIIGS, following Ireland, for 2009.

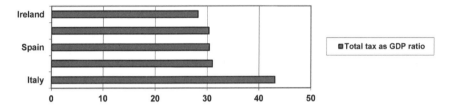

Figure 2.5 **Total tax to GDP ratio including social security contributions in PIIGS for 2009 (EC data)**

Greece was also suffering from a serious weakness in collecting taxes because of its large shadow economy. Figure 2.6 portrays its size as a GDP percentage and shows that it was larger in this country compared to Ireland, Italy, Portugal and Spain.[58]

The real amount lost due to tax evasion can hardly be calculated. According to an Alpha Bank study, the revenue loss was considered to be €12 billion per year in Greece. The study suggests €5 billion derived from VAT and €7 billion from income and property taxes lost.[59] Another analysis of scholars based in prestigious American institutions, however, gives much higher numbers.[60] Their research

---

56   Annual Report of the General Inspector of Public Administration 2009. Available at: http://www.gedd.gr/article_data/Linked_files/79/Ekthesh2009GEDDfinal.pdf [accessed August 2011], 6.

57   Ibid., 12.

58   The study of Professor Friedrich Schneider: Size and Development of the Shadow Economy of 31 European and 5 other OECD Countries from 2003 until 2011 [September 2011]. Available at: http://www.econ.jku.at/members/Schneider/files/publications/2011/ShadEcon31.pdf [accessed November 2011]. The data of 2012 are based on estimations of Professor Schneider.

59   Alpha Bank weekly report on Economic Developments 2011, 27 January.

60   N. Artavanis, A. Morse and M. Tsoutsoura. 2012. Tax evasion across industries: soft credit evidence from Greece. Chicago Booth Paper No. 12–25 [25 June]. Available at: http://greekeconomistsforreform.com/uncategorized/tax-evasion-across-industries-soft-credit-evidence-from-greece/ [September 2012].

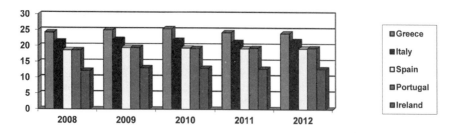

Figure 2.6   Size of shadow economy in the PIIGS as GDP percentage (OECD data, 2008–2012)

found €28 billion in evaded taxable income just for the self-employed in 2009. The highest tax evaders are doctors, engineers, private tutors, financial services agents, accountants, lawyers, artists and journalists.[61]

An additional crucial parameter in relation to the Greek public sector reported in 2009 was that of overspending in the national health system, particularly concerning medical supplies. According to OECD data, expenditure on pharmaceuticals as a GDP percentage, for instance, was higher in Greece than countries like Britain, France, Germany, Japan and the USA.[62] Figure 2.7 demonstrates that the Hellenic Republic along with Portugal have the lead in relation to Ireland, Italy and Spain regarding total expenditure on health and pharmaceuticals in particular.

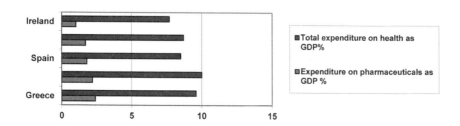

Figure 2.7   Expenditure on health and pharmaceuticals as GDP percentage (OECD data for 2007)

---

61   Ibid., 25.
62   Health Expenditure and Financing 2009. Available at: http://www.oecd-ilibrary.org/docserver/download/fulltext/8109111ec071.pdf?expires=1330370023&id=id&accname=guest&checksum=EE85D8BD4ED3EF0B61DD98E7BE164313 [accessed April 2011].

A public administration watchdog report raised an issue of possible corruption in the co-operation network between medical companies and doctors, by deliberately raising expenditure and distorting appropriate prescriptions.[63] The same report also concentrated on the tendency of various doctors to avoid using appropriate equipment in public hospitals in order to lead patients to private health centres:[64] in this way, valuable equipment in public hospitals was either abandoned or used for private health centre purposes. Overspending was a pathogeny dominating not only the Greek health system but also in other public sector areas. The National Electricity Company, for instance, was regularly financing its trade union, namely the General Federation of Working Staff (GENOP) with high amounts of money. After an investigation by Mr Leandros Rakintzis, the public administration watchdog, it was revealed that the total amount spent in 2009 was over €1.5 million.[65] This investigation also concluded that this financing activity was illegal.[66] Other examples of overspending included procurements in the military sector. Greek Former Minister of Defence Akis Tsochatzopoulos was imprisoned after being involved in a complex corruption case with the purchase of submarines and missile systems and money laundering through offshore accounts.[67] According to World Bank data, the country's military expenditure for 2009 as a GDP percentage was higher (3.3 per cent) compared to that of Portugal (2.1 per cent), Ireland (0.6 per cent), Italy (1.8 per cent) and Spain (1.2 per cent).[68] Of course, this difference can be – in theory – explained on the basis of Greece's geographical position, its problematic relations with Turkey and the unsolved Cyprus Question, but it still provides evidence as to the problem of overspending in Greece.

All in all, Greece entered the crisis suffering from a particularly high debt as its GDP percentage, compared to the euroarea average and to other PIIGS, in Figure 2.8 highlights.

---

63 Annual Report of the General Inspector of Public Administration 2009. Available at: http://www.gedd.gr/article_data/Linked_files/79/Ekthesh2009GEDDfinal.pdf [accessed August 2011], 12.

64 Ibid., 12.

65 Inspection Report 2011 [April]. Available at: http://www.gedd.gr/article_data/Linked_files/83/PorismaGENOP.pdf, [accessed August 2011].

66 Ibid., 33.

67 Other less important cases of overspending – such as the waste of energy in public buildings – were also frequent in Greece. The loss for the state was worth €450,000 in 2009. G. Elafros. 2009. Energeiaki spatali 450,000 euro to hrono (Energy loss 450,000 euros per year) [22 March]. Available at: http://news.kathimerini.gr/4Dcgi/4Dcgi/_w_articles_civ_11_22/03/2009_308353 [accessed September 2011].

68 World Bank Data on military expenditure 2012. Available at: http://data.worldbank.org/indicator/MS.MIL.XPND.GD.ZS [accessed September 2012]. Additional data for 2009 (3.2 per cent for the case of Greece instead of 3.3 per cent) are also provided by the Stockholm International Peace Research Institute (SIPRI).

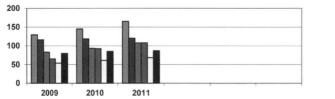

Figure 2.8   Debt of PIIGS in 2009, 2010 and 2011 as GDP percentage (Eurostat data)

On a parallel, Greece had also to deal with its imports–exports imbalance. Its current account deficit reached 11.2 per cent in 2009.[69] The most significant decline was seen in industrial products, fuel exports, raw materials and to a lower extent in agricultural products.[70] Figure 2.9 highlights that the country was suffering more compared to other PIIGS.

Figure 2.9   Balance of the current account as GDP percentage for the PIIGS in 2009, 2010 and 2011 (Eurostat data)

Finally, Greece entered the crisis period in recession. Its GDP contracted by 2 per cent in 2009 and projections for the years to come were worse. The decline of GDP was due to the drop in investment and the decrease in household consumer spending.[71] Recession had spread to various sectors such as construction, retail, wholesale trade and manufacturing.[72] As a result, labour conditions were

---

69   Bank of Greece Summary of the Annual Report 2009 [April]. Available at: http://www.bankofgreece.gr/BogEkdoseis/Summary_Annrep2009.pdf, [accessed August 2011], 16. OECD Report. 2010.

70   IOBE Quarterly Bulletin 2009. The Greek Economy. Available at: http://www.iobe.gr/media/engoik/IOBE_econ_04_09_eng.pdf, 58 (4/09) [accessed September 2011], 57.

71   Ibid.

72   National Bank of Greece Monthly Economic Outlook 2009 [Novembers/December]. Available at: http://www.nbg.gr/wps/wcm/connect/5f789b8040b0f66ebb31bfdd20353c80/Monthly_November09_3.pdf?MOD=AJPERES&CACHEID=5f789b8040b0f66ebb31bfdd20353c80 [accessed August 2011].

deteriorating. In 2009 total employment declined by 1.1 per cent, the number of employees fell by 1.6 per cent and the unemployment rate rose to 9.5 per cent.[73]

What Response?

A careful look at the Greek chaos in 2009 as well as at its roots causes dizziness. Many questions subsequently arise. The common element in all of them is the lack of understanding on how the Hellenic Republic managed to enter the eurosystem and why its democratically elected leadership was continuously ignoring future generations. Nevertheless, time to ponder on faults, mistakes and omissions of the past was an issue for political analysts. Starting from October 2009, the newly elected government had to immediately deliver. The state required a restructuring and the country a reboot. Greek politicians were in a desperate need to co-operate in order to tackle domestic pathogenies they had tolerated – if not fomented – for many years. The new mission of Greek politicians would be an almost impossible one, taking their historical performance into account. Only a thin margin for success existed. That is because the Hellenic Republic was placed under particularly high pressure by its European partners. In theory, the EU was determined to save the country and block any expansion of the crisis. The marathon would be run under European rules. Its future outcome, however, would not be a single one. Greece and the EU could either win together or lose together.

---

73   Bank of Greece Summary of the Annual Report 2009, 11.

Chapter 3
Between Scylla and Charybdis

The period which began in October 2009 and is currently in progress in Greece is one of the most painful and turbulent in decades. The problem the country triggered also risks leading the eurozone down the road to dissolution. To avoid bankruptcy, the Hellenic Government signed the Memorandum of Understanding with the European Commission (EC), the European Central Bank (ECB) and the International Monetary Fund (IMF) in May 2010 and essentially came under close international scrutiny for the next years. Greece received a loan of €110 billion and embarked on an attempt to stabilise its public finances, reform its economy and restore market confidence. Its main obligations included budget cuts, a reduction in wages and pensions and tax increases.[1]

The new conditions and in particular the impact of austerity measures, however, led to an explosion of social anger expressed by continuous strikes, occupation of public buildings and protest marches in Athens and other cities of the country. Along with domestic instability, and in spite of the initial optimism that Greece would escape default, the bailout package was soon proved inadequate. In the first months of 2011 the Greek crisis kept unfolding and spreading and uncertainty for the future started to dominate in the euro and market atmosphere. In June 2011 things took a dramatic turn. The Greek Government failed to deliver on most parts of its obligations and its reform progress was rather anemic.[2]

Without further financial support from the EU and the IMF, chaotic default would be almost unavoidable. In return, Greece had to approve a new memorandum known as the Medium Term Fiscal Strategy Plan (MTFSP) which was voted amid chaotic demonstrations and strikes in Athens. One month later, the EU organised an extraordinary summit in Brussels in order to avert a potential metastasis of the Greek crisis to other countries and opted for a second bailout package worth €109 billion. For the first time in eurozone history, the private sector was involved and Greek sovereign bonds lost part of their value. The terms of the second bailout package as they were decided in July 2011 changed in the following months. A higher haircut was decided in two different phases: in October 2011 and February 2012 in order to make the Greek debt sustainable, at least in theory. The amount of

---

1 International Monetary Fund (IMF) website 2010. Europe and IMF agree €110 billion Financing Plan with Greece [2 May]. Available at: http://www.imf.org/external/pubs/ft/survey/so/2010/CAR050210A.htm [accessed July 2011].

2 V. Monastiriotis. 2011. *The Greek Crisis in Focus: Austerity, Recession and Paths to Recovery: Special Issue*. Available at: http://www2.lse.ac.uk/europeanInstitute/research/hellenicObservatory/pdf/GreeSE/GreeSE%20Special%20Issue.pdf [accessed July 2011], 1.

the new bailout package was worth €130 billion, the future of the country uncertain and bondholders were the main losers of the game. All in all, Greece became the first Western nation to have its debt restructured in 60 years.

Unprepared for Bad Times

The euroarea is composed of 17 countries sharing a common currency. It is neither a state nor a strong political union. It brings together different economies as well as cultures aiming at achieving a high degree of co-ordination and fostering further integration. This commonplace observation explains why a problem born in its weakest link, Greece, has caused such trouble and highlights the practical difficulties and obstacles in the creation of a fiscal union. Although in a time of growth and prosperity the pathogenies of a small country had not been taken seriously into account, the outbreak of the world financial crisis led this convenient oversight to collapse. As Martin Feldstein puts it:

> When, in early 2010, the markets recognised the error of regarding all the eurozone countries as equally safe, interest rates began to rise on the sovereign debts on Greece, Italy and Spain [...] In particular, the fear that Greece might have trouble meeting its debt payments caused the interest rates on Greek debt on rise.[3]

What went wrong? Was the union unprepared to act decisively? Was it a victim of Greek authorities' unreliability? A flourishing debate exists. Jean Pisani-Ferry writes that the simplistic answer blames bad implementation of good rules.[4] From 2000 until 2007, for example, the Hellenic Republic violated the 3 per cent rule eight out of eight times.[5] As a whole, the eurozone failed – or was incapable – to prepare itself for bad times during good times. The asymmetric development of economic output and competitiveness had produced massive current account imbalances. Thus, banks in the core nations, namely Austria, Belgium, France, Germany and the Netherlands, had become stuffed with the debts of Portugal, Ireland, Italy, Greece and Spain.[6]

---

3 M. Feldstein. 2012. The Failure of the Euro: Little currency that couldn't. *Foreign Affairs*, January/February 2012, 91 (1), 105–16.

4 J. Pisani-Ferry. 2010. Eurozone governance: What went wrong and how to repair it, in *Completing the Eurozone Rescue: What More Needs to Be Done*, edited by R. Baldwin et al., London: voxEU.org Publication. Available at: http://www.voxeu.org/reports/EZ_Rescue.pdf [accessed February 2012].

5 R. Baldwin and D. Gros. 2010. Introduction: The euro crisis – What to do?, in *Completing the Eurozone Rescue: What More Needs to Be Done*, edited by Baldwin, R. et al. London: voxEU.org Publication. Available at: http://www.voxeu.org/reports/EZ_Rescue.pdf [accessed February 2012], 4.

6 Ibid., 4.

The EU budgetary surveillance system was also particularly problematic. The revision of the Greek figures in 2004, as we have seen, had not sent a clear signal to Brussels. Even in 2009, Europe avoided acting carefully and pre-emptively. *Financial Times* journalist Tony Barber, for example, writes that European authorities were already familiar with the Greek statistical deviation from real data from as early as the summer of that year. He argues that in a memorandum Mr Almunia publicised to finance ministers in July 2009 he expressed strong doubts about the reliability of the data that the Greek Government was supplying to Brussels and predicted the budget deficit was likely to soar above 10 per cent of GDP. His analysis concluded that EU governments took no action before then, perhaps because 'they deemed it inappropriate to embarrass a fellow government, especially one facing a hard election campaign'.[7]

The world financial crisis can be considered as an important pretext to the infection of the euroarea. Along with this, the exposure of European banks to the debt of the PIIGS was equally significant. According to data provided by the European Banking Authority in 2010, the EU sovereign debt exposure was estimated to be approximately €3 trillion, of which the PIIGS accounted for 25.6 per cent.[8] Richard Baldwin and Daniel Gros argue that this interconnectedness explains why European leaders could not afford to let Greece alone: they summed it up as: 'A failure in Greece [...] threatened a systemic banking crisis in the eurozone core nations, such as Germany and France'.[9]

It was not only the EU countries but also the USA who were interested in the Greek problem. From an American perspective the economic turmoil in Greece could have negative implications. US banks heavily exposed to Italian debt feared a possible contagion of the Hellenic crisis to other peripheral states. Washington's additional concern was that a slow growth in Europe might lead to a decreased demand of US exports in the eurozone and a subsequent increase of US imports, thus causing its trade deficit to widen.[10] In the final account, it was in America's national interest that Europe would not suffer from instability and would continue to co-operate with the USA in the defence of its global political and economic interests.[11]

---

7   T. Barber. 2010. Saving the euro: Tall ambition, flawed foundations [11 October]. Available at: http://www.ft.com/intl/cms/s/0/643daffa-d57a-11df-8e86-00144feabdc0.html#axzz1YJWFlqMo, [accessed August 2010].

8   R. Ayadi. 2011. A three pillar firepower to solve the European sovereign crisis: A last chance [19 October]. CEPS Commentary.

9   R. Baldwin and D. Gros. 2010. *Introduction: The Euro Crisis – What to Do?*, 13.

10 R. Nelson, P. Belkin and D. Mix,. 2011. Greece Debt Crisis: Overview, Policy Responses, and Implications. Available at: http://www.fas.org/sgp/crs/row/R41167.pdf, 18 August, Congressional Research Service [accessed September 2011], 14.

11 K.F. Kirkegaard. 2011. The Euroarea crisis: Origin, current status, and European and US responses [27 October]. Testimony before the US House Committee on Foreign Affairs Subcommittee on Europe and Eurasia. Available at: http://www.iie.com/publications/testimony/kirkegaard20111027.pdf [accessed February 2012].

Taking Measures

The economic play from October 2009 onwards had two interconnected dimensions: a Greek and a European one. Starting with the former, the newly elected Greek Government of PASOK had no other choice but to make difficult decisions which would become more unpopular within a recession environment. It thus embarked on an attempt to apply austerity measures even before asking for the activation of the bailout mechanism in April 2010. The Greek Government found itself in a position where it continuously needed to announce additional measures for reducing its fiscal deficit and calming down markets. Starting in mid-November 2009, it sent to parliament a draft budget for 2010, theoretically aiming at bringing down the deficit by 3.6 percentage points. As former Finance Minister George Papaconstantinou explained:

> The budget made choices such as reduction in primary expenditures in absolute terms; a 25 per cent decline in government consumption expenditures; a drastic cut in short-term government contracts; a civil service hiring freeze in 2010, and a gradual reduction in the civil service after that, where only one new workers will be hired in the public sector for every five who retire. At the same time, and within that deficit-reduction target, we have reallocated public resources to jump-start the economy and protect those hurt most by the recession. That means military expenditures are down, expenditures for health, education and public investment, are up.[12]

Mr Papandreou outlined policies to further cut the budget deficit of the country and regain investors' confidence on 14 December 2009. In his speech, entitled 'a national social agreement', he announced the abolishment of various allowances in the public sector and a reduction of salaries of state high-ranking officials.[13] One month later he unveiled the government's 'Stability and Growth Programme'. Examples of specific measures described in this programme for 2010 included a 10 per cent cut in wage entitlements in the public sector, a hiring freeze for 2010 followed by a 5:1 rule[14] from 2011 onwards, the termination of a large number of short-term contracts in the public sector, a 10 per cent reduction in the budget item relating to social security and pension funds as well as a significantly declining path for military expenditures up to 2013. On the revenue side, the 'Stability and Growth Programme' foresaw important tax revenue increases from the abolition

---

12 G. Papaconstantinou. 2009. The Greek Problem [30 November]. Available at: http://www.minfin.gr/portal/en/resource/contentObject/id/d4ab026b-a1cd-4024-b634-12b2b385e116 [accessed August 2011].

13 Speech by George Papandreou on a national social agreement 2009 [14 December]. Available at: http://www.primeminister.gov.gr/2009/12/14/440 [accessed August 2010].

14 This means that one person is hired for every five retirements.

of autonomous taxation, as well as of tax exemptions in the new tax bill, and increases in the excise tax for alcohol and tobacco.[15]

At the beginning of the following month the Greek Government went further. Specifically, on 2 February, Mr Papandreou elaborated on the importance of the 'Stability and Growth Programme' by addressing the Greek public.[16] In so doing, he announced a set of reforms to its pension system. The main aim was to postpone the average retirement age by two years, to 63, by 2015.[17] The day after, the European Commission adopted a series of recommendations to ensure that the budget deficit of Greece would be brought below 3 per cent of GDP by 2012.[18]

Important as it was, the attempt by Greek authorities to apply austerity measures was not sufficient. A new round would soon be announced by Premier Papandreou. On 3 March, he revealed an additional plan to reduce the budget deficit to over 2 per cent of GDP. Two days later the Hellenic Parliament passed the Economic Protection Bill, expecting to raise an extra €4.8 billion for the country. Until March 2010, for example, wages and salaries in Greece had been paid in 14 instalments but in March 2010 the 13th and the 14th salaries paid to civil servants were abolished.[19] Easter and Christmas bonuses were also reduced for civil servants.

First EU Response

In March 2010, as long as Greece was unable to access international markets, a political poker game was playing in Brussels. German Chancellor Angela Merkel was reluctant to include a potential rescue package for Greece in the agenda of European negotiations. Referring to a potential bailout mechanism, she asserted in an interview on *ARD* public television: 'This is out of question'.[20] Further to this, Ms Merkel made the inclusion of the IMF a condition for her approval of any EU aid plan for Athens. In opposition to the German Chancellor, former French President Nicolas Sarkozy was rather positive in providing assistance to prevent

---

15 Greek Ministry of Finance website 2010. Stability and Growth Programme [15 January]. Available at: http://www.minfin.gr/portal/en/resource/contentObject/id/4b0500ea-0f9f-4a58-858f-c43f5f38753e [accessed August 2011].

16 Announcement by George Papandreou 2010 [2 February]. Available at: http://www.primeminister.gov.gr/2010/02/02/816 [accessed September 2011].

17 OECD Report 2010. Greece at a Glance: Policies for a Sustainable Recovery, 6.

18 EU website 2010. Commission assesses Stability Programme of Greece; makes recommendations to correct the excessive budget deficit, improve competitiveness through structural reforms and provide reliable statistics [3 February]. Available at: http://europa.eu/rapid/pressReleasesAction.do?reference=IP/10/116 [accessed August 2011].

19 Matsaganis and Leventi, 9.

20 Bundesregierung website 2010. 'Merkel: Tarifabschluss im öffentlichen Dienst beispielhaft' [28 February]. Available at: http://www.bundesregierung.de/nn_1272/Content/DE/Artikel/2010/02/2010-02-28-merkel-ard-bericht-aus-berlin.html [accessed September 2011].

a potential bankruptcy of Greece: after his Paris meeting with Mr Papandreou on 10 March, for instance, he asserted eurozone members he would act if necessary in order to finance Greece.[21]

Market pressure on Greece and its bonds, however, was increasing and a drastic solution was required. On 25 March 2010, European leaders finally decided to take political ownership of the crisis. They agreed to provide financial support to Greece if the country would be unable to access financial markets. The IMF would participate in this safety network, as in the statement of the eurozone heads of state: 'as part of a package involving substantial IMF financing and a majority of European financing, euroarea member states are ready to contribute to co-ordinated bilateral loans'.[22] The details of the proposed financial assistance package were released in mid-April 2010. A financing package of €110 billion would be given to Greece. Eurozone countries pledged to contribute €80 billion and the IMF €30 billion. According to a Eurogroup statement of 11 April euroarea member states would be ready to contribute a three-year loan worth €30 billion in the first year of the programme.[23]

The period which followed the European agreement was rather a nervous one for markets. April and May were particularly crucial months because Athens was confronted with sizeable financial needs.[24] The initial will of Greece was to avoid asking for its bailout. Investor jitteriness, however, was spiking again and spreads on Greek bonds were rising (Figure 3.1).

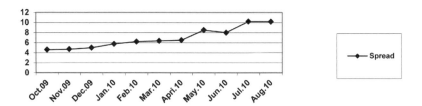

Figure 3.1   10-year spreads of Greek Government Bonds from October 2009 until August 2010 (Bloomberg Data)

---

21   French Presidency website 2010. Conférence de presse conjointe – M. Georges Papandreou, Premier Ministre de la République Héllénique [10 March]. Available at: http://www.elysee.fr/president/les-actualites/conferences-de-presse/2010/conference-de-presse-conjointe-m-georges.8035.html?search=mars&xtmc=&xcr= [accessed September 2011].

22   Statement by the Heads of State and Government of the euroarea 2010 [25 March]. Available at: http://www.consilium.europa.eu/uedocs/cms_data/docs/pressdata/en/ec/113563.pdf, Brussels [accessed August 2011].

23   Statement by eurogroup on the support to Greece by euroarea member states 2010 [11 April]. Available at: http://www.consilium.europa.eu/uedocs/cms_data/docs/pressdata/en/ec/113686.pdf [accessed August 2011].

24   Directorate-General for Economic and Financial Affairs 2010. *The Economic Adjustment Programme for Greece* [May] Occasional Papers, 8, 61.

Being under extreme pressure, the Greek Government formally requested financial assistance from the IMF and other eurozone countries on 23 April. On that day, Mr Papandreou considered as imperative the activation of the support mechanism. Being on the island of Kastelorizo he – inter alia – said:

> The moment has come for us to obtain the time that markets do not give us from the decision made by all the leaders of European countries together to support Greece. We must, this is a national and imperative need, to officially ask our partners to activate the support mechanism that we have jointly created in the EU. I have already instructed the Finance Minister to take the necessary action.[25]

Former IMF Managing Director Dominique Strauss-Kahn responded to this request by saying the Fund was prepared to move expeditiously on this request.[26] The programme's immediate objectives were an additional cut to public spending and enhanced revenue growth through tax increases. Most spending cuts would be related to the civil service, while the government also decided to raise VAT. Further to this, the Greek Government aimed to raise additional revenues by tackling the tax evasion problem. The Hellenic Parliament voted in favour of this EC-ECB-IMF programme on 6 May 2010.

After the Memorandum of Understanding was signed, the Greek economy immediately came under international scrutiny and disbursements would only depend on its progress. From May 2010 onwards, staff teams from the EC, the ECB and the IMF regularly visited Athens in order to inspect the performance of the government. In June 2010, their first statement confirmed policies were implementing as agreed.[27] Two months later, during their first review mission to Greece, they also saw the programme 'had made a strong start' and observed contraction had been in line with predictions.[28]

In the first months after May 2010, the Greek Government indeed began to implement healthcare and pension reforms. In July 2010, authorities of the country, for instance, decided to simplify the structure of the pension scheme, reduce the generosity of the system and increase the effective retirement age.[29] In the same month, the Greek Government also demonstrated its decisiveness to increase

---

25   Statement by George Papandreou 2010. [23 April]. Available at: http://www.papandreou.gr/papandreou/content/Document.aspx?d=6&rd=7739474&f=-1&rf=-1&m=12893&rm=20504593&l=1 [accessed September 2011].

26   Press Release No. 10/168, 2010 [23 April]. Available at: http://www.imf.org/external/np/sec/pr/2010/pr10168.htm [accessed September 2011].

27   Press Release No. 10/246, 2010 [17 June]. Statement by the EC, ECB and IMF on the interim review mission to Greece [17 June]. Available at: http://www.imf.org/external/np/sec/pr/2010/pr10246.htm [accessed September 2011].

28   Press Release No. 10/308, 2010 [5 August]. Statement by the EC, ECB and IMF on the first review mission to Greece [5 August]. Available at: http://www.imf.org/external/np/sec/pr/2010/pr10308.htm [accessed September 2011].

29   OECD Report for Greece 2011, 97.

competitiveness in the economy by liberating the so-called closed professions. In so doing, it decided to remove barriers to entry in the road transportation industry. Until this legislation was passed, firms wanting to enter needed to pay high licence fees up to €200,000.[30]

The beginning of Greece's fiscal consolidation attempt was rather promising. The two new visits by staff teams from the EC, the ECB and the IMF confirmed this progress, although they pushed for further action by the Greek Government. In particular, in November 2010, when they visited Athens for the second review of the government's economic plan, they assessed the programme was remaining on track but underlined that more structural reforms were needed.[31] Similarly, during their third mission to Greece in February 2011, representatives from the Troika still believed the economic programme was making progress but focused on the delays of the Greek state.[32] In 2010, the first year of the EC-ECB-IMF programme, the Greek budget deficit was reduced by almost 5 per cent of GDP. This was mainly achieved through cuts in wages and pensions, a freeze in public sector hiring, the slashing of operating costs and grants, increases in indirect taxes, the imposition of extraordinary levies on businesses and individuals and the collection of revenue from back tax settlements.[33] At the same time, a significant recovery in exports was observed as they increased by 3.8 per cent.[34] Only in the last quarter of 2010 did their increase reach 12.8 per cent.[35]

Second EU Response

The Memorandum of Understanding can be possibly considered as a 'life-jacket' which saved Greece from default. It did not succeed, nevertheless, in reversing the tendency of investors to distrust the ability of the Greek Government to meet its targets. In June 2010, a *Bloomberg* survey suggested 73 per cent believed Greece

---

30 C. Meghir, D. Vayanos and N. Vettas. 2010. The Economic crisis in Greece: A time for reform and opportunity [5 August]. Available at: http://greekeconomistsforreform.com/wp-content/uploads/Reform.pdf, [accessed July 2011], 24.

31 Press Release No. 10/454, 2010. Statement by the EC, ECB and IMF on the second review mission to Greece [23 November]. Available at: http://www.imf.org/external/np/sec/pr/2010/pr10454.htm [accessed September 2011].

32 Press Release No. 11/37, 2011. Statement by the EC, ECB and IMF on the third review mission to Greece [11 February]. Available at: http://www.imf.org/external/np/sec/pr/2011/pr1137.htm [accessed September 2011].

33 Bank of Greece Summary of the Annual Report 2010 [April]. Available at: http://www.bankofgreece.gr/BogEkdoseis/Summary_Annrep2010.pdf, [accessed September 2011], 8.

34 IOBE Quarterly Bulletin 2011. The Greek Economy [March]. Available at: http://www.iobe.gr/media/engoik/IOBE_Greek_econ_02_11_en.pdf, 63, [accessed September 2011], 46.

35 Ibid., 46.

would default.[36] This percentage was lowered by 2 per cent in November of the same year.[37] In the first months of 2011, numbers were even higher. In January of this year, 74 per cent believed Greece would default[38] and in May 85 per cent deemed such as scenario possible.[39] Furthermore, since March, spreads on 10-year bonds over German bonds soared to record highs (Figure 3.2). They exceeded 2650 bps and 1400 bps respectively, while rating agencies downgraded Greece to near-default status.[40]

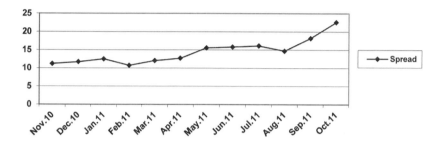

Figure 3.2   **10-year spreads of Greek Government Bonds from November 2010 until October 2011**

Developments – in spite of the above-presented achievements – were worrying in 2010. The real economy performed worse than expected. As the 2010 annual report of the Bank of Greece summarised:

---

36   R. Miller. 2010. Greek default seen by almost 75 per cent in poll doubtful about Trichet [8 June]. Available at: http://www.bloomberg.com/news/2010-06-08/greek-default-seen-by-almost-75-in-poll-of-investors-doubtful-on-trichet.html [accessed July 2011].

37   D. Lynch. 2010. Ireland default predicted by majority in global investor poll [12 November]. Available at: http://www.bloomberg.com/news/2010-11-12/ireland-s-debt-default-predicted-by-majority-of-investors-in-global-poll.html [accessed July 2011].

38   S. Kennedy. 2011. Greece default with Ireland breaks euro by 2016 in global poll [26 January]. Available at: http://www.bloomberg.com/news/2011-01-25/greece-default-with-ireland-breaks-euro-by-2016-in-global-poll.html [accessed August 2011].

39   S. Kennedy. 2011. Greece defaulting on debts anticipated by 85% in global poll of investors [13 May]. Available at: http://www.bloomberg.com/news/2011-05-13/greece-defaulting-on-debts-anticipated-by-85-in-global-poll-of-investors.html [accessed September 2011].

40   Rating for Greece included: CCC (Standard & Poors), Caa1 (Moody's) and B+ (Fitch). See the IMF Country No. 117/175, 2011 [July]. Greece: Fourth review under the stand-by arrangement and request for modification and waiver of applicability of performance criteria. Available at: http://www.imf.org/external/pubs/ft/scr/2011/cr11175.pdf [accessed September 2011], 4.

> The drop in domestic demand, which was to be expected due to the necessary fiscal adjustment, was the key factor behind the recession; GDP contracted by 4.5 per cent in 2010, exclusively weighed down by domestic demand, in particular declines of 4.5 per cent in private consumption, 6.5 per cent in government consumption and 16.5 per cent in gross fixed capital formation.[41]

The recession also led to a further increase of unemployment. Its rate reached 14.2 per cent of workforce. In the last quarter of 2010, 180,000 jobs were lost.[42] In addition, the potential growth rate was dropping and net national saving was -13.9 per cent of GDP in 2010.[43]

In the spring of 2011, it became evident that the Greek economy was contracting more severely than expected. Specifically, recession was shaping at 7.3 per cent in the second trimester of the year and predictions for the months to follow were not optimistic. According to the assessment of the Foundation for Economic & Industrial Research, fiscal developments in the first five months made clear the important deviation from the yearly target of the tax revenue. This was mostly the result of low efficiency of revenue collection mechanisms as well as of the deeper recession in relation to the original predictions.[44] The same assessment also concentrated on the deviation from the target of the primary expenditure of the Regular Budget and the drastic reduction of the Public Investments Programme (PIP) by circa 40 per cent during the first five months of 2011.[45]

Being under heavy pressure from markets once again, Greece had to negotiate a new tranche of financial help to cover its borrowing needs after 2012. In June 2011, the Troika stated that 'reinvigoration of fiscal and broader structural reforms' were necessary in order to further reduce the deficit.[46] The spectre of default once again threatened Athens. The government of the country had to apply an extensive programme of privatisations defined in the Medium Term Fiscal Strategy Plan (MTFSP). This consolidation plan worth €28 million would last for the period 2012–15. It predicted extra measures of almost €6.7 billion for the second semester for 2011 in order to approximate the primary target of the 2011 deficit and the general government targeted deficit of 1.7 per cent of GDP for 2015.

The Greek Parliament approved an additional round of austerity measures in order to secure a second bailout package. After the MTFSP was passed, the EU went further and decided on a second bailout package. On 21 July 2011, heads of state of

---

41 Bank of Greece Summary of the Annual Report 2010 [accessed September 2011], 7.
42 Ibid., 8.
43 Ibid., 10.
44 IOBE Quarterly Bulletin 2011. The Greek Economy. Available at: http://www.iobe.gr/media/engoik/IOBE_Greek_econ_02_11_en.pdf 64 (02/11) [accessed September 2011], 8.
45 Ibid., 8.
46 Press Release No. 11/212, 2011. Statement by the EC, ECB and IMF on the fourth review mission to Greece [3 June]. Available at: http://www.imf.org/external/np/sec/pr/2011/pr11212.htm [accessed September 2011].

the euroarea agreed to support a new programme for Greece which would amount to an estimated €109 billion.[47] For the first time in the history of the eurozone, however, the private sector would also have to contribute voluntarily. Members of the Institute of International Finance (IIF) welcomed this decision and expressed their will to take part in the voluntary plan.[48] The majority of Greek sovereign bonds, which would be exchanged, would be collateralised by 30-year zero coupons purchased using funds from the European Financial Stability Facility (EFSF).[49] This agreement certainly included elements of a debt-restructuring because the instruments involved in the exchange of Greek bonds would lead either to a prolongation of their maturities or a haircut. Thus, rating agencies such as Fitch downgraded Greece to restrictive default.[50]

A new opportunity was certainly created for Greece in spite of rating agencies' assessments.[51] On the basis of the agreement of 21 July 2011, the country would have its borrowing costs covered until 2020. Further to this, the maturity of future loans from the EFSF would be extended along with the previous one of May 2010 and lending rates would be approximately 3.5 per cent. The President of the European Commission also took the initiative of proposing a comprehensive programme of technical assistance to the country to support the delivery of the new adjustment plan by creating a 'Task Force'.[52] This 'Task Force' started working on 1 September 2011 in Athens.

So was it the end of the Greek drama? The answer is negative and the opportunity was missed due to the incompetence of Greek political personnel. As the OECD 2011 country report explains, the success of the new austerity plan – which is the prerequisite for the second bailout package – was subject to many risks.[53] Its implementation required a series of domestic and organisational issues Greece lacked in the previous months: for example, the materialisation of the privatisation programme and use of state land, worth €50 billion, until 2015 could

---

47 Statement by the Heads of State or Government of the euroarea and EU institutions 2011 [21 July]. Available at: http://www.consilium.europa.eu/uedocs/cms_data/docs/pressdata/en/ec/123978.pdf [accessed July 2011].

48 Press Release of the IIF, 2011. Greece Financing Offer: Statement by the IIF Board of Directors [21 July]. Available at: http://www.iif.com/press/press+198.php [accessed July 2011].

49 Ibid.

50 V. Pop. 2011. Greece to face restricted default as bailout details emerge. Available at: http://euobserver.com/9/32653 [accessed August 2011].

51 According to the Institute of International Finance, Greece's debt profile would be improved substantially with the exchange and roll-over program extending average maturities of privately held claims from 6 to 11 years. The stock of debt will be reduced by €13.5 billion through the bond exchange program and potentially by €24.3 billion (or 10.6 per cent of current GDP), including through a debt buy-back program (estimated to be €20 billion). Available at: http://www.iif.com/press/press+198.php [accessed July 2011].

52 Memo/11/599, 2011 [13 September]. Questions and answers on the Task Force for Greece [13 September]. Available at: http://europa.eu/rapid/pressReleasesAction.do?reference=MEMO/11/599&type=HTML [accessed September 2011].

53 OECD Economic Survey on Greece, 2011.

be considered the catalyst for the decrease of public debt as percentage of GDP below 130 per cent in 2015. This scenario was rather ambitious.[54] Moreover, the Greek Government was continuously showing a weakness in curtailing the public sector; it was mainly focusing on increasing revenue by imposing taxes and its tax-collecting mechanism was still problematic. Along with this scepticism, the numbers were creating a new nightmare. In July 2011, the IMF argued that the Greek public debt increased substantially between 2010 and 2011, from 143 per cent to 166 per cent of GDP. It also forecast that Greece's debt would rise again in 2012 to 172 per cent of GDP.[55]

Third EU Response

Only one month after the European Summit of 21 July 2011, the Greek Government was again under pressure. Representatives of the Troika visited Athens to discuss the implementation of the programme. The new Greek Finance Minister, Mr Evangelos Venizelos, who had taken the position of Mr Papaconstantinou in a cabinet reshuffle, failed to agree and talks broke down. The Troika departed from the Greek capital but left there the spectre of default. The government had no other choice but to apply new austerity measures. A new property tax, which would be incorporated into electricity bills, was the immediate response. Greek people who would not pay this tax might see electricity cut off in their houses.

Creditors of Greece were particularly concerned that the debt of the country could not be sustainable on the basis of measures agreed in July. Their main objective was that this debt would not exceed 120 per cent of the country's GDP in 2020. The European Summit of 26–27 October 2011 attempted to correct miscalculations of that of July. EU leaders agreed thus on a much deeper haircut. This time they 'invited Greece, private investors and all parties concerned to develop a voluntary bond exchange with a nominal discount of 50% on Greek debt held by private investors'.[56] This decision was a rather drastic one as it implied particularly heavy losses for bondholders as opposed to the velvet compromise of July.

In a repetition of its previous attempts to pass austerity measures, the Hellenic Parliament had to vote for a new memorandum full of austerity measures on 12 February 2012. These included further cuts in salaries and pensions as well as a

---

54 IOBE Quarterly Bulletin 2011. The Greek Economy [July]. Available at: http://www.iobe.gr/media/engoik/IOBE_Greek_econ_02_11_en.pdf 64 (02/11) [accessed September 2011], 8.

55 IMF Country No. 117/175, 2011. Greece: Fourth review under the stand-by arrangement and request for modification and waiver of applicability of performance criteria [July]. Available at: http://www.imf.org/external/pubs/ft/scr/2011/cr11175.pdf [accessed September 2011], 10.

56 Euro Summit Statement 2011 [26 October]. Available in: http://www.consilium.europa.eu/uedocs/cms_Data/docs/pressdata/en/ec/125644.pdf [accessed November 2011].

22 per cent reduction in the minimum wage. The IMF, however, was not confident Greece would meet its targets and expected its debt to reach 129 per cent of GDP in 2020 instead of 120 per cent. Therefore, the EU agreed on a rescue package for Greece which would now be higher, worth €130 billion. The agreement also included a haircut amounting to 53.5 per cent of the nominal value of bonds:[57] private bondholders had to suffer even more from Greece's inability to pay back its debts while the real danger of default did not disappear.[58]

Political Dissensus

Important as they are, numbers and the recession parameter cannot satisfactorily explain the Greek drama. Crucial domestic factors have to be taken into account. A particularly problematic dimension in Greek politics, especially from May 2010 until November 2011, was the lack of political consensus. Although European leaders had decided on a bailout mechanism in March 2010 and the Greek Premier had asked for its activation on 23 April, the Hellenic Parliament was divided in the critical vote of 6 May. On that day, Greek MPs voted on a bill with new austerity measures as we have seen. The release of the €110 billion loans would only be subject to the approval of this bill. However, only 172 MPs voted in favour while 121 voted against.[59] MPs of PASOK – with the exception of three[60] – as well as MPs of the right-wing party LAOS, approved the new bill. MPs of ND – with the exception of Ms Dora Bakoyannis[61] – along with MP's from the communist party (KKE) and the left-wing SYRIZA, voted against.

In June, 13 months after the important vote of May 2010, the Hellenic Parliament had to face a similarly crucial test. Specifically, on 29 June, it was the Medium Term Fiscal Strategy Plan which had to be approved in order for Greece to receive a second bailout package. This plan was passed with 155 deputies

---

57 Eurogroup Statement 2012 [21 February]. Available at: http://consilium.europa.eu/uedocs/cms_data/docs/pressdata/en/ecofin/128075.pdf [accessed February 2012].

58 According to a press release of the International Institute for Finance (IIF), the plan of 14 February 2012 seeks to reduce Greece's debt burden by €107 billion. Bondholders will need to exchange 31.5 per cent of their principal into 20 new Greek Government bonds with maturities of 11 to 30 years and the rest into short-dated notes issued by the EFSF. The same report explains that the coupon on the new bonds was set at 2 per cent until February 2015, 3 per cent for the following five years and 4.3 per cent until 2042. IIF Press Release, 2012. [28 February]. Available at: http://www.iif.com/press/press+231.php [accessed March 2012].

59 Parliamentary Proceedings 2010. [6 May]. Available at: http://www.hellenicparliament.gr/UserFiles/a08fc2dd-61a9-4a83-b09a-09f4c564609d/es20100506_1.pdf [accessed September 2011], 6783.

60 Ms Sofia Sakorafa, Mr Ioannis Dimaras and Mr Vassilios Economou voted against the bill and were expelled from the parliamentary group, Ibid., 6781.

61 Following her decision, Ms Bakoyannis was expelled from the parliamentary group of ND, Ibid., 6786.

voting in favour and 138 against.⁶² In this case, PASOK lost one vote from its own members but gained one from ND members.⁶³ As opposed to 6 May 2010, on 29 June 2011, MPs of LAOS voted against the Medium Term Fiscal Strategy Plan as also happened with deputies from ND, KKE and SYRIZA.

The lack of consent in Greek political elites regarding the Memorandum of Understanding and the MTFSP has created scepticism in Brussels. A few days before the second one had to be passed in the Hellenic Parliament, various European politicians encouraged Greek MPs to approve it. President of the European Commission, José Manuel Barroso, for example, met with ND's leader, Antonis Samaras, on 8 June 2011 and 'used this opportunity to urge [him] to show his commitment to reach a broad national consensus so that Greece can face in the most determined and effective manner its present historical challenges to address the situation of its public finances'.⁶⁴ Nonetheless, no positive results yielded. An attempt by Mr Papandreou and Mr Samaras to co-operate and form a national coalition government completely collapsed on 15 June 2011.

In the first two years of the crisis, political dissensus was not only related to disagreement among different political parties but also to the lack of cohesion within PASOK itself. Various voices heard by its members were regularly testing its unity. The ruling party lost four of its parliament seats during the aforementioned voting procedures. Furthermore, its policy often reflected a division among reformists and old guards of the movement. While the former pushed for change, the latter were not keen on agreeing with the Troika's demands and stuck to the socialist principles of PASOK's founding father, Andreas Papandreou. This distinction also led to personal clashes within the party. On 7 June 2011, for instance, during an economic affairs meeting its MP, Ms Vasso Papandreou, criticised the economic policy of Mr George Papaconstantinou – who was appointed Minister for the Environment, Energy and Climate Change after 20 months in the Ministry of Finance – by saying no appropriate plan had been set up by the government and that he 'had treated her as a UFO'.⁶⁵ A few days later the new Finance Minister, Evangelos Venizelos, embarked on an attempt to persuade MPs of the party to vote

---

62 Parliamentary Proceedings. 2011. [29 June]. Available at: http://www.hellenicparliament.gr/UserFiles/a08fc2dd-61a9-4a83-b09a-09f4c564609d/es20110629-30.pdf [accessed September], 13029.

63 Mr Panagiotis Kourouplis from PASOK and Ms Elsa Papadimitriou from ND were the ones who voted against and in favour respectively. Following their decisions, the first was expelled from the parliamentary group of PASOK and the second announced her independence from ND.

64 Memo/11/393, 2011. President Barroso's meeting with Mr Andonis Samaras, leader of the main Greek opposition party [8 June]. Available at: http://europa.eu/rapid/pressReleasesAction.do?reference=MEMO/11/393&type=HTML [accessed September 2011].

65 Intervention of Ms Vasso Papandreou 2011 [7 June]. Available at: http://www.tovima.gr/politics/article/?aid=405168 [accessed August 2011].

in favour of the new austerity plan because a few of them had publicly announced they would reject it.⁶⁶

A problematic feature in PASOK's politics had been that the pre-election agenda of the party was continuously contradicting the economic policy it followed after it came to power in October 2009. On these grounds, almost all of its MPs were under pressure by their voters in their constituencies because they could not keep their promises. According to a survey conducted in April 2010, for instance, 79.6 per cent of the ruling party voters argued that measures taken by the government opposed its pre-election promises.⁶⁷ Within this context, various PASOK MPs were facing a serious dilemma. They had to decide either to satisfy their voter's demands by rejecting austerity measures and reforms or to align themselves with the Troika policies and naturally risk their political survival in the next national elections.

After the Referendum

In the autumn of 2011, the government of PASOK was isolated domestically and almost dissoluted internally. The September decision of Finance Minister Venizelos to apply the new property tax to be paid through electricity bills had generated waves of political and public reaction. After the European Summit of October and the 50 per cent haircut, Mr Papandreou shocked the world economy by announcing on 31 October his decision for a referendum on the bailout terms. Commenting for *Associated Press*, I considered his choice as marking the end of his political career.⁶⁸ At the same time, although he cancelled this decision three days later, he did not avoid losing the confidence of his member parties. PASOK was gradually losing its cohesion and the government could hardly remain in power for many more days.⁶⁹ Indeed, Mr Papandreou resigned and one week later a unity government under technocrat Lucas Papademos was formed. The

---

66 PASOK's MPs Mr Alekos Athanasiadis and Mr Thomas Robopoulos said publicly they would vote against the Medium Term Fiscal Strategy Plan but after Mr. Venizelos' intervention they changed stance and finally voted in favour.

67 GPO Poll 2010 [26 April]. Available at: http://www.eklogika.gr/uploads/files/Dimoskopiseis/GPO-Mega26-4-2010.pdf [accessed August 2011], 10.

68 I supported the thesis on the 'political death' of Mr George Papandreou in an interview with Associated Press which was conducted on 3 November 2011. Excerpts of the interview are available at: http://www.aparchive.com/OneUpPrint.aspx?xslt=1p&showact=results&sort=relevance&page=1&sh=1180&kwstyle=and&adte=1323256334&rids=851468e0f1e7dbb1a30e996a0fca31fc&dah=-1&pagez=20&cfasstyle=AND& [accessed February 2012].

69 G. Tzogopoulos, interview for *Associated Press* 2011 [1 November]. Available at: http://www.aparchive.com/OneUpPrint.aspx?xslt=1p&showact=results&sort=relevance&page=1&sh=1180&kwstyle=and&adte=1320376045&rids=67d537728f568c3757336669bdb239ed&dah=-1&pagez=20&cfasstyle=AND& [accessed January 2012].

conservative New Democracy and the right-wing party LAOS co-operated with PASOK and supported the unity government.

The main mission of the Papademos government was to conduct negotiations between Greece and its creditors on the basis of the so-called PSI (Private Sector Involvement). This government also passed a new painful adjustment programme in the Parliament, including a 22 per cent minimum wage cut. Nevertheless, the agreement upon which this unity government was formed was that a new election would take place after the exchange of bonds. Indeed, this date was set for 6 May. Because PASOK had been already exhausted, ND could in theory easily win the election. Its percentage, however, was a historical low record. It only gathered 18.85 per cent of the vote. At the same time, PASOK (13.18 per cent) did not even manage to take second place which was captured by the leftist SYRIZA with 16.78 per cent. The neo-Nazi party Golden Dawn (6.97 per cent) also entered Parliament. From that moment no coalition government could be formed, so Greece had to organise a second election round on 17 June 2012.

The period from mid-May until mid-June 2012 was marked by increased political instability. The leader of SYRIZA, Alexis Tsipras, embarked on an attempt to persuade Greek public opinion that the country could survive without necessarily applying the terms of the bailout. He also enriched his rhetoric by inventing in populism and using the tone and style of Andreas Papandreou. His party managed to increase its power by gathering 26.89 per cent of the vote – compared to 16.78 per cent on 6 May – but ND won with 29.66 per cent. In the first three days after the new election, the conservative party co-operated with PASOK (12.28 per cent) and Democratic Left (6.26 per cent)[70] and formed a coalition government. It is remarkable that Golden Dawn preserved its power by receiving 6.92 per cent of the vote. The summer of 2012 was once again dramatic for Greece. The country needed to take additional painful measures worth €11.5 billion for the years 2013 and 2014 in order to receive further financing by the Troika. These measures included – inter alia – further reductions in salaries and pensions, the introduction of tuition fees for postgraduate studies, the abolishment of social benefits, additional taxes for self-employed people and a new retirement-age rise. Ironically, the leader of the ND and current Prime Minister, Antonis Samaras, would have to apply the same policy he had strongly opposed while being in the opposition!

Public Opinion

An additional important prerequisite for potential success of the Greek Government has been to persuade public opinion of the efficiency of its economic policy and the benefits of the bailout. Most Greek people started to familiarise themselves with the financial crisis the country was facing in the last months

---

70 The leader of Democratic Left is Mr Fotis Kouvelis.

of 2009. Various surveys conducted from December 2009 until March 2010 suggest the majority of respondents believed tough measures had been important for the country and that they trusted the newly elected government of PASOK. According to a Kapa Research poll published in Sunday newspaper *To Vima* on 7 February 2010, for example, 64.3 per cent considered austerity packages as necessary.[71] The new round of measures announced by Mr Papandreou on 3 March, however, caused frustration to Greek people. A survey conducted by GPO and presented on *Mega Channel TV* on 8 March demonstrated that 65.3 per cent saw them as unfair.[72]

As far as the Memorandum of Understanding is concerned most Greek people – although not happy – preferred this bailout mechanism than the country going alone. An Alco survey published in Sunday newspaper *Proto Thema* on 9 May 2010 shows that 54.2 per cent of respondents chose the first and 33.2 per cent the second option.[73] Nevertheless, this tendency was reversed one year later. Realising the consequences of austerity and the impact of recession, Greek public opinion expressed itself negatively towards the Memorandum and thought this was not the only alternative for the country and was not sufficient as a remedy. A VPRC poll organised by *Epikaira* magazine and published on 28 April 2011 suggests only 14 per cent saw this agreement as the only solution for the country while 63 per cent thought more alternatives had been available.[74] Further to this, another Public Issue survey published the following month revealed that 62 per cent thought the Memorandum had harmed the Greek economy and only 13 per cent thought it had benefited it.[75]

Most Greek people were also against the Medium Term Fiscal Strategy Plan. A June 2010 GPO survey outlined that only 23.4 per cent favoured it and that 66.3 per cent opposed it.[76] In parallel with this, most respondents believed the Troika would accept a possible re-negotiation of terms of the Memorandum while public opinion in the country was divided concerning the importance of the European agreement of 21 July 2011. According to a Kapa Research poll published in *To Vima* on 4 September 2011, 76.3 per cent urged the government to re-negotiate

71 Kapa Research poll 2010 [7 February]. Available at: http://www.tovima.gr/politics/article/?aid=313921 [accessed August 2011].
72 GPO poll 2010 [8 March]. Available at: http://www.eklogika.gr/uploads/files/Dimoskopiseis/GPO-Mega8-3.pdf [accessed August 2011], 31.
73 Alco poll 2010. *Proto Thema* newspaper, 9 May, 4.
74 VPRC poll 2011 [28 April]. Available at: http://www.vprc.gr/uplds/File/teleytaia%20nea/Epikaira/Political%20climate%20and%20governance_VPRC_April2011.pdf, [accessed August 2010], 8.
75 Public Issue poll 2011 [19 May]. Available at: http://www.publicissue.gr/wp-content/uploads/2011/05/mnimonio-debt-a-year-after-may-2011-all-survey-final.pdf [accessed August 2011], 4.
76 GPO poll 2011 [21 June]. Available at: http://www.eklogika.gr/uploads/files/Dimoskopiseis/Mega-GPO-22-6-2011.pdf, [accessed August 2011], 4.

with the Troika and 49.1 per cent considered the decision of 21 July as positive.[77] Finally, an overwhelming majority of Greek people were at that time pessimistic about the future, expressing agony and fear that their personal economic status, like that of the country, would deteriorate in the coming months.[78]

Within an atmosphere of depression and an environment of recession it is not surprising that Greek public opinion continued to disagree with the bailout terms after the European Summit of 26–27 October 2011. As a Kapa Research survey suggests, 58.9 per cent of the respondents considered the decisions as negative for Greece towards the end of the month.[79] Four months later, Greek citizens seemed to have lost their trust in the international rescue plan of their national economy even more. Specifically, 66.9 per cent of them did not believe the bailout could constitute the basis for the recovery of the country.[80] In the following months, while the public confidence in the Memorandum almost collapsed, Greek people strongly supported its participation in the euro and opposed its return to the drachma.[81] This tendency was not reversed in May and June 2012 while SYRIZA was fighting for an electoral win. According to a RASS survey conducted on 1 June 2012, 88.9 per cent of the respondents favoured Greece's stay in the eurosystem.[82] In spite of public support for the common currency, however, trust in the European Union had already started to decline.

The Greek Government's attempt to implement the necessary measures has become harder due to public disappointment. This disappointment has been often transformed into public ire against politicians. A credibility deficit has been rising in the country. Greek citizens did not easily trust politicians, considering them responsible for the crisis and urging them to share the burden of failure. In June 2011, an 'angry people movement' was created and thousands of people gathered in various cities to express their frustration. This movement was endorsed by Greek public opinion and was mainly formed by young people.[83] The youth of the Greek

---

77 Kapa Research poll 2011. *To Vima tis Kyriakis*, 4 September, A10-A11.

78 A survey conducted by *Metron Analysis* and published in *Eleftheros Typos* newspaper on 21 July 2011 shows that 80.9 per cent of the respondents are not optimistic for the personal plans. See the Metron Analysis poll. 2011. [21 July]. Available at: http://www.eklogika.gr/uploads/files/Dimoskopiseis/MetronAnalysis-Etypos21-7-11.pdf [accessed September 2011].

79 Kapa Research poll. 2011 [30 October]. Available at: http://www.eklogika.gr/uploads/files/Dimoskopiseis/KapaResearch-Vima27-10-11.pdf [accessed September 2012].

80 MRB poll 2012 [19 February]. Available at: http://www.eklogika.gr/uploads/files/Dimoskopiseis/realnews-mrb_19-2-12.pdf [accessed September 2012].

81 75.8 per cent of the respondents in March 2012 favoured the European orientation of Greece. See: Marc poll 2012 [24 March]. Available at: http://www.eklogika.gr/uploads/files/Dimoskopiseis/Marc-Ethnos_24-3-12.pdf [accessed September 2012].

82 Rass poll 2012 [1 June]. Available at: http://www.eklogika.gr/uploads/files/Dimoskopiseis/Rass-eltypos_1-6-12.pdf [accessed September 2012].

83 A survey conducted by Marc and published in *Ethnos* newspaper on 27 June 2011 demonstrated that the angry people movement was supported by 74 per cent of

population have been among the disadvantaged groups in the Greek labour market, with their unemployment rate exceeding the OECD average even before 2010 and 2011.[84] Under current circumstances they face even more painful repercussions because unemployment and poverty have been on the rise. Their disappointment is reflected in the results of various surveys which demonstrate that many of them were ready to leave the country and look for a job in a foreign one.[85] Additionally, their disillusionment is often expressed by protests, creating an additional issue of concern for the Greek Government and its attempt to apply its fiscal consolidation policies. It is a normal reaction and, further, the unemployment of young people exceeded 50 per cent in autumn 2012 and 60 per cent at the beginning of 2013.

Opposition to Change

A significant parameter of the crisis has also been related to the lack of social consensus and the continuous reaction to a policy of change. Some oppose reforms on the grounds that they are misguided or that they imply a loss of national sovereignty.[86] However, the driving force behind the opposition to various reforms has been the stance of trade unions. The Greek Government is much more hesitant in proceeding with structural reforms and privatisation of state-owned enterprises because of their behaviour. Trade unions have been prepared to fight for their own interests by mobilising public support and organising rolling strikes.

There are two significant trade unions in Greece which organise strikes and demonstrations.[87] The first is the private sector General Confederation of Greek Workers (GSEE) and the second one the public sector Civil Servants' Confederation (ADEDY). Their leaders are party cadres of the old PASOK and had supported it in the national election of 4 October 2009. Trade unions have relied on funds

---

respondents and that 35.9 per cent of its participants were young people from 15 to 34 years old. See the Marc poll 2011 [27 June]. Available at: http://www.eklogika.gr/uploads/files/Dimoskopiseis/MarcEthnos26-6-11.pdf [accessed September 2011].

84   See the OECD Report 2010.

85   According to an Alco poll conducted in September 2011 and published in *Proto Thema* newspaper, 75 per cent of young Greek people were prepared to leave Greece. See the Alco poll 2011. *Proto Thema*, 4 September, 1.

86   C. Meghir, D. Vayanos and N. Vettas. 2010. *The Economic Crisis in Greece: A Time for Reform and Opportunity*.

87   Kostas Milas, Finance Professor at Keele University, writes that the Greek situation brings to his mind the School of Athens – one of Raphael's most famous frescoes painted on the walls of the Room of the Segnatura, in the Vatican City: 'In the centre of the fresco, Greek policymakers – like modern versions of Plato and Aristotle – debate with extraordinary slack, a series of necessary economic measures to put Greece's public finances in order. The agreed economic measures, such as the drastic reduction of the public sector through privatisations or the opening up of "closed" professions, are then delayed or opposed by members of the Socialist ministerial cabinet and trade unions'.

distributed by the Ministry of Labour for their economic survival. Under current circumstances, however, their relationship with the government has been ruined because of the latter's reform agenda and its spending cuts policy. Both GSEE and ADEDY have strongly opposed the Troika's demands and have been keen on calling general strikes. On the one organised on 5 May 2010 three people died in the centre of Athens.

A plethora of examples outline that Greek trade unions often make decisions illegally, thus disrupting public service. The general federation of working staff in the public electricity company (GENOP DEI) is also one of the most powerful syndicates in Greece. Its representatives have not agreed with plans by the Greek Government to privatise the company and have shown their opposition by following a policy of power supply cuts. On 11 June 2011, for instance, its board of directors decided to start a series of 48-hour strikes by blocking the access of Greek people to electricity in various locations.[88] A few weeks later a Greek court judged these strikes as illegal. Furthermore, in July 2011 the pan-Hellenic federation of taxi drivers and owners opposed government plans to issue new taxi licenses and called for rolling strikes. They also went a stage further by occupying main roads, bridges and access to ports and airports in Athens and various other cities. As a result, tourism in the country suffered a serious blow.

The communist trade union federation PAME belongs to the groups which have often caused disruption in public services. PAME has a record of blocking the port of Piraeus as well as the access to Acropolis, the archaeological site. It has also expressed its contradiction to the government by occupying public buildings such as the Finance Ministry. According to a press release it issued on 7 September 2011, the ambition of its members has been 'to become the destroyers not only of the current government and the measures it takes but of any anti-popular policy or government – of the capitalist development itself and the barbarity it brings for working people'.[89]

Along with trade unions, a new dimension in the Greek public's opposition to the EC-ECB-IMF adjustment programme has been added through the creation of a 'non-payment campaign'. Members of this campaign have invented various techniques in order to avoid paying public fees where necessary. One of their activities, for example, is related to protesting against paying tolls on national roads by pushing barriers aside. Another one has been using public transportation without validating their tickets. The main strategy of the 'non-payment campaign'

---

88 GENOP DEI Decision 2011 [11 June]. Available at: http://www.genop.gr/index.php?option=com_content&view=article&id=985:2011-06-11-18-48-52&catid=1:2009-08-08-10-27-00&Itemid=2 [accessed August 2011].

89 PAME press release 2011. Available at: http://www.pamehellas.gr/fullstory.php?lang=1&wid=1915, 7 September [accessed September 2011].

has been to 'fight having free social goods for unemployed and young people as well as for pensioners'.[90]

The lack of social consensus and opposition to change is a crucial parameter in Greek politics. The subsequent question, nevertheless, is whether the political personnel has been prepared or even capable of tackling this problem. The performance of PASOK and the unity government was rather disappointing in the first two and a half years of the crisis. Various laws were passed in Parliament but were not enforced because of continuous reactions: the unsuccessful enforcement of laws regarding the liberalisation of 'closed professions' has perfectly mirrored the inability of politicians to practically implement policies. As a whole, demonstrations which have taken place in the country have often turned out to be useful for the ones who have participated and protested. Their will has been imposed many times due to the weakness of the Greek Government and the inefficiency of state mechanisms.

Only a Greek Fault?

The main responsibility for the outbreak and the painful continuation of the crisis in Greece certainly lies with its government and the weakness of national politicians to take the necessary actions and deliver. A broader discussion, nevertheless, has to include a particular reference to the EU and its role after the Greek national election of October 2009. The Hellenic Republic can hardly be considered solely culpable within the eurozone and its financial crisis, although its case is the most problematic one. Ireland and Portugal have activated the bailout mechanism in order to receive loans worth €78 and €112 billion respectively. At the same time, Italy and Spain have also suffered from a rise in their spreads, thus needing to apply tough austerity measures. In June 2012 the latter asked for a bailout to save its banks. At the beginning of 2013 Cyprus also needed a rescue package.

In the view of former Prime Minister Papandreou, the Greek crisis goes hand-in-hand with that of the eurozone. As he explained to the President of Europe, Jan Claude Juncker, in July 2011: 'no matter what Greece does [...] if Europe does not make the right, collective, forceful decisions, we risk new, and possibly global, market calamities due to a contagion of doubt that will engulf our common union'.[91] According to Loukas Tsoukalis, Greece 'served as the catalyst for the

---

90   Blog of 'non-payment campaign'. Available at: http://denplirono.wordpress.com/about/ [accessed January 2011].

91   Letter by Prime Minister George Papandreou to the President of the Eurogroup and Prime Minister of Luxemburg, Jean Claude Juncker 2011 [11 July]. Available at: http://www.primeminister.gov.gr/english/2011/07/11/letter-to-the-president-of-the-eurogroup-and-prime-minister-of-luxembourg-jean-claude-juncker/ [accessed July 2011].

crisis' which is also the result of colossal failures in markets and institutions.[92] Following the dramatic turn of developments after October 2009, the Hellenic Republic became a crucial case in testing the unity of the eurozone, its will for further integration and its investment on the common currency.

Europe most assuredly has found itself in the midst of a crisis that goes beyond its institutional framework and borders.[93] The Union has certainly been hesitant in providing quick and efficient solutions to the Greek debt crisis and in blocking its possible contagion. In the first months of 2010, for example, inertia was marking its stance. Former British Prime Minister Gordon Brown concentrated on the impact of Europe's slowness in agreeing on the Memorandum of Understanding and argued: 'In 2010 because of delays in decisions to help Greece the cost [to its government] of avoiding default grew from an estimated 30 billion euros to around 120 billion'.[94]

It is not a hard task to find negative comments for the modus operandi of the EU within the economic crisis. A research paper published by the European Council on Foreign Relations (ECFR) in December 2010, for instance, asserted that European leaders failed to provide a shield to protect the eurozone and restore investors' confidence.[95] As Olaf Cramme wrote: '… if politics, if processes or outcomes fall below expectations or even fail, someone is supposed to be culpable'.[96] Germany has received strong criticism. Many have singled out German Chancellor Angela Merkel and Finance Minister Wolfgang Schäuble for failing to promote a vision of Europe.

Berlin has arguably responded to the crisis quite roughly and aggressively. This stance has maybe reflected its economic supremacy in the euroarea. It has also mirrored the tendency of its elites to see their own economic and monetary model as the only solution for overcoming the crisis.[97] Berlin's will to urge southern states and especially Greece to become more like Germany has been an almost

---

92   L. Tsoukalis. 2011. The JCMS Annual Review Lecture: The Shattering of Illusions – And What Next. 26.

93   L. Tsoukalis. 2011. *The Delphic Oracle on Europe: Is There a Future for the European Union*, edited by L.Tsoukalis and Y.A. Emmanouilidis, Oxford and New York: Oxford University Press, 205–6.

94   G. Brown. 2010. *Beyond the Crash: Overcoming the First Crisis of Globalization*, New York, London, Toronto, Sydney: Free Press, 183.

95   T. Klau and Fr Godement, with J.I. Torreblanca. 2010. [December]. Beyond Maastricht: A New Deal for the EurozoneEurozoneEurozoneEurozoneEurozone. Available at: http://www.ecfr.eu/page/-/ECFR26_BEYOND_MAASTRICHT_AW(2).pdf [accessed July 2011].

96   O. Cramme. 2011 'In Search of Leadership', in *The Delphic Oracle on Europe: Is There a Future for the European Union*, 30.

97   U. Guérot and M. Leonard. 2011. The New German Question: How Europe can get the Germany it needs [April]. ECFR Policy Brief. Available at: http://www.ecfr.eu/page/-/ECFR30_GERMANY_AW.pdf [accessed November 2011].

impossible request.⁹⁸ The Hellenic crisis has also reflected a traditional 'rivalry' between Germany and France as to the role of the European Central Bank. Any move towards economic governance within the eurozone which would entail a 'soft euro' has not been seen positively by the former. There is no question that Greece has had almost no say in negotiations for the new European economic governance.

Criticism on the reaction of Germany has been on the rise since the aftermath of the outbreak of the crisis in Greece. It is always convenient for analysts to assess and judge developments because they are not being involved in day-to-day politics. From the moment the eurozone was not a state, however, Angela Merkel and her government had to take additional issues into account: domestic factors. German people have been frustrated regarding the economic support provided to the Hellenic Republic. A poll organised by French company IFOP in March 2010 crystallised their view along with that of other European citizens (Figure 3.3).⁹⁹

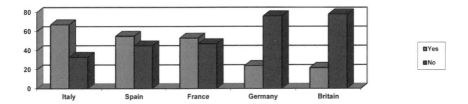

Figure 3.3   IFOP poll results on the first Greek bailout. The question asked is: should France/the UK/Germany/Spain/Italy provide Greece with financial aid in the interests of European solidarity?

The IFOP survey clearly suggests that citizens from two countries of the PIIGS, Italy and Spain, along with French people saw the Greek problem sympathetically while German and British people did not. An additional survey organised by a *Financial Times* opinion produced similar results.¹⁰⁰ If the stance of British citizens can be placed within the framework of a traditional euroscepticism, then that of Germans significantly derives from their view that Greek governments had failed to efficiently manage the country's economics. The second bailout for

---

98   S. Bulmer and W.E. Paterson. 2010. Germany and the European Union: from tamed power to normalized power. *International Affairs* 86 (5), 1051–73.

99   *IFOP* Research Report 2010. Europeans and the Greek Crisis [20 March]. Available in: http://www.ifop.fr/media/poll/1118-2-study_file.pdf [accessed April 2011].

100   R. Atkins and Q. Peel. 2010. Germans oppose Greek aid, poll shows [21 March]. Available at: http://www.ft.com/cms/s/0/ee055e82-3529-11df-9cfb-00144feabdc0.html#axzz1EIkc3yii [accessed November 2011].

Greece received similar judgement in Europe. An IFOP poll organised in June 2011 demonstrated that 20 per cent of the respondents in Great Britain, 41 per cent in Germany, 58 per cent in Spain, 59 per cent in France and 73 per cent in Italy considered further financial help to Greece important in the name of European solidarity.[101]

Domestic restraints have been of high importance for the leading economic power of the eurozone. Democratic countries like Germany also have parliamentary rules which they have to respect. Important decisions made in Brussels, such as bailout packages to support Greece, need parliamentary approval which cannot be always taken for granted. The German Government is not only formed by the party of Ms Merkel (Christian Democratic Union), but is a coalition one with the participation of the Christian Social Union of Bavaria and the Free Democratic Party. Bavarian Finance Minister Markus Söder and Vice-Chancellor and leader of the Free Democratic Party Philip Rössler, for instance, have criticised steps towards further European integration and have been much more aggressive vis-à-vis the Hellenic Republic. As opposed to Merkel's critics, however, Josephy Nye has developed a rather different view. Specifically, he argues:

> Merkel has proceeded cautiously on saving the euro. She faced public scepticism about using German funds to bailout the Greek economy. Her coalition was divided on the issue, and her party lost state elections. If she had acted more boldly, she might have lost even more support, but the steps that she agreed to remain insufficient to reassure markets.[102]

In the final account, Germany is gradually transforming economic governance in the EU, attempting to promote integration. The creation of European Stability Mechanism (ESM) indicates its intention. Whether the future of the euroarea will be interwoven into that of a political and fiscal union and eurobonds will be issues to be seen in the next years. This goal, however, cannot be achieved if discipline in problematic countries like Greece will not be guaranteed. Lessons from the past when discipline had been largely absent are now learnt.

What is particularly problematic with the Greek case is that the country's inability to deliver has caused frustration not only among European political elites but also in the European public opinion. An Ifop poll conducted in June 2012 highlights that even citizens in countries like Italy and Spain had almost lost their patience with the weaker chain of the eurozone.

---

101 *IFOP* poll. 2011. Europeans and the Euro Crisis [29 June]. Available at: http://www.ifop.com/media/poll/1562-2-study_file.pdf [September 2012].

102 J.S. Nye. 2011. Angela Merkel's vision thing [7 November]. Available at: http://www.project-syndicate.org/commentary/nye100/English [accessed February 2012].

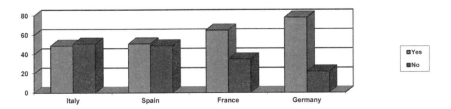

Figure 3.4   IFOP poll results after Greek national elections of June 2012. The question asked is: Wish to exclude Greece from the eurozone in the event of default of payment?

Likewise, a survey conducted by Harris Interactive and published in the *Financial Times* in September 2012 demonstrates that European citizens did not warmly support Greece's stay in the common currency. With the exception of respondents in Italy (59 per cent), only 24 per cent in Great Britain, 27 per cent in Germany, 39 per cent in France and 45 per cent in Spain believe that Greece should remain a member of the eurosystem. In parallel with this, 21 per cent in Great Britain, 25 per cent in France, 26 per cent in Germany, 43 per cent in Italy and 46 per cent in Spain agree that eurozone members should do more to help the Hellenic Republic remain in the eurozone.[103]

'Know Thyself'

The Greek crisis and its immediate contagion on Portugal and Ireland, but also Spain and Italy, has revealed various weaknesses in the eurosystem. Nevertheless, the Hellenic Republic has arguably entered an impasse because the common currency area is struggling to find a new orientation. The country has completely failed to implement the necessary reforms, efficiently deal with powerful trade unions, earn money from privatisation, tackle corruption, limit bureaucracy and eliminate illegal activities within the state. In parallel with this, its society has showed a strong opposition reaction to any drastic change suggested by the so-called Troika. In order to cover the widening financial gap, the Hellenic Government has principally followed a painful policy based on reductions in salaries and pensions as well as on tax rises, almost exhausting the majority of the population. By contrast, it did not hesitate to make decisions such as further financing of political parties in 2011 and expanding the haircut on ordinary citizens holding sovereign bonds. The Greek drama should not be attributed to the EU or Germany. Even if they suddenly decide to immediately write off the debt of Greece – as a matter of respect to its ancient civilisation – the problem of the country will not be solved.

---

103   *Financial Times/Harris* Poll 2012 [August]. Available at: http://www.ft.com/intl/cms/eb1b2004-f542-11e1-b120-00144feabdc0.pdf [accessed September 2012].

The Hellenic Republic needs to spend as much as it earns and create surpluses. The main reason it is navigated between Scylla and Charybdis is located internally and not externally. Self-knowledge is a crucial element to understand the Greek crisis. The phrase 'Know Thyself' used for the first time by the Chilon of Sparta seems to have particular resonance in modern Greece.

Chapter 4
A New Trend in Journalism

The work of journalists covering international affairs is a particularly challenging one. It requires knowledge of different cultures but also gives them the opportunity to prepare interesting stories relevant to developments in foreign countries. These developments can be synthesised around politics and economics but also other themes such as cultural and social life, tourism and sport. In calm times, foreign news is of relatively limited interest to the audience which is keen on closely following domestic news items. By contrast, in turbulent times, especially when elite interests are at stake, they become important and their volume is significantly increased. During wars and military operations abroad, for example, the work of journalists covering them often dominates the agenda and attracts the attention of the audience.

The narration of the Greek story by the media from October 2009 onwards is similar to that of a war of long duration. The main difference is that this war is not being fought by conventional weapons. Its battleground cannot be defined because no single geographic place is involved. And, enemies in the battles are not men or governments. In particular, a new type of war has emerged: an economic one. Main adversaries are deficits and debts while national governments and the EU seem unable to control markets. At the same time, an unelected group, the so-called Troika, is dictating austerity measures to democratic societies as is happening not only in Greece but also in Ireland and Portugal. The Hellenic Republic, however, has been the first and continuous target, being the most vulnerable and weakest link within the context of the eurozone crisis.

Media Attention towards Greece

Greece is a country which can certainly attract the attention of foreign journalists in calm times. The history of the country and its contribution to civilisation have been issues often discussed internationally on the occasion of various cultural events, publication of books and references by intellectuals, politicians and scholars. Furthermore, Greece does constitute an attractive tourist destination and, therefore, stories regarding suggestions for holidays and comparison of prices have been of interest to readers. As far as news items are concerned, information on economic issues such as the budget deficit, inflation, investments and unemployment have also been important for a country which is a member of the eurozone and taking the impact of globalisation into account. This said, it was expectable for foreign journalists to deal with Greece even before the financial crisis and not to suddenly 'discover' the country in its aftermath.

A quantitative analysis of the volume of articles published before and after the outbreak of the Greek crisis shows that the media had indeed shown an interest in the Hellenic Republic. Five different tables on the basis of the nationality of newspapers demonstrate the volume of articles published by each title from the beginning of 2005 until the end of 2011.

Table 4.1   British newspapers

	2005	2006	2007	2008	2009	2010	2011
Times	1014	909	792	801	704	1408	2020
Guardian	1606	1712	1721	2332	1854	3303	3974
Financial Times	687	758	717	827	1294	7217	4549
Sun	617	618	423	554	625	915	1080

Table 4.2   French newspapers

	2005	2006	2007	2008	2009	2010	2011
Le Figaro	865	955	787	1027	824	2779	3395
Le Monde	571	450	409	628	527	1754	2301

Table 4.3   German newspapers

	2005	2006	2007	2008	2009	2010	2011
Frankfurter Allgemeine Zeitung	998	851	807	1109	868	3153	4102
Süddeutsche Zeitung	1390	1382	1430	1744	1534	3910	4749
Handelsblatt	492	438	326	558	538	2966	3844
Bild	n/a	108	202	399	288	999	1170

Table 4.4   Italian newspapers

	2005	2006	2007	2008	2009	2010	2011
Il Corriere della Sera	726	673	700	798	723	1786	2119
La Repubblica	1092	930	948	1017	802	1701	2218

Table 4.5   US newspapers

	2005	2006	2007	2008	2009	2010	2011
Washington Post	329	339	312	357	235	506	678
New York Times	331	381	391	438	486	1466	1794
Wall Street Journal	498	500	546	518	1615	3759	4940

The data suggests that although foreign journalists had dealt with Greece in the years before the outbreak crisis, they mainly concentrated on it in 2010 and 2011. Many newspapers published more articles on the country in these two years than in the previous five, from 2005 until 2009. The examples of *Handelblatt*, *Le Monde*, *The New York Times* and *Bild* are characteristic as Figure 4.1 outlines.

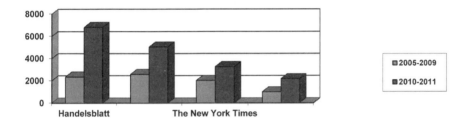

Figure 4.1   Volume of articles from 2005 until 2009 and from 2010 until 2011

The explosion of articles in 2010 and 2011 was the result of the tendency of foreign journalists to regularly focus on Greece and its economic problem after the national election of 4 October 2009. The *Financial Times*, for instance, published almost half of its articles on the Hellenic Republic for 2009 after October. Their volume in the last three months of that year was 637 while it had been 657 for the previous nine months.

Concentrating on the data of 2010 and 2011, Figure 4.2 presents the volume of articles published by all newspapers. The *Financial Times* and *The Wall Street Journal* have the lead in dealing with Greece compared to other titles. This finding is not surprising. Both the *Financial Times* and *The Wall Street Journal* are English-language international newspapers which were continuously paying particular attention to the possibility of a Greek sovereign default and a potential exit from the eurozone. Furthermore, the interest of the media in Greece has been an ongoing one as almost all titles published more pieces in 2011 than in 2010.

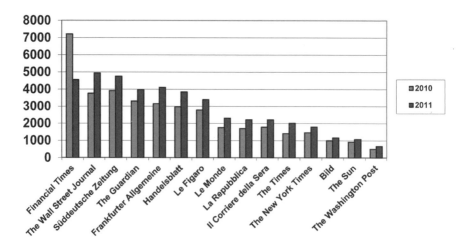

Figure 4.2 Volume of articles on Greece in 2010 and 2011

As far as the nationality of the media is concerned, the German newspapers focused on the Hellenic Republic to a larger extent. Figure 4.3 presents data per country from the ten political opinion-forming newspapers accessed.

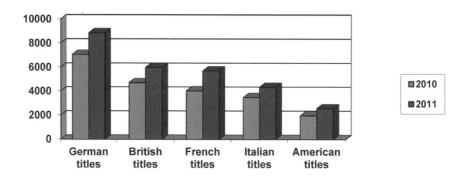

Figure 4.3 Articles published by political opinion-forming newspapers per country

The higher interest by the German *Frankfurter Allgemeine Zeitung* and *Süddeutsche Zeitung* compared to other titles can be attributed to the role Berlin has played in the eurozone debt crisis. Germany is certainly the driving force behind Europe's economic recipe for Greece and its national newspapers could not but extensively deal with its policy priorities.

Following German newspapers, British and French ones demonstrated relatively similar interest in Greece. Here, attention is mainly turned towards *The Guardian*. This title published over 7.000 pieces, more than *The Times*, *Le Figaro* and *Le Monde* respectively. The tendency of *The Guardian* to extensively deal with developments in the country is a not a new phenomenon and one completely inspired by the economic crisis. Even before its outbreak, the British liberal newspaper used to show a large interest in the country. Continuity is rather observed in its stance.

The Italian print media are placed fourth in the list as far as their volume of articles is concerned. In their case, an equivalent distribution of pieces marks the coverage of *Il Corriere della Sera* and *La Repubblica*. Finally, the comparatively limited attention paid to Greece by *The Washington Post* and *The New York Times* can be explained on the basis of the distant angle through which American titles covered developments in a European country. For their part, *The New York Times* confirms its highly international character as its number of articles was almost triple than that of *The Washington Post*.

Writing About Greece

The coverage of the Greek crisis has been principally an affair of either foreign editors or correspondents. Many of the accessed newspapers have indeed correspondents in Greece or in the region of South Eastern Europe in general. The *Financial Times*, *Handelsblatt* and *The Wall Street Journal* do co-operate with Ms Kerin Hope,[1] Mr Gerd Höhler and Mr Alkman Granitsas[2] respectively. As far as the other print media are concerned, Philip Pangalos works for *The Times*, Helena Smith for *The Guardian*, Niki Kitsantonis for *The New York Times*, Allain Salles for *Le Monde*, Alexia Kefalas for *Le Figaro*, Michael Martens[3] for *Frankfurter Allgemeine Zeitung* and Kai Strittmatter and Christiane Schlötzer for *Süddeutsche Zeitung*.[4]

Newspapers which do not have permanent correspondents in Greece do often send their foreign editors into the country on an ad hoc basis. Journalist of *Bild* Paul Ronzheimer, for instance, regularly travels to Athens in order to cover developments. For its part, *Il Corriere della Sera* sent journalist Benedetta Argentieri to Greece before Christmas of 2011 in order to report if people were not celebrating because of austerity measures. It also noteworthy that *Handelsblatt*

---

1 Mr Dimitri Kontoyannis also co-operates with *Financial Times*.
2 Dr Nick Skrekas co-operated with *The Wall Street Journal* in the first months of the Greek crisis.
3 Mr Michael Martens is based in Istanbul and also covers developments in Turkey along with Greece.
4 Mr Kai Strittmatter also covered developments in Turkey before moving to China.

sent a group of 20 journalists to the country in October 2011 in order to complement the work of correspondent Gerd Höhler and closely monitor the Greek crisis.

Journalists dealing with the Greek crisis have been particularly busy on days of demonstrations and strikes. Examples include the tragic events of May 2010, when three people died in the centre of Athens. They also include violent clashes in June 2011 on the occasion of a crucial voting procedure in the Hellenic Parliament to pass the Medium Term Fiscal Strategy Plan. Nevertheless, the juncture when Greece attracted the highest attention was after former Prime Minister George Papandreou decided to call a referendum, shaking the world economy.

The case of the Greek crisis confirms that international politics are normally covered by foreign editors and correspondents. The main difference here, however, is that the role of additional journalists and columnists becomes important. Specifically, a significant number of stories were written by journalists not particularly familiar with the matter. In parallel with this, various comments were published by scholars who are experts in politics as well as in economics and they attempted to explain the Greek problem and suggest possible remedies.

A Timeline of Coverage

The coverage of the Greek crisis by international media is an ongoing process. Nevertheless, there are eight different phases which can better mirror its pattern up to September 2012. The first one starts in October 2009 and ends in mid-January 2010. In this period, foreign journalists approached the economic problem of the country for the first time. They attempted to realise its importance and provided various figures on the budget deficit and future prospects for recovery. Nonetheless, a potential bailout of the Hellenic Republic rarely became part of the media agenda. All in all, this phase can be considered as the initial contact of foreign journalists with the Greek reality.

The second stage includes the period from mid-January 2010 until mid-May 2010. This is a critical one because it is synthesised the way the EU had to deal with the Greek problem. Although in the previous months the media had not largely discussed this perspective, they changed their stance and proceeded to continuously elaborate on it. At the beginning, the main question they asked was whether Brussels had to save Greece, but this question was soon transformed into 'how' the financial assistance had to be provided. A potential involvement of the IMF was the main issue the international media concentrated on.

The third phase starts in mid-May 2010 and ends in mid-November 2011. After the Memorandum of Understanding was signed, foreign journalists discussed the efforts of the Hellenic Republic in applying the austerity measures and implementing the necessary reforms. Their interest in the country was relatively limited compared to previous months. That is because the Greek Government had started its fiscal consolidation attempt in a promising way. It was thus demonstrating

– at least theoretically – a strong political will to keep its promises and respect the international agreement it had signed with its creditors in May 2010.

The fourth period refers to the coverage of the Greek crisis from mid-November 2011 until the end of July 2011. As opposed to their stance in previous months, foreign journalists realised that the performance of the Hellenic Republic had not been quite to the standard set by the so-called Troika. Therefore, they criticised the government for its delays in implementing reforms and put forward the question whether the first Memorandum of Understanding was sufficient for the economic needs of the country. The grace period for Greece seemed to have already expired and the possibility of a debt-restructuring gained ground in addition to the emphasis for the need for further austerity measures.

The fifth stage is of shorter duration. It includes the three months from between the European Summit of 21 July and the EU Council of 26–27 October 2011. The international media expressed their doubt on the efficiency of the haircut of 21 per cent as was agreed on 21 July. They thus explained that a more drastic debt restructuring might be required. In parallel with this, foreign journalists criticised once again the Hellenic Republic for delays in applying austerity measures and carrying out reforms and for its decision to oust the Troika from the country at the beginning of September.

The sixth phase started at the end of October 2011 and concluded in March 2012. Its highlight was Mr Papandreou's decision to call a referendum, thus shaking the world economy. In this period, the international media covered the formation of a new unity government in the Hellenic Republic and deliberated over whether it could finally restore the credibility of the country. The media agenda was also dominated by international negotiations on the private second involvement and the successful exchange of Greek bonds on the basis of the 53.5 per cent haircut on the name value agreed on 13 February 2012. These negotiations were successfully concluded on March 2012. This result, however, was not sufficient to calm concerns.

The seventh period included the coverage of both elections which took place in the country, on 6 May and 17 June 2012. It lasted approximately three months, from the end of March until the end of June, and mainly focused on the climate of political uncertainty prevailing in the Greek society and Europe. Journalists did develop various scenarios as to the consequences of a potential 'Grexit' and published many stories on the leftist SYRIZA party and the reliability of its economic policy. Finally, the eighth stage started after the formation of a coalition government in the Hellenic Republic and is currently in progress. The tinge of the coverage will depend on the extent to which new austerity measures will impact on Greek society as well as on Europe's decisiveness to act united in enforcing stronger economic governance.

Greece and the PIIGS

All international newspapers paid particular attention to Greece in 2010 and 2011. The significant increase in the volume of articles in these two years in relation to previous ones suggests that they extensively dealt with the Hellenic crisis. Important as it is, however, the economic problem of the country is not the only one in the common currency area. A small group of five countries – the so called 'PIIGS' – have put into question the existence of the eurozone because of their poor economic performance. Therefore, a fair analysis of the coverage requires a comparison of the interest paid by the media on the other problematic countries, mainly Ireland and Portugal.

There is an important common denominator which links the Greek case to the Irish and Portuguese ones. Both Ireland and Portugal are small European states which asked for the activation of the bailout mechanism, being unable to borrow from international markets. Therefore, it could be expected that the media would show similar attention towards these countries.[5] Nonetheless, the data in Figure 4.4 suggests that their interest was significantly lower, with the exception of the British press and Ireland.[6]

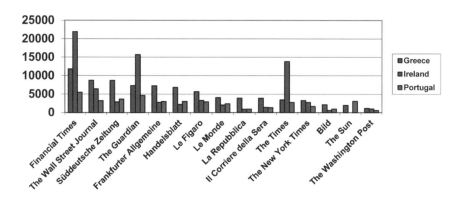

Figure 4.4   Volume of articles on Greece, Ireland and Portugal published by each title for both 2010 until 2011 (in total)

---

5 Names used in search engines were: 'Irlande' (French), Irland (German), Irlanda and Portogallo (Italian).

6 In the case of Ireland, British newspapers are excluded from the analysis due to cultural, geographical and historical reasons. *The Sun*, for example, published over 125,000 articles in 2010 and 2011. The *Financial Times* (21,945), the *Guardian* (15,658) and *The Times* (13,793) published much less articles on the country but still much more than on Greece and Portugal. If these results were included in the bar chart, conclusions reached might be distorted because of the expectable 'bias' of the British titles towards Ireland.

The special interest of the British media is obviously related to cultural, geographical and historical reasons and therefore it cannot distort the general conclusion about attention paid to Greece.

With the exception of the British newspapers, almost all other titles concentrated more on Greece than on Portugal and Ireland. The only exception comes from the *The Sun* which published a higher number of articles on Portugal. This result can be attributed to the tendency of the British tabloid to closely follow the personal achievements and private lives of two Portuguese stars with a remarkable career in English football: manager José Mourinho and striker Christiano Ronaldo. Indeed, 2,880 out of its 3,802 articles on Portugal contain the name of either the first or the second. The exception of *The Sun*, however, does not influence the general trend of the media. As a summary, Figure 4.5 outlines the volume of articles published by all newspapers on the three problematic countries.[7]

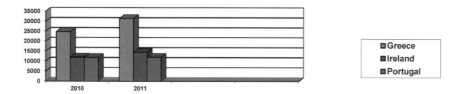

Figure 4.5 Volume of articles on Greece, Ireland and Portugal published by all titles for 2010 and 2011 together (British newspapers excluded)

In parallel with Portugal and Ireland, Italy and Spain also belong to the problematic eurozone states, being members of the PIIGS team. Their case, however, is rather different for three main reasons. First, Italy and Spain did not ask for European economic assistance because they were able to cover their financial needs by accessing international capital markets in 2010 and 2011. Second, their GDP is much higher compared to that of smaller countries like Greece, Portugal and Ireland and therefore their role in the eurozone is particularly important. And third, they constitute elite nations being continuously present in the international arena, have large populations and show a significant record in areas such as culture and sports.

A quantitative comparison of the interest shown by the media in Greece, Italy and Spain seems a risky decision. As opposed to Portugal and Ireland, Italy and Spain do routinely receive high international attention. In the case of Italy, for example, foreign journalists often deal with the country, covering and commenting on the erotic adventures of its former Prime Minister Silvio Berlusconi. Likewise,

---

7   Here, British newspapers are again excluded to make the analysis doable.

for Spain, foreign journalists regularly report on its regional problems as well on the performance of its national football team and clubs such as Real Madrid FC and Barcelona FC, which have admirers and supporters worldwide. To sum up, there are numerous reasons explaining the media interest in Italy and Spain which go far beyond the economic crisis itself.

Acknowledging the special features of Italy and Spain, economic newspapers can offer a useful tool for analysis. In particular, the *Financial Times*, *Handelsblatt* and *The Wall Street Journal* principally cover financial issues and hence their attention towards specific countries in 2010 and 2011 can be largely placed within their interest in the European debt crisis. The bar chart of Figure 4.6 depicts the volume of articles published on all PIIGS by these newspapers from the beginning of 2010 until the end of 2011.[8]

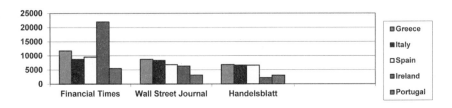

Figure 4.6 Volume of articles on Greece, Italy and Spain published by the economic newspapers for 2010 and 2011 together

Acknowledging the expectable exception of the *Financial Times*, the data suggests that the economic titles concentrated more on the Hellenic Republic, not only in comparison to Portugal and Ireland but also to Italy and Spain. Although the difference in the volume of articles in the latter case is relatively limited, especially for the coverage of *Handelsblatt*, this finding is also indicative of the tendency of the newspapers to largely focus on the Greek problem in 2010 and 2011.

Emphasis on the Greek Case

The European debt crisis is an issue of particular interest for the media. Starting in the last months of 2009 and continuing in the following years, they have attempted to investigate the roots and special features of this crisis by analysing – inter alia – the most problematic countries in the eurozone: Portugal, Ireland, Italy, Spain

---

8   In the German newspaper *Handelsblatt*, the names 'Italien' and 'Spanien' were used in the electronic search engine. Furthermore, the *Financial Times* is excluded from the analysis of the Irish case. As footnote 5 also mentioned, the numbers of articles published by the British economic newspaper containing the name Ireland was 21,945.

and Greece. As a result, a new trend in international journalism seems to have emerged. Covering the new, multidimensional economic war, journalists have shown a high interest in exploring current affairs in vulnerable eurozone countries, dealing not only with economic and political issues but also with the everyday lives of ordinary citizens. Their work has elements of a brief, modern history of the PIIGS, mirroring and analysing developments on a continual basis.

Greece has the lion's share in the media discussion on the PIIGS. Without ignoring other states of the European periphery – mainly Italy and Spain – journalists have emphasised the Hellenic case. Their tendency to largely focus on this specific country is confirmed by the data which compares the attention paid to other problematic countries of the eurozone by the media. It is also outlined by the significant increase in articles containing the name 'Greece' in 2010 and 2011 in relation to previous years.

All in all, the international media have demonstrated a preference for covering developments in the Hellenic Republic within the context of the European debt crisis. This raises questions as to the reasons foreign journalists emphasised the Greek cause. What have they found particularly interesting in this specific case? And how did they interpret the effort of the government of the country to adapt austerity measures and their impact on citizens? The next crucial step is to analyse the qualitative nature of articles published in order to sketch out how the name 'Greece' was constructed in the media discourse during the current economic war.

Chapter 5
Poleconomics in Unreliability

The economic problem of Greece was not suddenly created in the aftermath of the national election of 4 October 2009. It had been an existing one which was deepening over the years but only came to surface with the outbreak of the world financial crisis. The Greek statistic agency, for instance, was continuously publishing wrong data for the course of the economy. We only learned in October 2011 that the national economy had started to contract from 2008 onwards. Data presented earlier had suggested that it was growing normally in this year, thus creating a false image of its real performance. Media reports published before October 2009 had not extensively dealt with the economic status of the Hellenic Republic. Although references to it had been made by journalists, especially in *Financial Times*, *The Wall Street Journal* and *Handelsblatt*, the country had not been stigmatised. In general terms, it had been regarded as a normal peripheral state, suffering from widely known problems hitting countries such as Ireland, Italy, Portugal and Spain. However, Greece had not been considered as a special case within the common currency area.

The acknowledgment of some economic difficulties along with the coverage of a few catastrophic events, for example the wildfires of August 2007, had partly influenced the image of Greece in international newspapers. Nevertheless, stories published had not dominated the agenda and had not been reported on a continuous or frequent basis. At the same time, the country had preserved its traditional label as the cradle of democracy and a beautiful place for holidays in the media discourse. In a remarkable article published by *The New York Times* in May 2007, for instance, Athens was considered as a 'city reinventing itself where antiquity meets edginess'.[1] How did all this change in a period of only two years? The coverage of economics and politics in the Hellenic Republic after the outbreak of the crisis gives an initial but convincing response.

It's the Economy

The Greek crisis principally derives from the serious financial problem the country is encountering. It has therefore been expected that international media would cover in detail developments concerning the economy. Their main job has been to report the news. In so doing, they paid attention to several summits and meetings on the matter which took place in various cities such as Athens, Berlin, Brussels,

---

1   J. Kakissis. 2007. 36 hours in Athens, Greece. *The New York Times* [4 May]. Available at: http://travel.nytimes.com/2008/05/04/travel/04hours.html [accessed September 2012].

Cannes, Paris and Washington. They also dealt with statements issued by Greek and European authorities, the IMF and rating agencies, namely Fitch, Moody's and Standards & Poor's, and conducted interviews with investors and scholars familiar with the European debt crisis. Journalists have mainly focused on issues such as the budget hole and the current account deficit, the high public debt, the lack of competitiveness, the huge public sector and the status of the recession.

The Hellenic Republic has been portrayed as a bankrupt country[2] and one which consumes more than it spends.[3] A plethora of different expressions have been used in the media discourse to mirror the problem. *The Times*, for example, reported a 'parasite economy'[4] and *The Sun* of chaos in 'debt-drenched Greece',[5] associating the country with the adjectives: 'insolvent, bust and kaput'.[6] *Frankfurter Allgemeine Zeitung* considered it a 'Greek nightmare'[7] and *La Repubblica* a 'Greek tragedy'.[8] The problematic status of the economy has often become a recurrent feature in the coverage. There were cases in the coverage where journalists took it for granted, even in articles exploring different themes: *The Wall Street Journal*, for instance, published a piece on 31 December 2010 which mentioned that Greece was on the brink of a fiscal catastrophe in an article about Portuguese novelist José Saramago.[9]

The Metastasis Effect

National Sensitivities

All newspapers have agreed on the unacceptable status of the Greek economy. In so doing, they started to concentrate on its impact and principally on the danger for the

---

2   See for example: *The Wall Street Journal*. 2010. The Greek Economy Explained [7 May]. Available at: http://online.wsj.com/article/SB10001424052748703961104575226651125226596.html [accessed April 2011].

3   See for example: F. Van de Velde. 2010. Quelle dette Grecque. *Le Monde* [6 May]. Available at: http://www.lemonde.fr/idees/article/2010/05/06/quelle-dette-grecque-par-franck-van-de-velde_1347660_3232.html [accessed April 2011].

4   B. Maddox. 2010. Parasite economy lies behind Greek financial tragedy. *The Times* [6 January]. Available at: http://www.thetimes.co.uk/tto/opinion/columnists/bronwenmaddox/article2052930.ece [accessed January 2012].

5   S. Hawkes. 2011. The UK never joined the euro. You're in control. It's fantastic. *The Sun*, 2 July, 18,19.

6   S. Hawkes. 2011. Acropolis now. *The Sun*, 28 June, 46.

7   H. Steltzner.2010. Ein Griechischer Albtraum. *Frankfurter Allgemeine Zeitung* [24 April]. Available at: http://www.faz.net/aktuell/wirtschaft/europas-schuldenkrise/finanzhilfen-der-eu-ein-griechischer-albtraum-1574875.html [accessed January 2011].

8   R. Niri. 2011. Economia, una tragedia greca, la crisi has cambiato il mondo. *La Repubblica* [11 December]. Available at: http://ricerca.repubblica.it/repubblica/archivio/repubblica/2011/12/11/economia-una-tragedia-greca-la-crisi-ha.html [accessed January 2012].

9   J.S. Marcus. 2010. In Lisbon Writers Dies but Art Lives on. *The Wall Street Journal* [13 December]. http://online.wsj.com/article/SB100014240527487042784045760378815064 25842.html?KEYWORDS=Greece [accessed April 2011].

stability of the common currency and, further, the expansion of the Hellenic crisis on the eurozone and the world economy. The main term used in the media discourse to portray this potential contagion is 'domino'. *Handelsblatt*, for instance, published an article entitled: 'Experts fear a domino effect'.[10] For its part, *The Wall Street Journal* echoed the view of a contagion by publishing an article by MIT Professor Simon Johnson and Peter Boone from LSE and Salute Capital Management who commented: 'Financial markets are telling us the eurozone is under threat, but the real message is much broader: Unsustainable debt dynamics can undermine us all'.[11] Similar examples can be found in other newspapers as well.[12]

It is interesting that in the American, French and Italian print media, the coverage has reflected a slight fear that the Greek crisis might affect the national economies of their countries respectively and not only the body of the eurozone in general. In the case of France, for instance, Aurélien Véron, president of the Democratic Liberals, published a comment in *Le Monde* in which he argued that 'the challenge hitting Greece today can approach us tomorrow'.[13] *Le Monde* also published an article by Pierre Ecoiffier and Thanos Conthargis suggesting that the case of Greece was a necessary lesson.[14]

Expressing their concern for the possibility of a domino effect, some columnists have embarked on an attempt to show to readers that their economies were not

---

10 *Handelsblatt*. 2010. Experte fürchten Domino-Effekt [20 February]. Available at: http://www.handelsblatt.com/politik/international/experten-fuerchten-domino-effekt/3373726.html?p3373726=all [accessed November 2010].

11 S. Johnson and P. Boone. 2010. The Greek Tragedy that Changed Europe. *The Wall Street Journal* [13 February]. Available at: http://online.wsj.com/article/SB10001424052748703525704575061172926967984.html [accessed November 2010].

12 N. Dennis. 2010. Greek debt woes spread to Portugal and Spain. *Financial Times* [4 February]. Available at: [http://www.ft.com/intl/cms/s/0/953bfda8-117d-11df-9195-00144feab49a.html#axzz1k6mVMEQu [accessed November 2010] and B. Maddox. 2010. A Greek crisis may well become Germany's problem [18 January]. Available at: http://www.thetimes.co.uk/tto/opinion/columnists/bronwenmaddox/article2052937.ece [accessed November 2010]. For the French press, see: P. Rousselin. 2010. Grèce: Merkel et l'Effet Domino. *Le Figaro* [28 April]. Available at: http://www.lefigaro.fr/conjoncture/2010/04/28/04016-20100428ARTFIG00671-grece-merkel-et-l-effet-domino-.php [accessed November 2010] and A. De Tricornot and S. Dumoulin. 2010. Grèce: Le danger, c'est la contagion à l'ensemble de la zone euro. *Le Monde*. Available at: http://www.lemonde.fr/economie/article/2010/02/08/grece-le-danger-c-est-la-contagion-a-l-ensemble-de-la-zone-euro_1302840_3234.html [accessed November 2010]. For the Italian press see: M. Mucchetti. 2010. La Grecia e l'Europa a tre velocità. *Il Corriere della Sera* [28 April]. Available at: http://www.corriere.it/economia/10_aprile_28/grecia-europa-velocita-mucchetti_f08835c4-528b-11df-82ed-00144f02aabe.shtml [accessed November 2010].

13 V. Aurélien. 2010. Grèce: aide-toi, l'Europe t'aidera. *Le Monde* [5 March]. Available at: http://www.lemonde.fr/idees/article/2010/03/05/grece-aide-toi-l-europe-t-aidera-par-aurelien-veron_1314802_3232.html [accessed April 2011].

14 P. Ecoiffier and T. Conthargis. La Grèce nous donnera toujours des leçons essentielles. *Le Monde* [17 May]. Available at: http://www.lemonde.fr/idees/article/2011/05/17/la-grece-nous-donnera-toujours-des-lecons-essentielles_1523220_3232.html [accessed January 2011].

in as difficult a position as the Greek one and would thus be able to withstand the expansion of the crisis. In so doing, they have drawn comparisons with the Hellenic case. In *The Washington Post*, for instance, Fareed Zakaria explained that Greece had been different from the USA. He – inter alia – argued:

> We are not like Greece. Greece has a deficit that is 12 percent of its gross domestic product, with no prospect of economic growth that would reduce that deficit in the next few years. The US budget deficit is 10 per cent of GDP, but using reasonable assumptions made by Alan Auerbach and William Gale for the Brookings Institution, it will fall to less than 5 per cent in four years [...] Greek debt as a percentage of GDP is about 115 percent; U.S. debt is about 60 per cent of GDP.[15]

For its part, *Le Figaro* took a clear position on the matter by publishing a piece entitled: 'France is not Greece or Ireland'.[16] Finally, *Il Corriere della Sera* and *La Repubblica* have also 'protected' their country. While the first explained that Rome – as opposed to Athens – had benefited through privatisation,[17] the second emphatically rejected any comparison, asserting that Italy had not been like Greece.[18]

Additionally, the exposure of world banks to the Greek debt has been widely discussed, especially by economic newspapers. *The Wall Street Journal*, for instance, had put into question whether the French and German banking system could withstand a Greek default.[19] The *Financial Times*, for its part, was continuously observing market reactions to the Greek debt crisis and – inter alia – published an interesting article in July 2011 suggesting that funds had cut their investments in the euroarea as a preventive economic choice to avoid deeper losses in the future.[20] Two months later, the same newspaper explained that German

---

15 F. Zakaria. 2010. America is no Greece – for now. *The Washington Post* [24 May]. Available at: http://www.washingtonpost.com/wp-dyn/content/article/2010/05/23/AR2010052303824.html [accessed January 2012].

16 A. Bouilhet. 2010. La France n'est pas la Grèce ou l'Irlande. *Le Figaro Magazine*, 29 November, 25.

17 M. Muccheti, 2010. La Grecia e l'Europa a tre velocità. *Il Corriere Della Sera* [28 Apil]. Available at: http://www.corriere.it/economia/10_aprile_28/grecia-europa-velocita-mucchetti_f08835c4-528b-11df-82ed-00144f02aabe.shtml [accessed November 2010].

18 R. Amato. 2011. La crisi ha distrutto il welfare e i diritti Società disgregata, disuguaglianze record. *La Repubblica* [7 June]. Available at: http://www.repubblica.it/economia/2011/06/07/news/rapporto_sui_diritti_globali_2011-17353030/ [accessed November 2011].

19 V. Fuhrmans and S. Moffet. 2010. Exposure to Greece weighs on French, German banks. *The Wall Street Journal* [17 February]. Available at: http://online.wsj.com/article/SB10001424052748703798904575069712153415820.html [accessed December 2010].

20 D. McCrum and P. Jenkins. 2011. Money market funds cut euro bank exposure. *Financial Times* [24 July]. Available at: http://www.ft.com/intl/cms/s/0/1cda4056-b495-11e0-a21d-00144feabdc0.html#axzz1oEERGUZP [accessed August 2011].

banks would not experience insuperable problems in the case of a deeper haircut.[21] By contrast, French banks would suffer more losses.[22]

European newspapers have certainly shown a national interest in the coverage of the impact of the Greek crisis on the banking sector. *Frankfurter Allgemeine Zeitung*, for instance, concentrated on Hypo Real Estate, Eurohypo and Postbank.[23] *Le Figaro* published a highly analytical article on the issue, emphasising such corporations as BNP Paribas, Société Général and Crédit Agricole,[24] while *Le Monde* also shared this concern in a similar piece.[25] British and Italian newspapers, however, discussed the problem to a lower degree because their banks had not been largely exposed. According to a report by *The Guardian* in April 2010, the UK's banks accounted only for 3 per cent of the exposure to Greek bonds.[26] For its part, *Il Corriere della Sera* anticipated a limited loss for Italian banks as opposed to French ones.[27] All in all, however, the problem has been a global one. As *The New York Times* successfully commented, 'it's all connected'.[28] The metastasis effect would seriously hit bondholders holding European debt, and principally that of problematic countries, with Spain and Italy having the lion's share.

International newspapers have also demonstrated national sensitivities concerning who would pay for the Greek bailout. For the *Wall Street Journal*,

---

21   C. Bryant. 2011. German banks can stomach Greek debt. *Financial Times* [29 September]. Available at: http://www.ft.com/intl/cms/s/0/7cbdc3f4-e9f0-11e0-b997-00144feab49a.html#axzz1oEERGUZP [accessed December 2011].

22   D. Enrich and V. Gauthier. 2011. Struggling French banks fought to avoid oversight. *The Wall Street Journal* [21 October]. Available at: http://online.wsj.com/article/SB10001424052970204485304576641561540266494.html [accessed November 2011].

23   C. Siedenbiedel. 2010. Warum Darf Griechenland Nicht Pleitegehen. *Frankfurter Allgemeine Zeitung* [28 April]. Available at: http://www.faz.net/s/Rub3ADB8A210E754E748F42960CC7349BDF/Doc~ECB2665B27C654CD5AE7456EB8AC181FE~ATpl~Ecommon~Scontent.html, [accessed April 2011].

24   G. Errard. 2010. Les banques françaises très Exposées à la dette grecque', *Le Figaro* [11 May]. Available at: http://www.lefigaro.fr/societes/2010/05/06/04015-20100506ARTFIG00561-l-exposition-des-banques-francaises-a-la-dette-grecque.php [accessed November 2010].

25   *Le Monde*. 2010. 'L' exposition des banques françaises à la Grèce ne susciterait pas d'inquiétude particulière' [9 April]. Available at: http://www.lemonde.fr/economie/article/2010/04/09/l-exposition-des-banques-francaises-a-la-grece-ne-susciterait-pas-d-inquietude-particuliere_1331170_3234.html [accessed November 2010].

26   J. Treanor. 2010 Eurozone turmoil: British banks sitting on £100bn exposure to toxic euro debt. *The Guardian*, 29 April, Financial pages, 28.

27   M. Mucchetti. 2011. Banche, il conto della crisi è di 13 miliardi. *Il Corriere della Sera* [26 September]. Available at: http://www.corriere.it/economia/corriereconomia/11_settembre_26/mucchetti-banche-conto-crisi-miliardi_1ca7b5d2-e83e-11e0-9000-0da152a6f157.shtml [accessed November 2011].

28   B. Marsh. 2011. It's all connected: An overview of the euro crisis. *The New York Times* [22 October]. Available at: http://www.nytimes.com/interactive/2011/10/23/sunday-review/an-overview-of-the-euro-crisis.html [accessed November 2011].

the main issue was whether the USA would have to participate in the package, but the newspaper estimated that this participation would be relatively modest.[29] Moreover, European titles explored to what extent their taxpayers would have to share the burden of rescuing the Hellenic Republic.[30] In this case, the contribution of Berlin has been the most interesting affair because German newspapers and mainly *Bild* have raised serious concerns.[31] The tabloid, for instance, conducted an interview with a taxpayer who – seeing the Greek crisis unfolding – was not prepared to pay a cent for Greece and expressed his frustration.[32]

The anger of German taxpayers was discussed in other international newspapers as well. *The Guardian*, for instance, referred to the coverage of *Bild* and asserted:

> German taxpayers are still smarting from the multibillion-euro Greek bailout in May, which led to ugly headlines in the mass-market *Bild* about excessively profligate Greeks and how frustrated Germans were cancelling their holidays to Crete in protest at having to pay for their fellow Europeans' unchecked excesses.[33]

In a similar case, Clemens Wergin, foreign editor of *Die Welt*, prepared an editorial for *The Times*, not in his professional capacity but only as a simple German taxpayer.[34] In his piece he explained that German taxpayers had felt 'bad about Europe' and for the inability of the Hellenic Government to save itself and the country. To show that he was not biased against Greece, Mr Wergin he explained that his cousin had been married to a Greek. Finally, German people have been frustrated vis-à-vis Greece not only as taxpayers but also as small bondholders. In a dramatic article, a journalist of *Frankfurter Allgemeine Zeitung* – who had bought

---

29   B. Davis. 2010. Who is on the Hook for the IMF's Greek Bailout? *The Wall Street Journal* [5 May]. Available at: http://online.wsj.com/article/SB10001424052748704866204575224421086866944.html [accessed November 2010].

30   See for example: *Frankfurter Allgemeine Zeitung*. 2010. Höhe der Griechenland für Griechenland noch offen, 29 April and *Süddeutsche Zeitung*. 2010. Nicht Hinnehmbar, 12 April. Also: C. Calla. 2010. L'aide à la Grèce anime le débat politique en Allemagne *Le Monde*, 14 March, 8.

31   *Bild*. 2010. Haben wir jetzt ruhe vor den Pleiten-Griechen? [26 March]. Available at: http://www.bild.de/politik/2010/gipfel/eu-gipfel-bruessel-aufatmen-in-athen-11986622.bild.html [accessed January 2011].

32   *Bild*. 2011. Ich zahle keinen Cent für Pleite-Griechen Griechen! [22 September]. Available at: http://www.bild.de/politik/inland/euro-krise/steuerrebell-kein-cent-fuer-griechenland-20090790.bild.html [accessed November 2011].

33   K. Connolly. 2010. Ordinary Germans balk at second euro bailout. *The Guardian* [16 November]. Available at: http://www.guardian.co.uk/business/2010/nov/16/germany-balks-at-ireland-bailout [accessed December 2011].

34   C. Wergin. 2011. Why should tax-paying Germans bailout tax-dodging Greeks? *The Times* [16 September]. Available at: http://www.thetimes.co.uk/tto/opinion/thunderer/article3165811.ece [accessed January 2011].

bonds of the Hellenic Republic – expressed his anger for the haircut decision and insisted he would not be prepared to save the country again.[35]

Last but not least, the Greek crisis was perceived as challenging the policy of the European Central Bank. The *Financial Times*, for instance, analysed the important dilemma it had faced: either to support Greece at the cost of its own credibility or to pitch the euro into additional turmoil.[36] Although a problematic country like the Hellenic Republic should, in theory, be left to its own fate having violated all obligatory rules, such a decision might lead it to collapse. Therefore, the ECB had no other practical choice but to take immediate action by supplying liquidity.

Analysing the Crisis

Using False Statistics and Wasting Money

Portraying Greece as a country with an almost dead economy, foreign journalists became interested in investigating why it approached the brink of collapse and default. The unreliability of statistics has naturally attracted their attention. *The New York Times*, for instance, published a story on former head of the Greek statistics agency in which the following stereotype was reproduced: 'There are lies, damned lies and Greek statistics'.[37] In the view of the international media, the presentation of wrong data from the Hellenic Republic has been a significant cause of the problem, not only for the country itself but also for the eurozone. *Frankfurter Allgemeine Zeitung*, which investigated various lies of Greek politicians historically, did not hesitate to comment on an image of the Bank of Greece, 'that it only opened the door for the euro via wrong data'.[38]

The unreliability of Greek statistics has been perceived as a technique used by politicians of the country to hide the real expenses of the state. This said, international media have gone further as they have attempted to investigate the roots of the modern Hellenic drama by concentrating on overspending. *Le Figaro*, for instance, portrayed epigrammatically the problem, insisting on a Greek tendency 'of catastrophic and

---

35 P. Bernau. 2011. Ich rette die Griechen nicht! *Frankfurter Allgemeine Zeitung* [29 October]. Available at: http://www.faz.net/aktuell/finanzen/staatsanleihen-ich-rette-die-griechen-nicht-11510478.html [accessed November 2011].
36 R. Atkins. 2011. Frankfurt's dilemma. *Financial Times*, 25 May, 9.
37 D. Bilefsky and N. Kitsantonis. 2010. Statistician rejects blame for Greece's financial turmoil. Available at: http://query.nytimes.com/gst/fullpage.html?res=9C02E1D91F30F930A25751C0A9669D8B63&scp=2&sq=greek+statistics+%2B+lies&st=nyt, 13 February [accessed December 2011].
38 W. Mussler. 2010. Schwere Fehler in der griechischen Statistik. Frankfurter Allgemeine Zeitung [12 January]. Available at: http://www.faz.net/aktuell/wirtschaft/europas-schuldenkrise/staatsdefizit-schwere-fehler-in-der-griechischen-statistik-1908399.html[accessed November 2010].

even deceiving management of public expenses'.³⁹ The same newspaper has also elaborated on the Greek military budget, one of the larger budgets in the European Union, explaining that the crisis might be an opportunity for the Hellenic Republic not only to reduce it but also improve its relations with Turkey.⁴⁰

For its part, *The Times* has been more specific and focused on two particular cases: the Athens Olympic Games of 2004 and the purchase of swine flu batches in 2009. The newspaper interviewed a former Greek official who, remaining anonymous, argued that hosting the Games 'cost Greece more than 12 billion pounds, double what it would have been without money flying this way, that way and often under the table'. As far as the swine flu vaccination is concerned, the same official explained that the new health minister appointed after the October 2009 national election [Ms Marilisa Xenogianagopoulou] had to cancel unnecessary doses ordered by her predecessor [Mr Dimitrios Avramopoulos] and commented: 'It's a terrible waste of money' and 'this happens all the time as this is the Greek reality'.⁴¹

Dealing with overspending, foreign journalists have, moreover, dealt with the large public sector in the country and its cost for the state. *The New York Times* echoed the problem by asserting:

> Stories of eye-popping waste and abuse of power among Greece 'bureaucrats are legion, including officials who hire their wives, and managers who submit $38,000 bills for office curtains. The work force in Greece's Parliament is so bloated [...] that some employees do not even bother to come to work because there are not enough places for all of them to sit.⁴²

Defying as well as ignoring the danger of over-borrowing, the Hellenic Republic has also offered no-show jobs in the public sector for privileged groups of the population. Athletes have constituted such a category.⁴³ Additionally, it granted generous pensions for many years. Reflecting the German anger on the matter, *Bild* published a table comparing the privileges of Greek pensioners as opposed to German ones.⁴⁴

---

39   A. Cheyvialle. 2010 Un plan douloureux et à risques pour l'"économie grecque. *Le Figaro*, 4 May, 22.

40   C. Lacombe. 2010. Entretien; La Grèce est obligée de diminuer ses dépenses militaries. *Le Figaro*, 15 May, 5.

41   M. Campbell. 2009. Party's over for Greek gaspers. *The Sunday Times*. Available at: http://www.thesundaytimes.co.uk/sto/news/world_news/article193206.ece [accessed December 2011].

42   S. Daley. 2011. Bureaucracy in Greece defies efforts to cut it. *The New York Times* [17 October]. Available at: http://www.nytimes.com/2011/10/18/world/europe/greeces-bloated-bureaucracy-defies-efforts-to-cut-it.html?pagewanted=all [accessed January 2012].

43   J. Bones. 2011. Austerity in birthplace of Olympic forces athletes to choose between work and play. *The Times* [15 October]. Available at: http://www.thetimes.co.uk/tto/news/world/europe/article3195235.ece [accessed December 2011].

44   D. Hoeren and O. Santen. 2010. Warum Zahlen wir den Griechen ihre Luxus-Renten? *Bild* [27 April]. Available at: http://www.bild.de/politik/wirtschaft/griechenland/

In an additional striking example sketching out the tendency of statism and money wasting, *Handelsblatt* prepared a comprehensive video reportage in October 2011, explaining that various stadiums built for the Athens Olympic Games had been of no use at all. The conclusion of the German economic newspaper was that the Hellenic Republic had been unable to benefit from its public property, although it had spent high amounts of public money to construct various buildings, houses and stadiums.[45]

To sum up, the Hellenic Republic had not controlled its public finances benefitting from its participation in the common currency. Columnist Robert Samuelson explained in *The Washington Post* regarding the euro:

> For years, it enabled Greece to borrow at low interest rates, because the prevailing assumption was that the euro bloc wouldn't allow one of its members to default. It would be rescued by the others. These expectations constituted an implicit guarantee of the debt of Greece and other euro countries. If Greece defaulted, the guarantee would vanish and, possibly, trigger a flight from other countries' debt.[46]

This example by the American newspaper denotes that international media had acknowledged the responsibility of markets as well as of the eurozone itself for the outbreak of the crisis. Such an acknowledgment, however, does not entail they have endeavoured to justify Greek policy failure in the years before its bubble exploded. They have had rather been interested in paying attention to the general context.

Political Personnel

Interwoven into economics as a significant factor which has explained the Greek crisis in the media coverage has been domestic politics. Foreign journalists have had the opportunity to deal with the Hellenic political system and understand how Greek politicians work. In so doing, they have been struck by nepotism. Only one day after the national election of 2009, *Süddeutsche Zeitung* considered Mr Papandreou a member of a dynasty governing the country for approximately 50 years.[47] The idea that nepotism is a basic element in the Greek political culture became pretty clear

---

wir-zahlen-luxus-rente-mit-milliarden-hilfe-12338430.bild.html [accessed January 2011].

45 *Handelsblat*. 2011. Griechenland: Verfallende Olympiastadien [25 October]. Available at: http://videokatalog.handelsblatt.com/Sport/video-Griechenland-Verfallende-Olympiastadien-Video-News-Sportst%C3%A4tten-Spiele-132587.html [accessed November 2011].

46 R. Samuelson. 2010. Greece and the welfare state in ruins. *The Washington Post* [22 February]. Available at: http://www.washingtonpost.com/wp-dyn/content/article/2010/02/21/AR2010022102914.html [accessed December 2011].

47 K. Strittmatter. 2009. Griechenland am Abgrund. *Süddeutsche Zeitung* [5 October]. Available at: http://www.sueddeutsche.de/politik/parlamentswahlen-griechenland-am-abgrund-1.25816 [accessed September 2010].

in an interview by *Le Figaro* with a Greek student: although only 21 years old, the student explained to correspondent Alexia Kefalas that he had had enough of seeing members of the same families as well as tycoons reigning the country.[48]

Nepotism itself would not have necessarily been a pathogeny if politicians in power, and especially prime ministers, had performed well. Regrettably, this was not the case for Greece. When former Prime Minister George Papandreou decided to quit in November 2011, Thomas Landon Jr commented in *The New York Times*:

> His commitment to step down as prime minister is not only a devastating blow to one of the more enduring political dynasties in Europe. It may also force a major overhaul of the old-style socialist PASOK party that was created by Mr. Papandreou's father and which served as a major roadblock to many of the younger Papandreou's proposed economic and political changes.[49]

The excerpt of the editorial by Thomas Landon Jr denotes that nepotism in Greece has been linked to statism and opposition to any kind of reform in the country. It thus correctly highlights that politicians themselves are the only ones responsible for the crisis. However, although in his piece the columnist acknowledges the difficulty in pursuing drastic changes, he unsuccessfully isolates George Papandreou from the problem. Mr Papandreou may have developed a nice rhetoric, supporting reforms during his term, but he rarely moved from words into action. His failure to do so can certainly be attributed to strong reaction from supporters of the old-style socialist PASOK, but it is rather ungrounded to believe he himself had not endorsed this ideology being prime minister.

Nepotism has not been the only aspect the international media have explored in their coverage of Greek politics. They have also concentrated on the lack of reliability of politicians. This unreliability has not only been related to statistics and numbers but also to their inability to catch fiscal targets and their indifference to keeping promises. The tendency of foreign journalists to distrust Greek politicians became crystal-clear in February 2010. At that time, in an article discussing the potential involvement of China in the European debt crisis, the *Financial Times* made a suggestion about the then prime minister (in bold):

> To put it bluntly, few investors believe what Mr Papandreou has to say, either about the economy or the Chinese.[50]

---

48   A. Kefalas. 2011. Georges Papandréou joue son va-tout. *Le Figaro*, 17 June, 8.

49   T. Jr Landon. 2011. A Greek political scion undone by economics. *The New York Times* [7 November]. Available at: http://www.nytimes.com/2011/11/08/world/europe/prime-minister-george-papandreou-of-greece-undone-by-economics.html?_r=1 [accessed February 2012].

50   G. Tett. 2010. Bonds, Beijing and risk. *Financial Times* [10 February]. Available at: http://www.ft.com/intl/cms/s/0/f22721ea-1511-11df-ad58-00144feab49a.html#axzz1oEERGUZP [accessed November 2010].

Likewise, *Le Figaro* commented that the country 'was suffering from a real credibility deficit',[51] while *La Repubblica* echoed this view by seeing 'shadows in Greece's reliability'.[52] For its part, *Frankfurter Allgemeine Zeitung* explained that the default of the country had started with Mr Papandreou's promises in the pre-election campaign which were not followed by action but had served his need to become prime minister, attracting a sufficient number of votes in October 2009.[53]

A catalytic factor which has worsened Greece's credibility deficit in the perception of foreign journalists has been the inability of its politicians to co-operate. In their view it has been surprising that the Hellenic Parliament is so divided when voting for rescue packages for the country. When the attempt by Mr Papandreou and the main opposition leader Mr Antonis Samaras to build a national consensus collapsed in June 2011, the latter was strongly criticised. In the most remarkable example, *Süddeutsche Zeitung* portrayed him as a 'populist politician' whose decisions often reflected cynicism.[54] Other political leaders and political parties, mainly the ones of the left reacting to reforms, have been almost absent from the international media agenda

Shaking World Economy

Papandreou's Idea for a Referendum

The worst part in the drama of Greek unreliability was maybe played on 31 October 2011. On that day Mr Papandreou shocked his European partners as well as world leaders by announcing his decision for a referendum in the Hellenic Parliament. The referendum was to be related to the new rescue package decided only three days previously in Brussels, although the main question that would be asked was to remain unknown due to the referendum being cancelled. For approximately ten days, until the creation of a unity government, world attention turned towards domestic developments in the Hellenic Republic.

No one has yet successfully explained the decision by Mr Papandreou to announce a referendum. In theory, democracy can be enhanced when people vote. International media partly placed Mr Papandreou's idea within this context. Nevertheless, all

---

51 C. de Malet. 2010. Pour une agence européenne de la dette. *Le Figaro*, 11 February, 14.

52 F. Rampini. 2010. Wall Street ha aiutato Atene a truccare i conti pubblici. *La Repubblica* [15 February]. Available at: http://www.repubblica.it/economia/2010/02/15/news/rampini_grecia-2302829/ [accessed November 2010].

53 M. Amann. 2011. Postdemokrati.sch? *Frankfurter Allgemeine Zeitung* [6 November]. Available at: http://www.faz.net/aktuell/wirtschaft/europas-schuldenkrise/griechenland-postdemokratisch-11519476.html [accessed February 2011].

54 K. Strittmatter. 2011. Profiteur des Untergangs. *Süddeutsche Zeitung* [21 June]. Available at: http://www.sueddeutsche.de/politik/griechenlands-oppositionsfuehrer-samaras-profiteur-des-untergangs-1.1110743 [accessed November 2011].

newspapers did not hide their surprise and agreed that it had led to instability not only in the eurozone but also in the world economy. As *The Washington Post* mentioned, 'Europe's newly crafted plan to stem its debt crisis was in turmoil' after the decision for a referendum.[55] For its part, *The Sun* wrote on the day after:

> Greece was close to ruin last night after Premier George Papandreou lost his marbles and ordered a vote that could destroy the euro.[56]

In a similar example, a leading article in *The Times* entitled 'Athenian Democracy' asserted that Mr Papandreou's decision put the euro into danger and 'moved the eurozone beyond crisis and into chaos'.[57] Moreover, *Le Figaro* compared the political choice of the former Greek minister to a poker game[58] while *Le Monde* criticised him for playing with fire.[59] Furthermore, while the former considered him a 'non-gifted captain',[60] the latter wondered kind of fly Mr Papandreou was stung by![61] In additional examples of the way foreign journalists saw the referendum decision, *Il Corriere della Sera* perceived it 'a shocking announcement'[62] and *Handelsblatt* thought that the Hellenic Republic was risking its European participation in the common currency.[63]

The decision by Mr Papandreou to call a referendum was, finally, cancelled only three days after its announcement. His motivations remain unclear and only scenarios can be developed. In the final account, however, his idea was a wrong

---

55 H. Schneider and M. Birnbaum. 2011. Greek referendum calls upends euro-plans [2 November]. Available at: http://www.washingtonpost.com/business/economy/greek-referendum-call-upends-euro-plans/2011/11/01/gIQAxQGZdM_story.html [accessed January 2012].

56 S. Hawkes and N. Parker. 2011. Greece loses its marbles [2 November]. Available at: http://www.thesun.co.uk/sol/homepage/news/politics/3909249/Greece-loses-its-marbles.html [accessed January 2012].

57 T. Rice. 2011. Athenian Democracy [2 November]. Available at : http://www.thetimes.co.uk/tto/opinion/leaders/article3213531.ece [accessed January 2012].

58 G. De Capèle. 2011. Le dangereux poker grec. *Le Figaro*, 2 November, 2.

59 A. Lamassoure. 2011. M. Papandréou joue avec le feu! [3 November]. Available at: http://www.lemonde.fr/idees/article/2011/11/03/m-papandreou-joue-avec-le-feu_1598287_3232.html, [January 2011].

60 G. Renaud, 2011. Papandréou, un capitaine sans charisme. *Le Figaro*, 3 November, 16.

61 *Le Monde*. 2011. Editorial; La Grèce dans l'euro: la question se pose, 2 November, 1.

62 *Il Corriere della Sera.* 2011. Grecia: referendum sul piano degli aiuti fa scattare un vertice d'emergenza Ue [1 November]. Available at: http://www.corriere.it/economia/11_novembre_01/grecia-referendum-piano-aiuti_338fdca2-0468-11e1-89f9-a7d4dc298cd1.shtml [accessed December 2011].

63 *Handelsblatt.* 2011. Griechenland riskiert seine Euro-Mitgliedschaft [1 November]. Available at: http://www.handelsblatt.com/politik/international/geplantes-referendum-griechenland-riskiert-seine-euro-mitgliedschaft/5784286.html [accessed December 2011].

decision which was made at a wrong time. *The Washington Post* nicely refers to confusion, marking it:

> The Greek leader clearly mishandled his referendum call. Not only did he not tell Merkel and France's Nicolas Sarkozy, he did not even tell his own finance minister or allies at the International Monetary Fund that he was going to make the proposal. The referendum and Papandreou's hold on power, evaporated in the uproar from a public not ready to adopt austerity.[64]

Although the question to be asked was never clarified, *The Wall Street Journal* correctly commented that a referendum would lead anyway to an impasse. A 'yes' vote might deflate the massive street protests threatening to paralyse the country and a 'no' vote could bring down the government and cut off international funding.[65]

How Can Greece Make It?

International journalists have not only seen the Greek problem from the perspective of its roots, but from that of possible remedies. They have regarded it as a necessary pre-requisite for the Hellenic Republic to re-launch its national economy, implement reforms,[66] efficiently fight against tax-evasion and accelerate privatisations. The common denominator in the media discourse has been the consideration of the crisis as an opportunity for the country to modernise its economy, escape statism and rebuild the structure of public administration. Nevertheless, they also see this course as particularly hard and painful for the country. To illustrate the difficulty, the Greek words 'Odyssee' and 'marathon' have often been used in the analysis of this process.

Acknowledging the great danger stemming from the Greek crisis, the newspapers developed different economic theories on how the Hellenic Republic could be saved. The possibility for financial support came to the forefront in December 2009 onwards, especially in the first months of 2010. This theme led to a flourishing debate, especially in the German newspapers, as to whether the

---

64 J. Hoagland, 2011. We are all Greeks now – Hiding from tax truths. *The Washington Post* [10 November]. Available at: http://www.washingtonpost.com/opinions/we-are-all-greeks-now-hiding-from-tax-truths/2011/11/09/gIQADepS6M_story.html [accessed January 2012].

65 A. Granitsas, M. Walker and C. Paris. 2011. Greek vote threatens bailout. *The Wall Street Journal* [1 November]. Available at: http://online.wsj.com/article/SB10001424052970204394804577010091283798750.html [accessed December 2011].

66 An interesting article was published in the *Financial Times* by three Greek economists. See: C. Meghir, D. Vayanos and N. Vettas. 2010. Greek Reforms can yet stave off default. *Financial Times* [23 August]. Available at: http://www.ft.com/intl/cms/s/0/a39c6a50-aee8-11df-8e45-00144feabdc0.html#axzz1k0Won1bd [accessed April 2011].

EU had to save Greece. The only newspaper – as we will see – which completely opposed the decision of the Union to help Greece was *Bild*. With the exception of the German tabloid, articles clearly supporting the Greek bailout could be found in most other newspapers.

Starting with articles advocating the bailout idea first, an editorial from *The Times* published on 29 April 2010 considered this decision as difficult but essential.[67] Moreover, in January 2010, the *Financial Times* published a piece by the leading economist from the Centre for European Policy Reform, Simon Tilford, who concluded that the eurozone could not allow a Greek default. In particular, the columnist argued:

> If the eurozone fails to support Greece or makes the terms of any bailout politically impossible for the country's authorities to meet, Greece could default on its sovereign debt. The eurozone would then face a big problem.[68]

In a similar article, Tommaso Padoa Scioppa, at that time president of Notre Europe – before his unexpected death[69] – insisted that the eurozone could not leave Greece on its own.[70] For its part, *Handelsblatt* also echoed the view of the need for a Greek bailout[71] while *The Washington Post* was emphatic in an editorial by Robert Samuelson, asserting: 'We're all Greek now'.[72] In articles of similar content, *Frankfurter Allgemeine Zeitung* explained that 'if we do not help [Greece], the pressure by markets on the country will be heavier'.[73] For its part, *Süddeutsche Zeitung* was assertive in its approach advocating for a bailout in a

---

67 *The Times*. 2010. Greece is the Word: A debt crisis in Southern Europe threatens to spread financial contagion. 29 April, 2.

68 S. Tilford. 2010. Europe cannot afford to let Greece default. *Financial Times* [15 January]. Available at: http://www.ft.com/intl/cms/s/0/c5b67472-0174-11df-8c54-00144feabdc0.html#axzz1kH8dnNP2 [accessed January 2011].

69 Tommaso Padoa Schioppa passed away in Rome on 19 December 2010 at the age of 70.

70 T. Schioppa. 2010. Europe cannot leave Athens on its own. *Financial Times* [18 February]. Available at: http://www.ft.com/intl/cms/s/0/f1eef94a-1cc9-11df-8d8e-00144feab49a.html#axzz1kH8dnNP2 [accessed January 2011].

71 *Handelsblatt*. 2010. Griechenland Braucht Schnelle Hilfe [10 April]. Available at: http://www.handelsblatt.com/politik/international/griechenland-braucht-schnelle-hilfe/3408568.html?p3408568=1 [accessed January 2011]. See also: M. Maisch. 2010. Griechenland Braucht Ernsthafte Hilfe *Handelsblatt* [15 April]. Available at: http://www.handelsblatt.com/finanzen/boerse-maerkte/boerse-inside/griechenland-braucht-ernsthafte-hilfe/3412106.html [accessed January 2011].

72 R. Samuelson. 2010. We're all Greek now. *The Washington Post*, 22 February, A15.

73 B. Schulz. 2010. Griechenland Kämpft um Vertrauen. *Frankfurter Allgemeine Zeitung* [31 January]. Available at: http://www.faz.net/aktuell/wirtschaft/internationaler-finanzmarkt-griechenland-kaempft-um-vertrauen-1907934.html [accessed January 2011].

piece entitled: 'the Greek experiment'.⁷⁴ The same newspaper also encouraged European leaders to save the single currency and the eurozone.⁷⁵

In parallel with the aforementioned examples, Nicolas Bouzou supported European solidarity vis-à-vis Athens in an article he prepared for *Le Figaro*. In his piece he regarded the Greek crisis being at the same time a French one.⁷⁶ As far as *Le Monde* was concerned, the newspaper expressed its position by publishing an editorial entitled: 'Europe has no other choice: the Greek drama cannot end into a tragedy'.⁷⁷ Finally, Italian newspapers also expressed their sympathy towards Greece. On 18 February 2010, for example, Francesco Giavazzi urged the EU to show its solidarity by arguing: 'Do not play with Greece' in his column for *Il Corriere della Sera*.⁷⁸

As mentioned before, German newspapers, namely *Handelsblatt*, *Frankfurter Allgemeine Zeitung* and *Süddeutsche Zeitung*, followed a rather balanced approach concerning the Greek bail out. That is because they also published articles opposing this option. *Handelsblatt*, for example, gave floor to Chicago University Professor Harald Uhlig who insisted the Hellenic Republic had to make it alone.⁷⁹ Further, *Frankfurter Allgemeine Zeitung* expressed the view that Greece should not count on European support, even from December 2009.⁸⁰ In the same newspaper, a particular reference was additionally made to the German economist Joachim Starbatty who, along with his colleagues, planned a recourse to the Constitutional Court of Germany in case their country should participate in the bailout package. Their argument was that Greece would not be able to pay back the loans.⁸¹ Finally,

---

74   U. Schäfer. 2010. Das Griechische Experiment. *Süddeutsche Zeitung* [1 February]. Available at: http://archiv.sueddeutsche.de/sueddz/index.php [accessed January 2011].

75   *Süddeutsche Zeitung*. 2010. Dem Euro Retten, Europa Retten, 30 April.

76   N. Bouzou. 2010. La crise grecque est aussi française. *Le Figaro* [30 April]. Available at: http://www.lefigaro.fr/editos/2010/04/29/01031-20100429ARTFIG00629-la-crise-grecque-est-aussi-francaise-.php [accessed January 2011].

77   P. Briançon. 2010. L'Europe n'a pas le choix : le drame grec ne finira pas en tragédie. *Le Monde*, 1 February.

78   F. Giavazzi. 2010. Non scherzate con la Grecia. *Corriere della Sera* [18 February]. Available at: http://www.corriere.it/editoriali/10_febbraio_18/scherzare_grecia_01508468-1c56-11df-beab-00144f02aabe.shtml [accessed January 2011].

79   H Uhlig. 2010. Eine Griechische Tragödie. *Handelsblatt* [12 February]. Available at: http://blog.handelsblatt.com/oekonomie/2010/02/12/eine-griechische-tragodie/ [accessed January 2011].

80   W. Mussler. 2010. Griechenland muss sich selbst retten. *Frankfurter Allgemeine Zeitung* [11 December]. Available at: http://www.faz.net/s/Rub3ADB8A210E754E748F42960CC7349BDF/Doc~E7254A19463C54B7D895B9990C5046777~ATpl~Ecommon~Scontent.htm [accessed January 2011].

81   H. Steltzner. 2010. Griechen oder Mark. *Frankfurter Allgemeine Zeitung* [6 March]. Available at: http://www.faz.net/s/Rub3ADB8A210E754E748F42960CC7349BDF/Doc~E3E65E7BC0DE541D9969AD355852177BA~ATpl~Ecommon~Scontent.html [accessed January 2011].

Süddeutsche Zeitung opposed the will of the EU to assist the Hellenic Republic financially by publishing a piece entitled: 'Help? Rather, not!'.[82]

The coverage by *Bild* has to be examined separately from *Handelsblatt*, *Frankfurter Allgemeine Zeitung* and *Süddeutsche Zeitung* as it completely opposed the effort of the EU to help the Greek Government. On 10 February 2010, the German tabloid took a clear position by urging Berlin to forget the idea of assisting Athens.[83] Approximately two months later, on 26 April, its correspondent in Athens Paul Ronzheimer went even further by arguing that Greeks had not suffered from the crisis, and therefore they did not deserve to be rescued.[84] In this report the journalist visited such places as a casino venue and discovered that it had been crowded in spite of austerity measures. Although this analysis was not a deep one, it certainly sent a signal to readers of *Bild* that – in spite of the crisis – the party was going on in Greece. One year later, however, Mr. Ronzheimer – as we will see – would be one of the journalists who revealed the real, social dimension of the Greek crisis in the international media.

IMF or Europe?

An important parameter concerning the first Greek bailout package was the potential involvement of the IMF in the discussions. In the political arena, Germany was in favour and France against in the first months of 2010. The clash between Berlin and Paris was noted in the media coverage.[85] The coverage was, however, limited in news stories as many newspapers did not take a clear position on the issue. From those that took part in this debate, *The Wall Street Journal* and the German newspapers were in favour of an active IMF role, the *Financial Times* followed a balanced line while the French and Italian titles supported a European solution per se.

---

82   C. Gammelin, C, Hulverscheidt and S. Kornelius. 2010. Hilfe? Bloss nicht. *Süddeutsche Zeitung* [22 March]. Available at: http://www.sueddeutsche.de/geld/streit-um-griechland-hilfe-bloss-nicht-1.9595 [accessed January 2011].

83   *Bild*. 2010. Keine Finanzhilfe f'ür Griechenland [11 February 2010]. Available at: http://www.bild.de/politik/wirtschaft/griechenland/was-kostet-die-rettung-der-pleite-griechen-11433914.bild.html [accessed November 2010].

84   P. Ronzheimer. 2010. Krise? Welche Krise? *Bild* [26 April]. Available at: http://www.bild.de/politik/wirtschaft/pleite/machen-weiter-wie-bisher-von-krise-keine-spur-12327120.bild.html [accessed November 2010].

85   See for example: R. Berschens, T. Ludwig and M. Kurm-Engels. 2010. IWF-Hilfe für Griechenland spaltet EU und EZB [24 March]. Available at: http://www.handelsblatt.com/politik/international/iwf-hilfe-fuer-griechenland-spaltet-eu-und-ezb/3397592.html [accessed January 2011]. See also: S. Castle. 2010. IMF is more likely to lead efforts for aid to Greece. *The New York Times*, 30 March, Business/Financial Desk, 2.

To begin with, *The Wall Steer Journal* explained in its main article on 22 March 2010 that the German Chancellor had been 'right to resist an EU-led bailout'.[86] Furthermore, German economist Otmar Issing advocated an extended role of the IMF in *Frankfurter Allgemeine Zeitung*, saying that the only external solution would be the request to this Fund for help.[87] *Süddeutsche Zeitung* also agreed with the potential IMF involvement in the bailout. The excerpt from the article of Claus Hulverscheidt highlights the position of the German liberal newspaper:

> What can we do? The wiser way is to activate this institution which can provide a specific solution with payment problems: the International Monetary Fund (IMF). Many EU politicians oppose this idea, others because they are proud and others because they fear that the eurozone will show its weakness., if the support come externally. But would the reputation be larger? Larger than it is now? The IMF has not only an important experience in dealing with crisis but also the appropriate means to apply austerity measures as opposed to the European Commission.[88]

This article in *Süddeutsche Zeitung* also explained that the engagement of the IMF would not be new for Europe as it had already been involved with Hungary, Latvia and Romania.

Moving on to the relatively balanced stance of the *Financial Times*, the British newspaper published an article by Jean Pisani-Ferry and André Sapir from the Bruegel think-tank on 1 February 2010 supporting the need for Greece to call on the IMF.[89] The same title, however, gave floor in its comment pages to Alpha Bank Chief Economist Michael Massourakis, who explained that Greece and its European partners did not seek IMF involvement.[90] A piece with similar content was also written by Governor of the Bank of Greece, Georgios Provopoulos.[91]

---

86   *The Wall Street Journal*. 2010. Greece and the IMF [22 March]. http://online.wsj.com/article/SB10001424052748703775504575135793701057172.html [accessed February 2011].

87   O. Issing. 2010. Die Europäische Union Währungsunion am Scheidenweg. *Frankfurter Allgemeine Zeitung*, 29 January.

88   C. Hulverscheidt. 2010. Der Richtige Muss Helfen. *Süddeutsche Zeitung* [2 March]. Available at: http://archiv.sueddeutsche.de/sueddz/index.php?id=A46818504_EGTPOGWPOPPEPWGRAHOHSPR [accessed January 2011].

89   J. Pisani-Fery and A. Sapir. 2010. The best bourse for Greece is to call in the fund. *Financial Times* [1 February 2010]. Available at: http://www.ft.com/cms/s/0/01554c86-0f69-11df-a450-00144feabdc0.html#axzz1CoNW2LYD [accessed April 2011].

90   M. Massourakis. 2010. Privatisations offer Greece the best way to avoid a bailout. *Financial Times* [11 February]. Available at: http://cachef.ft.com/cms/s/0/816b0f86-173a-11df-94f6-00144feab49a.html#axzz1EUujJ2Dn [accessed January 2011].

91   G. Provopoulos. 2010. Greece will fix itself, from inside the eurozone. *Financial Times* [21 January]. Available at: http://www.ft.com/cms/s/0/018d0a1e-06cb-11df-b058-00144feabdc0.html#axzz1CoNW2LYD [accessed January 2011].

As far as French and Italian newspapers are concerned, the idea of IMF involvement was not desirable. In this case, *Le Figaro* and *Le Monde* revealed a slight anti-German tinge in their coverage or at least their frustration at Berlin's stance. Specifically, for *Le Figaro* the IMF involvement mirrored the policy of Germany to show that 'nothing in Europe can be done without this specific country'.[92] The editorial of *Le Monde* after the European Summit of 24–25 March 2010 was even more emphatic:

> Ms Merkel imposes her plan. In the case of financial difficulty the IMF will support Greece along with the European states. Who is to blame? First, Greece which is the 'enron' child[93] in the eurozone. And then, Germany as there was no real reason for the IMF participation except for domestic policy ones.[94]

Neither did *Il Corriere della Sera* support involvement from the IMF in the case of Greece.[95] This newspaper also reflected disappointment in Berlin's role as it criticised the German Chancellor Angela Merkel for her stance and urged for more efficient co-ordination from the EU.[96]

Predicting a Default

A Vicious Circle without Growth

The possibility of a sovereign default by the Hellenic Republic is an issue extensively discussed in the media discourse. Until Friday 9 March 2012, the day the swap of Greek bonds was officially declared a 'credit event' by ISDA (International Swaps and Derivatives Association), almost all international newspapers had expressed their distrust and believed Greece would arguably avoid bankruptcy. Even from the beginning of 2010, international newspapers, mainly the economic titles *Financial Times*, *Handelsblatt* and *The Wall Street Journal*, had started to elaborate on the view that the government of the country would not be able to make it and that its

---

92   J.J. Mevel. 2010. LEurope accouche d'un accord sur la Grèce. *Le Figaro* [26 March]. http://www.lefigaro.fr/conjoncture/2010/03/25/04016-20100325ARTFIG00734-grece-l-allemagne-impose-son-plan-.php [accessed January 2011].

93   This word refers to an economic scandal of an American company which defaulted in 2002. See for example: B.T. Cathy. 2002. Called to Account. Available at: http://www.time.com/time/business/article/0,8599,263006,00.html [accessed September 2010].

94   *Le Monde*. 2010. Euro et FMI, 27 March.

95   S. Romano. 2010. Grecia: Tre ipotesi per uscire dalla crisi, *Il Corriere della Sera* [25 March]. Available at: http://archiviostorico.corriere.it/2010/marzo/25/Grecia_tre_Ipotesi_per_uscire_co_9_100325003.shtml [accessed January 2011].

96   L. Offeddu. 2010. La Crisi di Atene Scuota l'Euro. *Corriere della Sera* [19 March]. Available at: http://archiviostorico.corriere.it/2010/marzo/19/crisi_Atene_scuote_euro_co_9_100319076.shtml [accessed January 2011].

public debt might prove to be unsustainable. Ironically, as opposed to statements by various Greek and European politicians, it was this approach by the media which realistically described the economic problem in the Hellenic Republic.

To begin with, *Handelsblatt* published an article by Professor of Cologne University Clemens Fuest on 10 January 2010 which analysed how the EU dealt with problematic states. He – inter alia – suggested that a special provision for a potential bankruptcy of problematic eurozone countries had to be included in the economic strategy of European leaders.[97] Moreover, a few weeks later *The Wall Street Journal* published a comment by AEI resident fellow Desmond Lachman entitled 'Greece's long road to default' which discussed public economics in the country. A representative excerpt is the following:

> Following many years of budget profligacy, can Greece in the end really avoid defaulting on its sovereign debt even if it does get the periodic European bailout? Sadly, a careful look at Greece's economic numbers does not give grounds for much optimism. There can be little question that Greece's public finances are on an unsustainable path.[98]

Along with Desmond Lachman, various scholars and columnists had not been convinced the first rescue package would be sufficient to save Greece. Irving Stelzer, for instance, considered it almost a certainty that a debt-restructuring would be decided. Assessing the support of €110 billion provided to Greece by the EU and the IMF, the columnist argued: 'the loans would do little more than buy some time before Greece is forced to restructure – the polite word for a partial default – on its massive and rising debt'.[99]

Wolfgang Münchau agreed with leading columnists in correctly thinking that a debt-restructuring would be unavoidable in the case of Greece. Mr Münchau published a prophetic editorial on 4 April 2010, arguing that 'Greece will default but not this year'.[100] Two weeks later he complemented this argument by underlining that the bailout package only delayed the inevitable.[101] In parallel to this, articles

---

97 C. Fuest. 2010. EU braucht ein Insolvenzverfahren für Staaten. *Handelsblatt* [10 January]. http://www.handelsblatt.com/meinung/gastbeitraege/fuest-eu-braucht-ein-insolvenzverfahren-fuer-staaten;2510303 [accessed January 2010].

98 D. Lachman. 2010. Greece's long road to default. *The Wall Street Journal* [1 February]. Available at: http://online.wsj.com/article/SB40001424052748704107204575038781822930608.html [accessed January 2011].

99 I. Stelzer. 2010. A successful restructuring in Greece may leave a weaker Europe economy. *The Wall Street Journal* [26 April]. Available at: http://online.wsj.com/article/SB10001424052748704627704575203940253330902.html [accessed April 2011].

100 W. Münchau. 2010. Greece will default but not this year. *Financial Times* [4 April]. Available at: http://www.ft.com/cms/s/0/372886dc-400d-11df-8d23-00144feabdc0.html#axzz1EOlF63dE [accessed January 2011].

101 W. Münchau. 2010. Greece's bailout only delays the inevitable. *Financial Times* [18 April]. Available at: http://www.ft.com/cms/s/0/da5b9516-4b1f-11df-a7ff-00144feab49a,s01=1.html [accessed January 2011].

written by John Dizard were of similar content. The financial editor explained on 16 May 2010, for example, that the crisis in the eurozone was postponed and asserted on the Greek case:

> Most of the lawyers, bankers, and emerging market investors who have worked on the dozens of sovereign defaults over the past three decades have not changed their view on the fundamentals of the distressed European sovereigns. Among them, the betting is that Europe and the International Monetary Fund have bought no more than another six months to a year before a restructuring.[102]

As far as the percentage of a potential haircut was concerned, Gillian Tett developed a scenario in May 2010 onwards, analysing the consequences a 50 per cent loss in the value of bonds might imply.[103] In July 2010, Mr Dizard attempted once again to show to readers that Greece had already started to restructure its debt by referring to an economic agreement settling the debt of the Greek state hospital system. According to this agreement, zero coupons bonds for the years 2007, 2008 and 2009 would be issued.[104] Likewise, in one of the most critical articles entitled 'Trust Greece … to default', Allen Mattich asserted emphatically: 'The Greek government has no credibility. Nor does it deserve any. And ultimately, it will default'.[105]

It is worth mentioning that figures such as Bert Flossbach,[106] Martin Feldstein,[107] Nouriel Roubini[108] and Carl Weinberg[109] often commented in economic newspapers on the necessity of a Greek default as the best solution. In April 2010, for instance,

---

102   J. Dizard. 2010. Eurozone crisis averted for now. *Financial Times* [16 May]. Available at: http://www.ft.com/cms/s/0/718569b8-5f83-11df-a670-00144feab49a.html#axzz1Dqko0ArR [accessed January 2011].

103   G. Tett. 2010. Greek bondholders jittery over haircuts. *Financial Times* [27 May]. Available at: http://www.ft.com/cms/s/0/3e2c01ec-69a8-11df-8432-00144feab49a.html#axzz1Dqko0ArR [accessed January 2011].

104   J. Dizard. 2010. It's no secret: Greece is restructuring debt. *Financial Times* [4 July]. http://www.ft.com/cms/s/0/2ac462f6-8600-11df-bc22-00144feabdc0.html#axzz1Dqko0ArR [accessed January 2011].

105   A. Mattich. 2010. Trust Greece … to default. *The Wall Street Journal* [17 September]. Available at: http://blogs.wsj.com/source/2010/09/17/trust-greeceto-default/ [accessed: January 2011].

106   Dr Bert Flossbach is owner of company Flossbach von Storch, along with Kurt von Storch. This is one of leading portfolio management firms in Germany.

107   Martin Feldstein is professor of economics at Harvard University.

108   Nouriel Roubini is professor of economics at Stern Business School (New York University). He is also the founder of Roubini Global Economics. This is an independent global economic and market strategy research firm offering its clients a view into the developments of the world economy. Its headquarters are located in New York and other offices are in London.

109   Dr Carl Weinberg is owner of Higher Frequency Economics and author of *Notes on the Global Economy*.

Carl Weinberg argued that only debt-restructuring could save the country,[110] while in the same month Bert Flossbach advocated this option.[111] On his part, Nouriel Roubini went further in June 2010 in an editorial he prepared for the *Financial Times*, elaborating on the nature of this bankruptcy and explaining that an orderly default would be ideal for the Hellenic Republic.[112]

Along with economic newspapers, all other titles linked Greece with default in their coverage in the first months of 2010. In particular, American, British and German media reflected assertiveness in their discourse. *The Washington Post*, for instance, saw Greece 'on the edge of default' in April,[113] and *The New York Times* explained in the same month that the country had remained at risk as it was not able to devaluate its currency.[114] For its part, *The Sun* echoed the same view by arguing that the country was 'spiraling towards bankruptcy in a circle of death',[115] while *The Guardian* saw the original bailout as being not 'enough to pull Greece decisively back from the brink of defaulting on its national debts'.[116] Moreover, the coverage did sometimes take an ironic and offending dimension, especially in German and British titles. In a striking case, *Frankfurter Allgemeine Zeitung* published a sketch with the Turkish flag on top of the Acropolis, selecting the following caption 'Good news: advert of the Greek state bankruptcy'.[117] This piece in the German conservative newspaper assumed that it was Turkey which had finally saved Greece.

French and Italian newspapers also expressed a continuous fear that the Greek Government would go bust. Their approach, however, was not that emphatic – especially in commentary stories – but it rather reflected an internal hope that the Hellenic Republic might make it. *Le Monde*, for instance, considered the scenario of

---

110   C. Weinberg. 2010. Only debt restructuring can save Greece. *The Wall Street Journal* [14 April]. Available at: http://online.wsj.com/article/SB10001424052702303695604575181421506589114.html [accessed January 2011].

111   J. Hackhausen. 2010. Griechenland muss pleitegehen. *Handelsblatt* [15 April]. Available at: http://www.handelsblatt.com/finanzen/anlagestrategie/bert-flossbach-im-interview-griechenland-muss-pleitegehen;2562021 [accessed January 2011].

112   N. Roubini. 2010 Greece's best option is an orderly default. *Financial Times* [28 June]. Available at: http://www.ft.com/cms/s/0/a3874e80-82e8-11df-8b15-00144feabdc0.html#axzz1Dqko0ArR [accessed January 2011].

113   A. Ahrens and A. Faiola. 2010. Greece moves closer to default situation. *The Washington Post* [23 April], A01.

114   C. Swann and N. Paisner. 2010. History is hardly on Greece's side. *The New York Times*, 13 April, Business and Financial Desk, 2.

115   *The Sun*. 2010. Another week. And another financial, 24 April, 13.

116   L. Mangan. 2010. Saturday: This week: people: no halting the defaulting: Greece. *The Guardian*, 1 May, Comment pages, 46.

117   G. Braunberger. 2010. Krückstock für den kranken Mann? *Frankfurter Allgemeine Zeitung* [29 April]. Available at: http://www.faz.net/aktuell/wirtschaft/europas-schuldenkrise/griechenlands-schuldenkrise-krueckstock-fuer-den-kranken-mann-1575521.html [accessed March 2012].

debt-restructuring a 'taboo' one.[118] French and Italian journalists clearly showed their concern for the Greek economic problem while conducting interviews with bankers and policymakers. Their questions often centred on the idea of Greece having to write off its debt and their will to provide a specific answer to their audience. *Le Figaro*, for instance, did so in an interview with former Prime Minister George Papandreou who excluded this possibility.[119] In a similar case, *Il Corriere della Sera* insisted on the view of former President of the European Central Bank, Jean Claude Trichet, that a Greek default had not been on the agenda, possibly expressing temporary relief that the danger had been far away, at least in April 2010.[120]

The 'Greek default' theme was mainly on the agenda of international media in the first months of 2010. After the Hellenic Republic came under international scrutiny in May 2010, the country gained a short grace period. The main reason is that its government seemed, at a first glance at least, determined to implement reforms and deliver. At the same time, the cases of Ireland and Portugal started to largely attract international attention. The expansion of the economic crisis in other countries did not mean the Hellenic Republic had persuaded markets it could deliver. Nevertheless, it rather gained temporary sympathy from a few journalists as it attempted to continue its hard fiscal consolidation effort. In July 2011, for example, *Le Monde* deemed the country the 'good pupil' of Europe[121] and the *Financial Times* argued it had make a strong start with reforms.[122]

It was mainly from November 2010 onwards when the spectre of Greek default returned to the forefront. The important difference in the coverage between the period after November 2010 and the first months of this year is that the credibility gap of the Hellenic Republic was continuously widening, leading even optimistic scenarios for an escape from bankruptcy to collapse. In the last months of 2010 and for the whole 2011, a potential reader of international newspapers might be familiar with the possibility of a sovereign default of the country. Foreign journalists, for instance, often reported on assessments of rating agencies relegating the status of

---

118 M. De Vergès, 2010. La restructuration de la dette, un scénario envisagé mais tabou. *Le Monde*, 28 April.

119 A. Kefalas. 2010. Grèce: La restructuration de la dette est hors de question. *Le Figaro* [16 November]. Available at: http://www.lefigaro.fr/conjoncture/2010/11/15/04016-20101115ARTFIG00702-grece-la-restructuration-de-la-dette-est-hors-de-question.php [accessed January 2011].

120 *Il Corriere della Sera*. 2010. Grecia: Trichet, tema default non si pone [8 April]. Available at: http://www.corriere.it/notizie-ultima-ora/Economia/Grecia-Trichet-Tema-default-non-pone/08-04-2010/1-A_000095812.shtml [accessed January 2011].

121 P. Briançon. 2010. Le point de vue des chroniqueurs de l'agence économique Reuters Breakingviews. *Le* Monde, 13 July, 13.

122 K. Hope. 2010. Greece makes strong start on reforms. *Financial Times* [18 July] Available at: http://www.ft.com/intl/cms/s/0/a5478676-927f-11df-9142-00144feab49a.html#axzz1pYLeDy1r [accessed November 2010].

Greek bonds.[123] It seemed like a common secret that it was only a matter of time for the Hellenic Republic to have its debt restructured. The main question on the media agenda was not whether a default would happen but how this could be organised.

From the moment Greece required a second bailout package having been unable to meet its fiscal targets, foreign journalists concentrated on the participation of the private sector in the new agreement.[124] In such a case, for example, *The Wall Street Journal* presented views of politicians and bankers discussing the pros and cons concerning this unprecedented development in eurozone history.[125] Having experienced the weakness of the Greek Government to successfully implement reforms in previous months, however, all international newspapers started to pose questions as to whether the public debt of the country could be sustainable even after the haircuts of 21 per cent and 50 per cent imposed in July and October 2011 respectively. The Hellenic economy sunk into recession and the country seemed adrift as its citizens made sacrifices which were not yielding results. Therefore, the option of debt-restructuring might not be sufficient per se to end the crisis.

All international newspapers considered growth a critical parameter which would help Greece overcome its serious problem.[126] As *The Guardian* nicely put it, with growth so low the country would be never able to pay back its debts.[127] For his part, Paul Krugman elaborated in *The New York Times* on areas the Hellenic Republic could invest in order to kick off its economy:

> A high-quality tourism sector will remain central in Greece's future, strengthened and complemented by more cultural activities, retirement communities from northern Europe and high-quality medical services at advantageous costs. High value-added agriculture will also be important. Greece should work on channelling

---

123   See for example: *La Repubblica*. 2011. S&P taglia ancora la Grecia [13 June]. Available at: http://www.repubblica.it/economia/2011/06/13/news/s_p_taglia_grecia_default_vicino-17648848/ [accessed November 2011].

124   See for example: M. De Vergès. 2011. Les trois options envisagées. *Le Monde*, 27 May, 15 and D. Kansas. 2011. Greek bond yield spreads widen, restructuring chatter grows. *The Wall Street Journal* [27 April]. Available at: http://blogs.wsj.com/marketbeat/2011/04/27/greek-bond-yield-spreads-widen-restructuring-chatter-grows/?KEYWORDS=greece+++haircut [accessed November 2011].

125   C. Forelle and B. Blackstone. 2011. Europe divided over Greek crisis. *The Wall Street Journal*, 25 May, 7.

126   It is interesting that German newspapers saw the Greek crisis and the perspective for a return to growth as an opportunity for national investments. *Bild*, for instance, extensively dealt with a potential co-operation between Athens and Berlin concerning solar energy, the so-called 'Helios project'. *Bild*. 2011. Pleite-Griechen wollen die Sonne anzapfen. [5 September]. Available at: http://www.bild.de/politik/ausland/griechenland-krise/griechenland-krise-jetzt-pumpen-sie-auch-die-sonne-an-19777402.bild.html [accessed November 2011].

127   I. Traynor. 2011. Europe in turmoil: Debt summit: European policymakers struggle for united front to save Greece. *The Guardian*, 19 July, Financial Pages, 22.

a greater portion of the revenues generated by shipping to its national economy. It should find niches in the high-technology sector and participate in its worldwide structure. Finally, with considerable potential for wind and solar energy, green technologies can, in the longer run, become a major source of growth.

Furthermore, in the view of *Handelsblatt*, Greece needed new courage[128] while *Le Figaro* commented on the vicious circle of a service-based economy being dangerously shrunk by various rounds of austerity measures:

> The reality is that the exit of Greece from the crisis does not only depend on the government of Athens in spite of the good intentions it seems to have. Based on tourism, maritime industry and small manufacturing industry, the Greek economy has no chance to recover if recession in the eurozone remains at this level. If the fall of the Greek GDP continues, the country will be not able to pay back its debt.[129]

As a whole, the impasse in the case of Greece was attributed to the lack of a clear and straightforward strategy which could, in theory, guarantee its return to normalcy and growth. On the occasion of the Hellenic crisis, the alleged absence of a strong European leadership was discussed in the media discourse.[130] Germany, in particular, was largely criticised for insisting on austerity measures and failing to realise the pain of Greek people. In July 2011, *Le Monde* deemed Chancellor Merkel as 'destabilised by the file of the Greek debt' and wondered what she actually wanted.[131] *La Repubblica*, for its part, asserted in September 2011 that she had adapted a 'hard line' on the Hellenic Republic.[132] It is interesting that signs of criticism of Angela Merkel's economic policy on Greece were also apparent in the press of her own country. In a remarkable example based on an interview with

---

128   *Handelsblatt*. 2011. Griechenland braucht neuen Mut [27 October]. Available at: http://www.handelsblatt.com/politik/international/griechenland-braucht-neuen-mut/5752022.html?p5752022=all [accessed November 2011].

129   R. Girard. 2011. Grèce: la spirale infernale, économique et politique. *Le Figaro* [7 November]. Available at: http://www.lefigaro.fr/international/2011/11/07/01003-20111107ARTFIG00696-grece-la-spirale-infernale-economique-et-politique.php [accessed February 2011].

130   See for example: P. Ricard. 2011. Le marasme grec illustre la défaillance du leadership européen. *Le Figaro*, 22 June, 14.

131   C. Boutelet. 2011. Angela Merkel déstabilisée par le dossier de la dette grecque. *Le Monde* [19 July]. Available at: http://www.lemonde.fr/europe/article/2011/07/18/angela-merkel-destabilisee-par-le-dossier-de-la-dette-grecque_1550210_3214.html [accessed November 2011].

132   M. Masciaga. 2011. Linea dura della Merkel sulla Grecia. *La Repubblica* [12 September]. Available at: http://www.repubblica.it/economia/2011/09/12/news/linea_dura_della_merkel_sulla_grecia_borse_in_calo_a_picco_i_titoli_bancari-21568560/index.html?ref=search [accessed November 2011].

Bild, former Chancellor Helmut Kohl said she had led the country to isolation.[133] In this case, the German tabloid selected the title 'dramatic appeal to Merkel' in order to signal the importance of Mr Kohl's message.

Leaving the Eurozone

The perspective of a Greek debt-restructuring was largely reported and commented on in the international media discourse. An additional scenario was that of a potential exit of the Hellenic Republic from the eurozone. Even before the decision of Mr Papandreou for a referendum in October 2011, economic newspapers along with opinion-forming titles from Britain, Germany and the USA had already started to analyse the possibility of Greece leaving the common currency. Their stories – mainly the commentary ones – largely included arguments seeing the future of the country outside the eurosystem. By contrast, French and Italian newspapers were hesitant in foreseeing a potential Greek return to its national currency and only reported on rumors. They seemed more sensitive concerning the stability of the euro[134] and generally advocated continuous support for the country as we have already seen.

Starting with pessimistic articles regarding the future of the eurozone, Dan Lewis, executive director of Economic Policy Centre, argued in *The Wall Street Journal* in February 2010 that only a division of the euro could save Greece.[135] In this piece, Dan Lewis proposed the establishment of a second European currency, undervalued by 20 per cent in comparison to the normal euro. In a similar case, four German professors, Wilhelm Hankel, Wilhelm Nolling, Karl Albrecht and Joachim Starbatty, insisted on this view in *Financial Times* approximately one and a half months later.[136] In the same economic title, 'a California type' solution was

---

133 *Bild*. 2011. Dramatischer Appeal an Merkel. [24 August] Available at: http://www.lemonde.fr/europe/article/2011/07/18/angela-merkel-destabilisee-par-le-dossier-de-la-dette-grecque_1550210_3214.html [accessed November 2011].

134 See for example: *Le Monde*. 2010. La Grèce dément les rumeurs sur la sortie de l'euro [9 June]. Available at: http://www.lemonde.fr/europe/article/2010/06/09/la-grece-dement-les-rumeurs-sur-sa-sortie-de-l-euro_1370194_3214.html [accessed January 2011] and *Il Corriere della Sera*. 2010. Crisi, Merkel: Troppe speculazioni. La CSU Bavarese: Via la Grecia dall' euro [24 April]. Available at: http://www.corriere.it/economia/10_aprile_24/grecia-merkel-germania-euro_190c0c4a-4f9a-11df-9c4e-00144f02aabe.shtml [accessed January 2011].

135 D. Lewis. 2010. One possible outcome of Greece crisis: Only splitting the euro will save it. *The Wall Street Journal* [17 February]. Available at: http://online.wsj.com/article/SB10001424052748704804204575069570005834614.html?KEYWORDS=Greece+++default [accessed January 2010].

136 W. Hankel, W. Nolling, K. Albrecht and J. Starbatty. 2010. A euro exit is the only way out for Greece. *Financial Times* [25 March]. Available at: http://www.ft.com/cms/s/0/6a618b7a-3847-11df-8420-00144feabdc0.html#axzz1AuRXYVYq [accessed January 2010].

also suggested for the case of Greece.[137] Furthermore, *Handelsblatt* was emphatic as it quoted in a headline from the President of the Bavarian Finance Centre, Wolfgang Gerke, asking the Hellenic Republic to leave the euro.[138]

Not only economic newspapers but also political ones have seen the future of Greece outside the common currency. In the German press, *Frankfurter Allgemeine Zeitung* took the lead in urging for the removal of Greece. In this centre-right title, economist Joachim Starbatty advocated so as well,[139] along with former member of the board of the European Central Bank, Otmar Issing.[140] Likewise, *Süddeutsche Zeitung* proposed serious consequences for undisciplined countries.[141] It is also worth mentioning that British media reflected frustration for Greece's participation in the eurozone, denoting that the country had not deserved to enter it. *The Times*, for example, published a piece by Charles Grant entitled 'Greece doesn't belong in the euro. It must go';[142] *The Guardian* explained that it might be finally possible for Greece to return to the drachma, however initial provisions of the eurozone did not allow such a development;[143] while *The Sun* reported on a local nostalgia in the country for its old currency.[144] As a whole, British newspapers have reflected relief and a posteriori satisfaction Britain did not left its currency to enter the eurosystem.

Columnists who have regularly discussed the possibility of an exit by Greece from the eurozone include Desmond Lachman from the American Enterprise Institute and Nouriel Roubini and Mark Weisbrot from the Centre for Economic and Policy Research. The first, for example, noted on 12 January 2010:

---

137 C. Goodhart and D. Tsomocos. 2010. The California solution for the club Med. *Financial Times* [24 January]. Available at: http://www.ft.com/cms/s/0/5ef30d32-0925-11df-ba88-00144feabdc0.html#axzz1EOlF63dE [accessed January 2011].

138 *Handelsblatt*. 2010. Griechenlans muss aus dem Euro raus [27 April]. Available at: http://www.handelsblatt.com/finanzen/boerse-maerkte/anleihen/anleihen-unter-druck-griechenland-muss-aus-dem-euro-raus/3421902.html [accessed November 2010].

139 M. Wohlgemuth. 2010. Denn sie werden es wieder tun. *Frankfurter Allgemeine Zeitung* [26 April]. Available at: http://www.faz.net/aktuell/feuilleton/buecher/rezensionen/2.1716/denn-sie-werden-es-wieder-tun-1971814.html [accessed January 2011].

140 *Frankfurter Allgemeine Zeitung*. 2011. Sollen die Griechen raus aus dem Euro? [8 October]. Available at: http://m.faz.net/aktuell/wirtschaft/europas-schuldenkrise/schaeuble-und-issing-im-streitgespraech-sollen-die-griechen-raus-aus-dem-euro-11486535.html [accessed December 2012].

141 A. Hagelüken. 2010. Liebe Griechen, so geht's. *Süddeutsche Zeitung* [30 December]. http://www.sueddeutsche.de/geld/euro-zone-estland-tritt-bei-liebe-griechen-so-gehts-1.1041245 [accessed June 2011].

142 C. Grant. 2011. Greece doesn't belong in the euro. It must go. *The Times* [20 June]. Available at: http://www.thetimes.co.uk/tto/opinion/columnists/article3067279.ece [accessed December 2011].

143 J. Treanor. 2011. Front. Eurozone crisis: Exit Strategy: How could Greece leave the euro. *The Guardian*, 22 June, 14.

144 S. Hawkes. 2011. The UK never joined the euro. You're in control. It's fantastic. *The Sun*, 2 July, 2.

This experience informs me that, much like Argentina a decade ago, Greece is approaching the final stages of its currency arrangement. There is every prospect that within two to three years, after much official money is thrown its way, Greece's euro membership will end with a bang.[145]

Likewise, the second encouraged Greece to leave the eurozone, explaining that 'a return to the national currency and a sharp depreciation would quickly restore competitiveness and growth'.[146] Finally, the third columnist called on the country to say 'goodbye to the euro', also considering the experience of the Argentina instructive.[147]

Last but not least, a few newspapers covered the scenario of a potential exit by Greece from the eurozone in a satirical way. In particular, *Bild* and *Frankfurter Allgemeine Zeitung* showed a mocking tendency. In April 2010, *Bild's* correspondent in Athens Paul Ronzheimer along with photographer George Kalozois met Greek people in the centre of Athens, mainly pensioners, distributing drachmas. For its part, *Frankfurter Allgemeine Zeitung* uploaded a video on its website depicting its journalist eating Greek food and calling on the country to leave the eurozone.[148]

The publication of articles suggesting that the Hellenic Republic had to leave the eurozone did not mean that opposite views did not appear in some international newspapers. New stories often presented the position of European and Greek politicians who continuously supported Greece remaining in the eurozone. Stories of this content can also be found. In such a case, Paul Krugman argued that it was difficult for Greece to exit the eurozone because it – inter alia – did not have drachmas in circulation as opposed to Argentina.[149] Additionally, in a rather moving piece he prepared for the *Financial Times*, former President of the European Commission Romano Prodi concluded: 'Europe's story is not over yet. This is a film that will run and run'.[150] In spite of some optimistic articles, however,

---

145 D. Lachman. 2010. Greece looks set to go the way of Argentina. *Financial Times* [12 January]. Available at: http://www.ft.com/intl/cms/s/0/5ffb0694-ff1b-11de-a677-00144feab49a.html [accessed January 2011].

146 N. Roubini. 2011. Greece should default and abandon the euro. *Financial Times* [10 September]. Available at: http://blogs.ft.com/the-a-list/2011/09/19/greece-should-default-and-abandon-the-euro/#axzz1pb11j1Ef [accessed December 2011].

147 M. Weisbrot. 2010. Why Greece should reject the euro. *The New York Times* [9 May]. Available at: http://www.nytimes.com/2011/05/10/opinion/10weisbrot.html?_r=1&hp [accessed November 2011].

148 *Frankfurter Allgemeine Zeitung*. 2010. Kein Euro den Griechen [4 March]. http://www.faz.net/s/Rub28EF38B483C94193A70B58D41ADA26A4/Doc~E85989C210 22F42FFA52F92A3F33A22E0~ATpl~Ecommon~SMed.html [accessed January 2011].

149 P. Krugman. 2011. The conscience of a liberal. *The New York Times* [10 May]. Available at: http://krugman.blogs.nytimes.com/2011/05/10/greek-out/ [accessed December 2011].

150 R. Prodi. 2010. A Europe under fire can still make its voice heard. *Financial Times* [12 December]. Available at: http://www.ft.com/intl/cms/s/0/a69c9eae-061e-11e0-976b-00144feabdc0.html#axzz1pbKEiWRH [accessed March 2011].

euroscepticism has certainly been a dominant element in the coverage of the Greek crisis, at least in American, British and German media.

Greece, Sell your Islands!

And the Acropolis!

International newspapers, mainly British and German ones, made their own suggestions on the way the Hellenic Republic would be able to pay back its debts. These mainly urged the country to sell part of its national property and give away part of its sovereignty. Media stories were first published in March 2010 after two German politicians, Josef Schlarmann and Frank Schäffler, proposed uninhabited islands or ancient artefacts that could be sold. The main headline of *Bild*, for instance, was: 'Bankrupted Greeks, sell your islands ... and the Acropolis along with them!'[151] Here, the German newspaper conducted interviews with Mr Schlarmann and Mr Schäffler who explained that bankrupted countries such as Greece had to sell their properties in order to serve their debt. *Süddeutsche Zeitung*[152] and *The Guardian* also[153] commented on the proposal by these German politicians.

Frankfurter Allgemeine Zeitung ironically wondered on 24 April 2010, on the same day Mr Papandreou had asked for the bailout mechanism, 'who should buy a Greek island?'[154] Two months later, in June, *The Guardian* went further: the newspaper asserted that the country had supposedly already started to look for buyers. Journalist Elena Moya wrote:

> *The Guardian* has learned that an area in Mykonos, one of Greece's top tourist destinations, is one of the sites for sale. The area is one-third owned by the

---

151 *Bild*. 2010.Verkauft doch eure Inseln, ihr Pleite-Griechen [27 October]. Available at: http://www.bild.de/politik/wirtschaft/griechenland-krise/regierung-athen-sparen-verkauft-inseln-pleite-akropolis-11692338.bild.html [accessed April 2011]. The article was updated on 27 October and for this reason this date appears in the link.

152 C. Schlötzer. 2010. Ich Kaufe eine Insel. *Süddeutsche Zeitung* [5 March]. Available at: http://www.sueddeutsche.de/geld/griechenland-in-not-ich-kaufe-eine-insel-1.1324 [accessed April 2011] and *Süddeutsche Zeitung*. 2010. Gepfefferte Ratschläge aus Deutschland [4 March]. Available at: http://www.sueddeutsche.de/geld/griechenland-in-der-krise-gepfefferte-ratschlaege-aus-deutschland-1.19557 [accessed April 2011].

153 J. Finch. 2010. Greece to sell off islands and artworks. *The Guardian* [4 March]. Available at: http://www.guardian.co.uk/world/2010/mar/04/greece-greek-islands-auction [accessed April 2011] and P. Inman and H. Smith. 2010. Greece should sell islands to keep bankruptcy at bay, say German MPs. *The Guardian* [4 March]. Available at: http://www.guardian.co.uk/business/2010/mar/04/greece-sell-islands-german-mps [accessed April 2011].

154 W. von Petersdorff. 2010. Wer kauft eine Griechische Insel? *Frankfurter Allgemeine Zeitung* [25 April]. Available at: http://www.faz.net/aktuell/wirtschaft/europas-schuldenkrise/staatsbankrott-wer-kauft-eine-griechische-insel-1969140.html [accessed April 2011].

government, which is looking for a buyer willing to inject capital and develop a luxury tourism complex, according to a source close to the negotiations.[155]

This article by Ms Moya was also reproduced by other newspapers such as *Le Figaro*[156] and *Il Corriere della Sera*.[157] Approximately one year later, while Greece was missing its fiscal targets, *Bild* raised once again the question of whether the country should sell the Acropolis.[158] Furthermore, *The Sun* reported on the fear of many Greek people that their famous ancient places and even some holiday islands like Corfu could end up in foreign ownership.[159] The British tabloid accurately covered in this case the xenophobia dominating the Hellenic society within the framework of the economic crisis.

No Mercy to Greece

From October 2009 onwards, Greece largely attracted the attention of international media. The detailed coverage of poleconomics confirms their strong interest in the modus operandi of the Hellenic state. It touches upon critical problems of the economy and political system. Journalists elaborated on the crisis in three stages. First, they portrayed the status of the Greek problem and assessed its impact on the stability of the EU and the eurozone. Second, they attempted to investigate its roots by making particular references to the role of Greek politicians and maladministration in the country. And third, they suggested remedies for the government to get out of the crisis and pay back its debts.

In the coverage of the Hellenic crisis, themes such as the large deficit, the huge debt, recession, over-borrowing and overspending in the public sector have been extensively discussed. At the same time, the unreliability of Greek politicians as well as their inability to co-operate, thus not putting the national interest of the country above their own personal survival has been stigmatised. In summary, the

---

155   E. Moya. 2010. Greece starts putting island land up for sale to save economy. *The Guardian* [24 June]. Available at: http://www.guardian.co.uk/world/2010/jun/24/greece-islands-sale-save-economy [accessed April 2011].

156   I. de Foucaud. 2010. La Grèce pourrait vendre des îles pour renflouer sa dette: *Le Figaro* [25 June]. Available at: http://www.lefigaro.fr/conjoncture/2010/06/25/04016-20100625ARTFIG00388-la-grece-pourrait-vendre-des-iles-pour-renflouer-sa-dette.php [accessed April 2011].

157   F. Tortora. 2010. Crisi economica: La Grecia mette in vendita le sue isole. *Il Corriere della Sera* [25 June]. Available at: http://www.corriere.it/economia/10_giugno_25/grecia-vendita-itol_7676922a-805e-11df-85d3-00144f02aabe.shtml [accessed April 2011].

158   *Bild*. 2011. Muss Griechenland die Akropolis verkaufen? [17 May] Available at: http://www.bild.de/politik/ausland/griechenland-krise/muss-griechenland-die-akropolis-verkaufen-17937616.bild.html [accessed November 2011].

159   T.N. Dunn and S. Hawkes. 2011. I owe Youzo; Euro Debt crisis: Things can only get feta. *The Sun*, 22 July, 8, 9.

general image of Greece has been that of a country which is responsible for its tragic fate and one which seems like a great problem for the EU, not only by cooking the books and providing false statistics but also by failing to implement reforms.

Shaping an extremely negative picture for Greece, international media subsequently put into question the ability of its government to avoid bankruptcy and doubted the sufficiency of the rescue packages provided by the EU and the IMF. On that basis, a sovereign default was highly anticipated in all newspapers while American, British and German titles sometimes saw the future of the country outside the eurozone. In parallel with this, growth has been considered as a catalytic factor which will possibly break the vicious circle of the Greek economy and thus contribute to a revival of hope for recovery. A few titles, mainly German and British ones, also mocked Greece by suggesting it sell its ancient sites and some islands in order to reduce its debt.

The comparison of the coverage of the Greek crisis by newspapers from five different countries reveals a remarkable degree of consensus in criticising the Hellenic Republic for its crisis. Although the approach of French and Italian titles was not as harsh as that of American, British and German ones, they – as a whole – agreed on their representation of poleconomics in the country. The stance of the former media certainly reflected a European sensitivity for the stability of the common currency. This sensitivity, however, rather derived from their concern that France and especially Italy might be future victims of the Hellenic crisis than from their commitment to European integration and the viability of the monetary union itself. It is characteristic that *Le Figaro* and *Le Monde* were particularly sceptical about the exposure of French banks to the Greek debt.

The coverage of poleconomics in the Hellenic Republic challenges, finally, utopian views hoping for a europeanisation of national media discourses in member states of the Union. Leaving the American press apart, it is straightforward that British, French and Italian newspapers lacked a common vision for the European future of Greece. Although they correctly blamed the country for mistakes, omissions and pathogenies, they hesitated to give it a new chance. By contrast, in times of crisis, the national media from different European countries demonstrated a strong interest in the future of their own states, denoting the important internal divisions not only in the euroarea but also within the EU. Analysing the Greek battleground, for instance, it is interesting that the French and Italian newspapers did not hide their frustration at the rise of German economic power in Europe.

Is Europe heading towards the right dimension when media from its member states view its weakest link in a hostile and ironic way? Can it sincerely achieve further integration and work towards tougher economic governance when foreign journalists from different European nationalities lack a common approach and have more to disagree over than to share? Or, is the media coverage of the Greek crisis a precursor for unprecedented developments which will see the euroarea dissolved and the project of European unification at risk? These questions will be answered by developments in the next years. The case of the Greek crisis, however, does not create a wave of optimism from the moment it revolved around not only poleconomics but also intolerable living conditions for ordinary citizens. As we will see, journalists were the first to discover and report it.

Chapter 6
How is It to Live in Greece?

The Greek crisis seems, at a first glance, like an economic and political problem per se. Within the context of the European debt explosion, the Hellenic Republic's weakness has been indeed the worst link in the chain of the 17 eurozone members in terms of specific statistics and numbers. That is why the solution of a voluntary debt-restructuring was finally qualified by EU leaders as the appropriate remedy which could maybe save the country and constitute its debts sustainable. The Troika itself has had to reconsider its projection many times on the course of the national economy of the country. Within this framework of instability, themes and issues such as the EU decision for a bailout mechanism, the announcement of austerity measures and tax rises, the downgrading of Greece's economy by rating agencies and obviously the decision by Mr Papandreou to call and then subsequently cancel his decision for a referendum could not but attract the attention of foreign journalists.

The Greek crisis, however, goes far beyond this as it is interwoven into additional parameters which explain the drama and influence the implementation of reforms as well as the quality of citizens' everyday lives. Although not particularly familiar with the structure of the Hellenic society and the modern culture of the country, the international media attempted gradually to understand and analyse it. Their correspondents were keen to explore the special features which made Greece and its crisis seem 'unique'. In parallel with this, they showed particular interest in sketching out the social dimension of the problem by publishing various stories based on personal interviews not only with authorities but also with simple people who were affronted with a plethora of problems, certainly rare ones for a theoretically civilised Western country.

A Tradition of Corruption

Corruption in Greece was a main issue that foreign journalists focused on in their coverage of the crisis. The view that the country was a corrupted one was reproduced in the media discourse while it was often connoted that such a tradition had been incorporated in the Hellenic Republic, thus affecting several areas of public life. These included the judiciary system, hospitals, the police and tax offices and the Greek people themselves. In the view of *Le Figaro*, corruption in the Hellenic Republic was 'endemic'[1] while *Le Monde* portrayed it as 'a state plagued' by this problem.[2]

La Repubblica went further and published in February 2010 a piece entitled 'the battle of Papandreou in Greece of corrupted people'. This article explained how difficult it was for the former prime minister to implement the necessary reforms.[3] Other newspapers such as *Süddeutsche Zeitung* located the modern roots of corruption in the years of his father, Andreas Papandreou, which were 'golden times for many Greeks' as cronyism flourished.[4] Indeed, during his years, citizens supporting his socialist party had enjoyed privileged treatment from the state. The newspaper was thus correct in its argument.

Dealing with corruption, journalists prepared different stories in order to explain the phenomenon. Markus Walker published a characteristic piece in *The Wall Street Journal*, arguing in his leading paragraph:

> Behind the budget crisis roiling Greece lies a riddle: Why does the state spend so lavishly but collect taxes so poorly? Many Greeks say the answer needs only two words: fakelaki and rousfeti.

Mr Walker nicely defined the word 'fakelaki' as a little envelope containing amounts of money aimed at bribing, and that of 'rousfeti' as a political favour.[5] Another interesting example came from *The Guardian* which dealt with corruption and the lack of transparency in finding jobs. Specifically, the British newspaper dispatched journalist Jon Henley to Greece. The correspondent interviewed ordinary people who had experienced cronyism and explained how jobs were often given in the country. In that case, the interviewee, Leonidas Pitsoulis, who studied in the UK and then returned to his country, said on the matter:

> I really hadn't been aware of the scale of everyday corruption here [...] You just don't pick up on that, as a kid. But coming back, and when you're used to another way of doing things, it really, really strikes you. Corruption pervades every corner of day to day life in Greece [...] From the doctor who takes his consultation fee without declaring it, to the bar-owner who buys his stock cash,

---

1 A. Cheyvialle. 2010. Athènes lance sa réforme fiscale. *Le Figaro*, 15 April, 21.
2 T. Ben Jelloun. 2010. Peurs. *Le Monde*, 6 June, 28.
3 G. Rampoldi. 2010. La sfida di Papandreou nella Grecia dei corrotti. *La Repubblica* [6 February]. Available at: http://www.repubblica.it/economia/2010/02/06/news/dossier-grecia-2204292/ [accessed April 2011].
4 A. Stefanidis. A. Highway to Hellas. 2010. *Süddeutsche Zeitung* [May edition of the magazine]. Available at: http://sz-magazin.sueddeutsche.de/texte/anzeigen/32559/ [accessed April 2011].
5 M. Walker. 2010. Tragic flaw: Graft feeds Greek crisis. *The Wall Street Journal* [15 April]. Available at: http://online.wsj.com/article_email/SB10001424052702303828304575179921909783864-lMyQjAxMTAwMDEwNjExNDYyWj.html [accessed December 2011].

no questions asked [...] It's just unthinking; the way it is [...] Nobody gets a job because they're the candidate best qualified and suited for it, he said: You get a job because you're the son or nephew or cousin or old schoolfriend of someone who knows someone who might want a little service.[6]

The example of *The Guardian* is of increased significance because the content did not derive from the journalist's main assessment but on the personal experience of a Greek person who had practically diagnosed cronyism. The trauma became larger because this person was able to compare the British with the Hellenic experience. Indeed, this was the main feeling many Greeks had when they needed to return to their country after having studied or worked in a well-organised country like Great Britain. In a similar example like the one of *The Guardian*, *Le Monde* interviewed a French-Greek girl who confessed: 'France has taught me respect for the state, democracy, equal opportunities and public service. In Greece cheats and clientelism do reign'.[7] This quote by the young girl once again highlighted the remarkable difference between Greece and other civilised countries of the Western world.

The only newspapers which did not extensively deal with corruption in Greece – with the exception of the aforementioned example of *La Repubblica* – were Italian ones. These titles mainly reported on results of international surveys which placed their country in a better position in comparison to the Hellenic Republic. As a whole, however, they avoided publishing long stories on the issue perhaps because their own country was significantly affected by corruption as well. It is interesting that foreign newspapers did not only consider the problem as an exclusive Greek one but also explored its Italian dimension. In such a case, *Le Monde* argued in its editorial that 'corruption and mafia infiltration had become a daily phenomenon in Italy'.[8]

German newspapers were fair and sincere in diagnosing involvement of German national companies in the development of Greek corruption. In a striking example, *Süddeutsche Zeitung* put forward a question as to whether bribe money coming from Berlin constituted an important aspect in the story. This article referred to Siemens, Man, Daimler, Ferrostaal and ThyssenKrupp and their alleged illegal co-operation with Greek politicians in order to expand their presence in the Hellenic

---

6   J. Henley. 2011. In Greece corruption pervades every corner of life. *The Guardian* [20 October]. Available at: http://www.guardian.co.uk/world/blog/2011/oct/20/europe-breadline-corrution-pervades-corner [accessed December 2011].

7   *Le Monde*. 2011. Crise grecque: Il ne nous reste que 300 euros par mois pour vivre [28 June]. Available at: http://www.lemonde.fr/europe/article/2011/06/28/crise-grecque-il-ne-nous-reste-que-300-euros-par-mois-pour-vivre_1542203_3214.html [accessed September 2011].

8   *Le Monde*. 2010. Italie: la fin du berlusconisme se joue sur fond de corruption, 4 August, 15.

Republic.⁹ Likewise, *Frankfurter Allgemeine Zeitung* explained that employees of the aforementioned companies had not been prepared to talk to journalists on the issue, being afraid of becoming suspects for participating in the supposed exchange of bribe money.¹⁰

A 4-4-2 Play

The National Sport of Tax Evasion

Tax evasion is another Greek pathogeny largely discussed in the media discourse. The international newspapers elaborated on the habit of various Greek citizens to hide their wealth as well as on the feeling of social injustice prevailing among others who normally paid their taxes.¹¹ To begin with, *Le Figaro* portrayed the situation in the country by arguing that 'frauds and cheats are common'. On that basis, the conservative French newspaper explained why an underground economy had accounted to 35 per cent of GDP. It also concluded that, as a result, revenues in the country had been lowered to between €18 and €20 billion per year.¹² For its part, *Bild* published a piece entitled: '14,000 Greek citizens owe to the state 36 billion euros'.¹³ The German tabloid reported that many of them had been doctors affording luxurious villas.

The successful attempt by some Greek citizens to hide their wealth in the years before the economic crisis has also been discussed. *The New York Times*, for instance, elaborated on it and asserted:

> Tax investigators studied satellite photos of the area – a sprawling collection of expensive villas tucked behind tall gates – and came back with a decidedly

---

9   K. Ott and T. Telloglou. 2011. Schöner wohnen mit deutschem Schmiergeld? *Süddeutsche Zeitung* [20 June].
Available at: http://www.sueddeutsche.de/wirtschaft/korruption-in-griechenland-schoener-wohnenmitdeutschem-schmiergeld-1.1110217 [accessed November 2011].

10   R. Herman. 2011. Griechen kaufen weniger deutsch. *Frankfurter Allgemeine Zeitung* [23 April]. Available at: http://www.faz.net/aktuell/wirtschaft/europas-schuldenkrise/konsum-in-der-krise-griechen-kaufen-weniger-deutsch-1970654.html [accessed April 2011].

11   See for example: N. Martens. 2010. Am Pranger im Dienste der Zahlungsmoral. *Frankfurter Allgemeine Zeitung* [29 July]. Available at: http://www.faz.net/aktuell/politik/ausland/steuerhinterziehung-in-griechenland-am-pranger-im-dienste-der-zahlungsmoral-11007640.html [accessed April 2011].

12   C. Lacombe. 2010. Athènes s'attaque à l'évasion fiscale, sport national. *Le Figaro*. Economie – Enterprises, 12.

13   *Bild*. 2011. 14,000 Griechen schulden dem Staat 36 Mr. Euro [14 July]. Available at: http://www.bild.de/politik/ausland/griechenland-krise/griechenland-krise-papandreou-14000-griechen-schulden-staat-36-milliarden-euro-steuern-18857554.bild.html [accessed February 2012].

different number: 16,974 pools. That kind of wholesale lying about assets, and other eye-popping cases that are surfacing in the news media here, points to the staggering breadth of tax dodging that has long been a way of life here. Such evasion has played a significant role in Greece's debt crisis, and as the country struggles to get its financial house in order, it is going after tax cheats as never before.[14]

The tendency to escape declaring taxes has not been perceived to be only a habit of various ordinary Greek people, but also of famous celebrities. *Il Corriere della Sera* introduced its readers to this tendency, reporting on the scandal of the resignation of former tourism minister Angela Gerekou. Ms Gerekou had to step down from her position because her husband, legendary singer Tolis Voskopoulos, was revealed as owing millions of euros in unpaid taxes to the Greek state.[15]

Tax evasion has been linked to corruption in the media discourse. Some newspapers, for instance, analysed the illegal way Greek taxpayers managed to avoid paying fines at the expense of the state and in favour of tax collectors. *The Sun* sketched out this dodgy method by referring to a senior Greek Government source who said:

> The problem with our country is some tax offices play 4-4-2. If an individual or company owes 10.000 euros in taxes, they slip 4.000 to the inspector, keep 4.000 and pay 2.000 to the state. Doctors and lawyers like to be paid in cash – it is estimated a quarter of all taxes owed in Greece are not paid. This helps to explain why, in a developed country of 11 million people, only around 15.000 declare an annual income of more than 100.000 euros.[16]

For its part, *Handelsblatt* commented negatively on the inability of the Greek state to conduct efficient tax controls on the economic activity of enterprises and citizens from 2000 until 2009. Instead of organising extensive audits, the government of the country decided in September 2009 to give them the opportunity to pay a flat rate. The German economic newspaper regarded this choice as an 'amnesty promise to taxpayers'.[17]

---

14   S. Daley. 2010. Greek wealth is everywhere but tax forms. *The New York Times* [1 May]. Available at: http://www.nytimes.com/2010/05/02/world/europe/02evasion.html?pagewanted=all [accessed November 2011].

15   *Il Corriere Della Sera*. 2010. Grecia: si dimette ministro il cui marito era accusato di evasione fiscale [17 May]. Available at: http://www.corriere.it/notizie-ultima-ora/Esteri/Grecia-dimette-ministro-cui-marito-era-accusato-evasione-fiscale/17-05-2010/1-A_000105138.shtml [accessed April 2011].

16   O. Harvey. 2011. Greece play 4-4-2. *The Sun* [18 May]. Available at: http://www.thesun.co.uk/sol/homepage/features/2976628/Cost-of-corruption-in-Greece.html [accessed December 2011].

17   G. Höhler. 2010. Steuer-Ablasshandel in Athen. *Handelsblatt* [23 September]. Available at: http://www.handelsblatt.com/politik/international/zahlungsmoral-der-griechen-

It is worth mentioning that in the case of tax evasion in Greece, as also with corruption, Italian newspapers *Il Corriere della Sera* and *La Repubblica* have not been particularly keen on discussing the problem, at least in detail. This reserved stance may mirror a national understanding of the tendency to not pay taxes. For their part, the international media have not been hesitant in associating this pathogeny not only with Greece but also with Italy. *The Washington Post*, for example, published a piece entitled: 'Amid crisis, Italy confronts a culture of tax evasion' in which it regarded it a 'solid business plan'.[18]

Doing Business?

Better to Be Patient

Bureaucracy is another problem analysed by the international media in their coverage of the Greek crisis. In this case, foreign journalists considered bureaucracy as a factor which prevented companies from inventing and hindered Greece from attracting foreign capital. They also saw it as an obstacle creating unnecessary trouble for ordinary citizens in their everyday lives. Alkman Granitsas gave an overview of bureaucracy by commenting in the *Wall Street Journal* on the modus operandi of the public sector:

> Its inefficiency is legend. For example, it takes between 14 and 18 painful steps to set up a business. And every Greek will tell you his own story of waiting a year to collect a state pension, or waiting three years for a building permit.[19]

Likewise, Philip Pangalos asserted in *The Sunday Times* that Greek bureaucracy was driving people crazy.[20] For its part, *The Washington Post* also used a characteristic phrase to portray the Greek pathogeny. Specifically, Anne Applebaum emphatically asserted in her editorial: 'The country has an unusually old-fashioned legal system, a bureaucracy straight out of a Kafka novel and a byzantine system of regulation'.[21]

---

steuer-ablasshandel-in-athen/3546168.html [accessed April 2011].

18 A. Faiola. 2011. Amid crisis, Italy confronts a culture of tax evasion. *The Washington Post* [24 November]. Available at: http://www.washingtonpost.com/world/amid-crisis-italy-confronts-a-culture-of-tax-evasion/2011/11/22/gIQAef4JtN_story.html [accessed February 2012].

19 A. Granitsas. 2009. Attacking Greece's bureaucratic beast. *The Wall Street Journal* [20 October]. Available at: http://online.wsj.com/article/SB10001424052748704500604574484972685756020.html [accessed December 2010].

20 P. Pangalos. 2011. Young talent flees stricken Greece. *The Sunday Times* [3 July]. Available at: http://www.thesundaytimes.co.uk/sto/news/world_news/Europe/article661584.ece [accessed January 2012].

21 A. Applebaum. 2010. America's Greek Tragedy. *The Washington Post*, A13.

Acknowledging the problem, the international media considered the limitation of Greek bureaucracy as a necessary prerequisite for the modernisation of the state. That is because, as Ian Bremmer explained in the *Financial Times*, Greece's bureaucracy was inspiring little confidence in success of the government.[22] Further, Christiane Schlötzer published a piece in *Süddeutsche Zeitung* suggesting in her main headline that its 'walls should fall down',[23] and *The New York Times* also explained that it would be helpful for the country if it 'could reap significant savings by reducing its bureaucracy, which employs one out of five workers and by some estimates could be trimmed by as much as a third without materially affecting services'.[24]

Criticising a Whole Nation

In their coverage of the Greek crisis the international media did not only focus on specific persons but sometimes dealt with the Greek society as a whole. Here, it was denoted that the population of the country had been responsible for the crisis. Within this context, international newspapers were often entrapped in the logic of overgeneralisation. 'Party's over for Greek graspers' was, for example, the title of an article written by Matthew Campbell in *The Sunday Times* on 20 December 2009. This piece also asserted:

> A black mood has settled upon Athens. After the bonanza of European Union development aid and the euphoria of hosting the Olympics, the Greeks are shocked to realise that their gravy train has rolled off the tracks.[25]

Likewise, the *The Sun* followed a similar path. Satirically commenting on the struggle by the EU to save the euro, it noted in an editorial: 'The cash would help

---

22   I. Bremmer. 2011. Greece escapes collapse, but is true problems are only just beginning. *Financial Times* [29 June]. Available at: http://blogs.ft.com/the-a-list/2011/06/29/greece-has-escaped-collapse-but-its-problems-are-only-beginning/#axzz1i3LQYFXm [accessed September 2011].

23   C. Schlötzer. 2011. Die Mauern der Bürokratie müssen fallen. *Süddeutsche Zeitung* [9 October]. Available at: http://www.sueddeutsche.de/politik/folgen-der-finanzkrise-fuer-griechenland-die-mauern-der-buerokratie-muessen-fallen-1.1157677 [accessed January 2012]. For a similar case: A. Véron. 2010. 'Grèce: aide-toi, l'Europe t'aidera' *Le Monde* [6 March]. Available at: http://www.lemonde.fr/idees/article/2010/03/05/grece-aide-toi-l-europe-t-aidera-par-aurelien-veron_1314802_3232.html [accessed March 2011].

24   S. Daley. 2011. Bureaucracy in Greece defies efforts to cut it. *The New York Times* [17 October]. http://www.nytimes.com/2011/10/18/world/europe/greeces-bloated-bureaucracy-defies-efforts-to-cut-it.html?pagewanted=all [accessed January 2012].

25   M. Campbell. 2009. Party's over for Greek gaspers. *The Sunday Times* [20 December]. Available at: http://www.thesundaytimes.co.uk/sto/news/world_news/article193206.ece [accessed December 2011].

prop up the eurozone's wasters like lazy Greece, where many retire on fat pensions in their 50s and tax dodging is a national pastime'.²⁶ For its part, *The Washington Post* argued:

> Greece represents a perverse aspiration – a society with (in the words of Wisconsin Republican Rep. Paul Ryan) more takers than makers, more people taking benefits from government than there are people making goods and services that produce the social surplus that funds government. By socialising the consequences of Greece's misgovernment, Europe has become the world's leading producer of a toxic product – moral hazard.²⁷

Furthermore, for *Frankfurter Allgemeine Zeitung*, its correspondent Michael Martens published an article entitled: 'The country needs new Greeks'.²⁸ This peace connotes that all Greeks are responsible for their crisis and unable to contribute to an exit from it although the journalist only wanted to paraphrase the title of the German song 'the country needs new men' as he explained me. Moreover, in *The Washington Post*, columnist Anne Applebaum also attempted to explain why Germans were angry with the bailout and referred to the Hellenic society as a whole without being specific. She wrote:

> The Germans are fed up with paying the bills of everybody in Europe, they don't want to bailout the feckless Greeks with their flagrantly inaccurate official statistics, they resent being Europe's banker of last resort, they object to the universal demand that they plug the vast holes in the Greek deficit in the name European unity [...] Sooner or later, Germans will collectively decide that enough sacrifices have been made and that the debt to Europe has been paid. Thanks to the ungrateful Greeks, with their island villas and large pensions, that day may arrive more quickly than we originally thought.²⁹

German newspapers, namely *Bild* and *Süddeutsche Zeitung*, also endeavoured to summarise their comments on Greece in the form of letters. *Bild*, for instance, sent a letter to former Greek Prime Minister Papandreou on 5 March 2010 on the occasion of his trip to Berlin to meet with Chancellor Merkel. This letter produced

---

26   *The Sun*. Eur a Joke. 2011, 29 September, 8.

27   G. Will. 2010. European Union: A coalition of irresponsibility. *The Washington Post* [16 May]. Available at: http://www.washingtonpost.com/wp-dyn/content/article/2010/05/14/AR2010051404279.html [accessed January 2012].

28   N. Martens. 2011. Neue Griechen braucht das Land. *Frankfurter Allgemeine Zeitung* [6 November]. Available at: http://www.faz.net/aktuell/politik/ausland/koalitionsverhandlungen-in-athen-neue-griechen-braucht-das-land-11519713.html [accessed January 2012].

29   A. Applebaum. 2010. Germany's tug-of-war with Greece. *The Washington Post* [9 March 2010]. Available at: http://www.washingtonpost.com/wp-dyn/content/story/2010/03/08/ST2010030803490.html?sid=ST2010030803490 [accessed January 2012].

various stereotypes, linking Greek people to laziness and making comparisons with the working standards of people in Germany. The main points of this letter, which, in the view of the newspaper, highlighted different habits between Germans and Greeks, were:

> – People work until they are 67 here. There is no longer a 14-month salary for civil servants.

> – Here, nobody needs to pay a €1.000 bribe to get a hospital bed in time.

> – And we don't pay pensions for the General's daughters who sadly cannnotfind husbands.

> – In our country petrol stations have cash registers, taxi drivers give receipts and farmers do not swindle EU subsidies with millions of olive trees that do not exist.

The same letter to Mr Papandreou also asserted that Germany could meet its debts as Germans 'get up reasonably early and work all day' and because in good times they 'always spare for bad times'. In the post-scriptum of the letter, *Bild* enclosed a stamped-addressed envelope to help Mr Papandreou in case he wanted to reply.[30] The letter, sent by the editorial of *Bild* to Mr Papandreou, was maybe the most ironic example of the way the international media viewed both the Greek crisis and the Greek people.

For its part, *Süddeutsche Zeitung* published a letter which was supposedly written by Mr Papandreou to his European partners, summarising his poor government progress in 2010:

> I thank you with all my heart as you have managed that we, Greeks can muddle through once again [...] Your billions have saved us. Although we have in all previous years not met even once the Stability and Growth Pact criteria, we only entered the Monetary Union using falsified statistics, with no consequences [...] You are indeed nearly as tolerant as a normal Greek who must buy a bed in the hospital or have a treatment via bribery because our system is so ramschakle. Dear Europeans, that's pretty cool.

> I ask you, however, not to let your helpfulness go into your head [...] We don't want to change various favourite habits we have such as the sensational early

---

30 *Bild*. 2010. Ihr griecht nix von uns [5 March]. http://www.bild.de/BILD/politik/wirtschaft/2010/03/05/griechenland-bild-schreibt-pleite-premier/keine-hilfe-fuer-griechen.html [accessed April 2011].

retirement on the basis of which Greeks go to pension and enjoy their life [...] So, please pay more. We love you for this.[31]

This letter, published in *Süddeutsche Zeitung*, was certainly written in a satirical way. It reflected, nevertheless, the main perception of the Greek society by the German media, especially concerning early retirement.

All in all, American, British and German newspapers were often 'hostile' vis-à-vis the Hellenic society. As opposed to their coverage, however, the French and Italian print media were much more careful in generally dealing with the Greek people. At least, they avoided blaming all citizens as one for corruption, tax evasion and laziness. Here, the stance of Italian journalists could certainly be attributed to their cultural proximity to their 'neighbours'. That of their French colleagues seems more complicated though. Their stance does maybe reflect an internal inclination for respecting the Greek demos, living in the country where a civilisation they admire had been created in classical times.

Melancholic Journalism

The Pain of Austerity

The international media have often criticised Greek society as a whole in their attempt to analyse the crisis. Nevertheless, this does not mean they have failed to realise the problems ordinary citizens have encountered within the era of unprecedented austerity. By contrast, they attempted to explore the impact of tough measures taken by the government on their everyday lives as well as the consequences of rising unemployment. This part is maybe the most interesting one in the coverage of the Hellenic problem. The work of foreign journalists has revealed the real dimension of the economic crisis which is often ignored in European summits and other top-class meetings at the international level.

A plethora of examples can be found in the media discourse highlighting the drama of the Greek people. Many stories dealt with the struggle by various families to survive after continuing drastic cuts in their salaries. *The Times*, for instance, concentrated on the families with children.[32] Within this context, *Bild* prepared an interesting story on the tendency of some parents to give their children to orphanages because of financial difficulties. The correspondent of this tabloid visited SOS village

---

31 *Süddeutsche Zeitung*. 2010. Weihnachtskarte, die geschrieben werden müssten: Ein satirischer Rundumschlag zum Jahr der Krisen [24 December]. Available at: http://archiv.sueddeutsche.de/sueddz/index.php?id=A48594658_EGTPOGWPOPOWWRGRHSTRASH [accessed April 2011].

32 P. Pangalos. 2011. Families battle to survive rising bills and falling incomes. *The Times* [17 June]. Available at: http://www.thetimes.co.uk/tto/news/world/europe/article3065121.ece [accessed January 2011].

in Athens and predicted that this had been a growing trend.[33] On this occasion, and noting the sensitivity of the issue, I called SOS village to cross-check information provided by *Bild* which was indeed confirmed.[34]

Along with Greek families, many newspapers discussed the problem of poverty and hunger in the country. Looking at the problem in more detail, it was synthesised around two main developments. The first was the increase in the numbers of homeless people in the centre of Athens and other cities of the country, and the second was the supporting role by organisations such as Orthodox Church and the Red Cross in providing a food service not only to homeless people but also to poor pensioners. According to a report published in *The Times*, approximately 1,000 people per day were looking for food, medication and clothing in Athens. As the newspaper explains, most of them were Greeks, although asylum seekers and immigrants had constituted the majority before the outbreak of the crisis.[35]

In a heart-breaking example of the media coverage, *La Repubblica* interviewed famous director Theodoros Angelopoulos who portrayed Athens in a grey colour. Approximately two months before his tragic car accident which cost him his life, he shared his experience with the Italian audience, saying that every time his he went back home from work he saw many people sleeping in the streets.[36] It was also interesting that *Bild* published a story presenting an heiress of the Onassis family being forced by the crisis to search for food in rubbish,[37] while *Frankfurter Allgemeine Zeitung* depicted conditions by asserting: 'no bread, no oil'.[38]

Another disappointing consequence of the crisis has been the impact of austerity on consumption in Greece, often leading to calamity. A service-based economy such as the Greek one has shrunk due to rising unemployment and cuts in salaries and pensions. *Frankfurter Allgemeine Zeitung* illustrated this development by noticing that people had been almost obliged to spend less because of tax rises and

---

33   P. Ronzheimer. 2011. Griechen geben ihre Kinder im Heib ab. *Bild* [11 November 2011]. Available at: http://www.bild.de/politik/ausland/griechenland-krise/griechen-geben-ihre-kinder-im-heim-ab-20951494.bild.html [accessed November 2011].

34   On 13 December 2011 Mr. Stergios Sifnios, head of social service at SOS village, confirmed the reliability of reports in a telephone interview.

35   R. Boyes. 2011. Greeks line up for lunch as new man sets terms. *The Times*, 8 November, 6, 7.

36   P. Russo. 2011. Angelopoulos dirige Servillo: Come è grigia la mia Grecia. *La Repubblica* [15 October]. http://www.repubblica.it/spettacoli-e-cultura/2011/10/15/news/intervista_anghelopoulos_servillo-23190339/index.html?ref=search [accessed November 2011].

37   P. Ronzheimer. 2011. Hier krammt eine Onassis-Erbin im Müll. *Bild* [20 October]. Available at: http://www.bild.de/politik/ausland/onassis-clan/hier-kramt-eine-erbin-im-muell-20543334.bild.html [accessed November 2011].

38   *Frankfurter Allgemeine Zeitung*. 2011. Kein Brot, kein Benzin [19 October]. Available at: http://www.faz.net/aktuell/wirtschaft/europas-schuldenkrise/generalstreik-in-griechenland-kein-brot-kein-benzin-11498150.html [accessed November 2011].

cuts in salaries and pensions.[39] As a result, various small shops have had to close down, unable to cover their expenses and the salaries of their employees. Peter Beaumont wrote a story for *The Guardian* on the consequences of the economic crisis on the local market. Passing through various streets in commercial districts of the capital, he realised how many shops were available to let.[40]

The media have also dealt with the lack of liquidity in Greece, explaining it has often led people to seek alternatives to borrowing money. Unable to cover their financial needs, a tendency to exchange gold and jewellery for instant cash has been observed in the country. Within this context, stores – pawnshops and gold dealers – have thrived. People have been prepared to exchange jewellery and other valuables in order not only to pay necessary taxes, such as the property one incorporated in the electricity bill, but also to buy food and clothes. Sketching out this unprecedented development in the Hellenic society, *The New York Times* reported that 90 per cent of the 224 officially registered pawnshops only opened up in 2011. The newspaper also denoted some of their activities had not been legitimate as they had expanded the illicit trade of gold.[41]

The financial crisis has increased the Greek suicide rate to record highs. International media have shown an interest in dealing with this sad trend. *Il Corriere della Sera* explained in October 2011 that an increase of approximately 40 per cent had been observed and wrote that an appropriate helpline received approximately 100 calls per day from desperate citizens.[42] Going even further, *The Wall Street Journal* prepared a personal story of a despairing Greek person who drank a poisonous brew of beer and gasoline. The American economic newspaper concluded that 'the economic crash has created a new phenomenon of entrepreneurs with no prior history of mental illness, who are found dead every other week'.[43] In parallel with the increase in suicide attempts, criminality has been also on the rise with thieves

---

39   R. Herman. 2011. Die Griechen geben weniger Geld aus. *Frankfurter Allgemeine Zeitung* [1 August]. Available at: http://www.faz.net/aktuell/wirtschaft/europas-schuldenkrise/schuldenkrise-die-griechen-geben-weniger-geld-aus-11106443.html [accessed November 2011].

40   P. Beaumont. 2011 Athens is plastered with one message: enoikiazetai. To let. *The Guardian* [4 August]. http://www.guardian.co.uk/world/2011/aug/04/athens-to-let-signs-are-everywhere[accessed December 2011].

41   N. Kitsantonis. 2012. In Greece's sour economy, some shops are thriving. *The New York Times* [2 January]. Available at: http://www.nytimes.com/2012/01/03/world/europe/as-greece-struggles-pawnbrokers-prosper.html?_r=1 [accessed February 2012].

42   *Il Corriere della Sera*. 2011. Grecia, è allarme suicidi per la crisi [20 September]. Available at: http://www.corriere.it/salute/11_settembre_20/grecia-crisi-suicidi-aumento_e91e128e-e391-11e0-bc23-ba86791f572a.shtml [accessed November 2011].

43   M. Walker. 2011. Greek crisis exacts the cruelest toll. *The Wall Street Journal* [20 September]. Available at: http://online.wsj.com/article/SB10001424053111904199404576538261061694524.html [accessed November 2011].

breaking into homes to take money. As *The Times* clarified in their report, they were amateurs doing it for food and unemployed people trying to keep their families.[44]

Brain Drain

Unemployment hitting Greece is a problem foreign journalists have often discussed. Their coverage has not only been limited to numbers and statistics but has gone deeper. The media attempted to explore the impact of the economic crisis on ordinary citizens, especially young ones. *Le Monde*, for example, concentrated on this problem even from December 2009. Its story was an interactive one based on video interviews. In particular, it illustrated that although young people in the country were the most educated in Europe, they had been the most affected by the crisis. The newspaper considered them as 'the generation of 700 euros'.[45]

It is maybe a tragic irony but the report by the French liberal newspaper and its reference to the salary of €700 would almost seem ideal for the country's economic standards in the following years. With unemployment on the rise and recession deepening, optimism has almost disappeared from the sky of the country. Obviously, young Greek people have not been the only ones suffering in Europe as Spanish citizens have also experienced a similar drama.[46] Nevertheless, the special attention paid to the former by the media is related to their increasing need to look for alternatives in pursuing a career in foreign countries, at least to a larger extent compared to their European friends. The so-called new wave of emigration from the Hellenic Republic to other states has gradually become an issue of high interest.

The harsh dilemma of young Greek people has been nicely illustrated by *Le Monde*. The opinion-forming newspaper asserted that they have had to consider either to remain unemployed or to leave their country. Germany is one of the main destinations for Greek emigrants.[47] *Handelsblatt*, for example, spoke of an 'exodus' and reported on two young girls who had attended a seminar in the Athens Goethe Institute to explore the opportunity of living 'in a country which is working'.[48]

---

44 J. Bone, 2011. Crime shows dark side of ancient capital. *The Times* [15 October]. Available at: http://www.thetimes.co.uk/tto/news/world/europe/article3195239.ece, [accessed December 2011].

45 *Le Monde*. 2009. Les jeunes Grecs ou la génération des '700 euros' [8 December]. Available at: http://www.lemonde.fr/europe/video/2009/12/08/les-jeunes-grecs-ou-la-generation-des-700-euros_1277507_3214.html [accessed April 2011].

46 See, for example: *Süddeutsche Zeitung*. 2011. Europas Jugend ohne Arbeit [11 August]. http://www.sueddeutsche.de/wirtschaft/jobmangel-in-der-eu-europas-jugend-ohne-arbeit-1.1130405 [accessed November 2011].

47 R. Müller. 2011. Die Krisenflüchtlinge. *Frankfurter Allgemeine Zeitung*. Available at: http://www.faz.net/sonntagszeitung/gesellschaft/arbeitsziel-deutschland-die-krisenfluechtlinge-11542594.html [accessed: December 2011].

48 M. Brüggman. 2011. Junge Griechen-Elite verlässt ihr Land. *Handelsblatt* [29 October]. http://www.handelsblatt.com/politik/international/exodus-der-akademiker-junge-

Britain and Australia are also among the favourite destination countries. In a story similar to that of *Handelsblatt*, *The Times* conducted an interview with a young electrician who had visited the Australian embassy in Athens in order to collect information to find a job in Sydney.[49] To sum up, the Hellenic Republic has been perceived as a state which could not benefit from its young and gifted workforce, kicking it out from its boundaries.

Uncertainty like in World War II

A potential default of the Hellenic Republic does not only create concern for banks and bondholders but also for ordinary citizens. As there is no recent paradigm of a bankrupted country – at least in Europe – Greek people feel unsafe and unsure for the future value of their money and properties. The international media have elaborated on this unprecedented uncertainty and have analysed various methods ordinary citizens found in order to protect their personal assets. These have, first, included transfers from domestic into foreign banks.[50] Destination countries have been principally Britain, Germany and Switzerland.[51]

Bank transfers, however, only represent one of the necessary choices Greek people have had to make during the crisis. Additional bizarre incidents have been also taken place. *Frankfurter Allgemeine Zeitung* wrote in May 2011, for example, that according to customs officers, 'many people with money in their luggage had been caught in airports'.[52] For its part, the *Financial Times* illustrated the tendency of Greek people to rush for gold. In a remarkable case, its correspondent Kerin Hope interviewed a computer technician, who explained that he had exchanged his euros for gold coins, keeping them at home just like his grandmother did in World War II.[53]

The international newspapers have generally correctly depicted the uncertainty of Greek citizens after the outbreak of the crisis. Unable to trust their politicians who were encouraging them to increase their deposits in national banks, they preferred

---

griechen-elite-verlaesst-ihr-land/5765892.html [accessed December 2011].

49 J. Bones. 2011. Jobs crisis forces thousands to seek a better life abroad. *The Times* [14 October]. Available at: http://www.thetimes.co.uk/tto/news/world/europe/article3193945.ece [accessed December 2011].

50 See for example: A. Salles. 2011. Des particuliers grecs retirent leurs dépôts des banques. *Le Monde*, 3 June, Economie – Enterpises, 14.

51 See for example: M. Maurisse, 2011. Avec la crise, la fuite de capitaux grecs vers la Suisse s'accélère. *Le Figaro*, 4 June, 20.

52 W. Mussler, M. Frühauf and R. Hermann. 2011. Griechen ziehen ihr Geld von Bankkonten ab. *Frankfurter Allgemeine Zeitung* [25 May]. Available at: http://www.faz.net/aktuell/wirtschaft/europas-schuldenkrise/furcht-vor-staatsbankrott-griechen-ziehen-ihr-geld-von-bankkonten-ab-1642173.html [accessed November 2011].

53 K. Hope. 2011. Grek savers rush for gold. *Financial Times* [21 June]. Available at: http://www.ft.com/cms/s/0/c986823e-9bf8-11e0-bef9-00144feabdc0.html#axzz1o8KgF71t [accessed November 2011].

old-fashioned but possibly safer solutions. Elaborating on the fear of people for the future, correspondent for *Bild* Paul Ronzheimer visited a branch of the National Bank of Greece three days before the critical European summit of 26–27 October 2011 and saw a large queue waiting in order to withdraw their money.⁵⁴

Public Ire

We Don't Want Foreigners!

Along with the impact of austerity measures placed on Greek citizens and the economic calamity, the international media have also concentrated on an additional aspect. Greek public opinion was one of frustration and especially ire against elected politicians who led the country to the brink of collapse and bankruptcy. Foreign journalists reported on the various reactions, such as the peaceful 'angry people movement' which developed in the spring of 2011. In this case, *The Times* reported:

> People filled with anger, disgust and a sense of despair flowed into Syntagma Square in the hot evening sun to stand before the Parliament in protest. The whole bunch of them should just go to jail, all 300 MPs, said Sophia, a 40-year-old unemployed secretary. First they robbed us and now they've sold us to the foreigners.⁵⁵

In an article looking at the anger of Greek people against national politicians, *Bild* elaborated on the various privileges of the latter such as special allowances and benefits. In the view of the German tabloid, public anger could be placed within this framework and there was a sentiment of social injustice prevailing in the Greek society. On this occasion, I was asked to comment for the *Bild* and I partly justified public reaction by saying: 'Politicians who led Greece into the crisis are now unable to save it'.⁵⁶

Greek people have not only blamed national politicians but also European ones for the economic crisis. The international newspapers realised this additional dimension and sometimes reported on public perceptions of the Troika, Chancellor

---

54 P. Ronzheimer. 2011. Hier plündern die Griechen ihre Konten. *Bild* [24 October]. Available at: http://www.bild.de/politik/ausland/griechenland-krise/angst-vor-schuldenschnitt-griechen-pluendern-ihre-konten-20624790.bild.html [accessed November 2011].

55 C. Bremmer. 2011. In Athens some whisper it: Revolution. *The Times* [18 June]. Available at: http://www.thetimes.co.uk/tto/news/world/europe/article3066434.ece [accessed December 2011].

56 P. Ronzheimer. 2011.Das Kassieren die Pleite-Politker. *Bild*. [5 May 2011]. Available at: http://www.bild.de/politik/ausland/griechenland-krise/demonstrationen-in-athen-20316842.bild.html [November 2011].

Merkel and President Sarkozy. The slogan: 'Nazi-Nazi, Merkel-Sarkozy', for example, often used in Athens demonstrations has been reproduced by foreign journalists.[57] In particular, the four German newspapers accessed seemed to be well aware of the hostile inclination of the majority of Greeks towards Berlin. Even from February 2010 *Süddeutsche Zeitung* had reported that Germany was regarded as a 'nazi country' and 'former occupying power'.[58]

A Country in Paralysis

Strikes and Bad Service

Covering the daily life of Greek citizens, foreign journalists also analysed the quality of public service within the crisis framework. Here, their attention was attracted to the continuous strikes, heavily disrupting public service. The frequent closure of the Parthenon, for instance, was an issue the media reported.[59] On the day of such a strike, *The Guardian* asserted emphatically: 'In a dramatic escalation of the anger unleashed by the economic crisis engulfing Greece, communist protesters stormed the Acropolis today'.[60] The occupation of one of the most important monuments in world history by Greek people themselves had a rather shocking and symbolic meaning in the coverage of the country by international media connoting that the situation was almost out of control.

Communist protesters also damaged the international image of Greece by occupying the port of Piraeus and causing chaos to transportation from Attica to islands. In June 2010, for example, they followed the same illegal strategy as with the closure of Acropolis, by blocking the harbour tiers and not letting tourists depart. On this occasion, *La Repubblica* uploaded a video in its website showing passengers waiting in Piraeus with no idea when they would board.[61] Furthermore,

---

57 P. Ronzheimer and R. Schuler. 2011. Warum machen die Griechen uns zum Buhmann, *Bild* [21 June]. Available at: http://www.bild.de/politik/ausland/griechenland-krise/deutschland-zahlt-und-wird-dafuer-beschimpft-18452080.bild.html [accessed July 2011]. See also: Salles, A. 2011. L'odyssée de Papandréou. *Le Monde*, 16 September, 19.

58 *Süddeutsche Zeitung*. 2010. Vorwürfe gegen ex-besatzer Deutschland [24 February]. Available at: http://www.sueddeutsche.de/wirtschaft/griechenland-der-ton-wird-rauer-vorwuerfe-gegen-ex-besatzer-deutschland-1.2839 [accessed April 2011].

59 See, for example, *Le Figaro*. 2010. Troisième matinée de grève à l'Acropole [15 October]. Available at: http://www.lefigaro.fr/conjoncture/2010/10/13/04016-20101013ARTFIG00366-l-acropole-bloque-par-des-fonctionnaires.php [accessed April 2011].

60 H. Smith. 2010. Greek protesters storm the Acropolis. *The Guardian* [4 May]. Available at: http://www.guardian.co.uk/business/2010/may/04/greek-protesters-storm-acropolis [accessed April 2011].

61 *La Repubblica*. 2010. Sciopero in Grecia: bloccati I tragheti dei touristi [23 June]. Available at: http://video.repubblica.it/dossier/grecia-crisi-economica/sciopero-in-grecia-

the image of Greece has acquired a particularly negative tinge during the strike of taxi-drivers in the summer of 2011. At that time, many tourists visiting the country faced serious difficulties due to the continuous opposition of taxi-drivers to government plans aimed at liberating their professions. In an ironic phrase, the British tabloid *The Sun* commented on the quality of service they provided, by asserting that 'taxis – when not on strike – are pricey'.[62] For its part, *Handelsblatt* reported on the strike by publishing an online story with a picture of a tourist carrying his luggage near taxis which had been unavailable.[63]

Foreign journalists had additional opportunities to deal with the strikes in the Hellenic Republic. Employees working in public transportations and national railway, also air traffickers, doctors, pharmacists and lawyers often demonstrated against governmental policies. Strikes organised by doctors working in public hospitals influenced the quality of services provided. In such a case, *The Guardian* elaborated on the problematic healthcare sector. Its correspondent in Athens, Peter Beaumont, visited a public hospital and interviewed a 50-year-old former port worker who was unemployed and diabetic and who explained to the British newspaper his painful experience.[64]

The weeks from Monday 10 until Friday 21 October 2011 were maybe among the most difficult ones for ordinary citizens. In this period, *Bild* dealt extensively with the strike of garbage collectors and published photos depicting the conditions in the centre of Athens due to uncollected litter.[65] One of the published stories was entitled: 'Greece stinks until the sky'.[66]

Violence and Teargas

International media attention was attracted to the organised demonstrations that took place in Athens and other cities of the country. The newspapers, especially in their electronic versions, extensively used multimedia in order to regularly update the content of their website and provide new material. In so doing, *Il Corriere*

---

bloccati-i-traghetti-dei-turisti/49443/48952 [accessed November 2010].

62 *The Sun*. 2011. Avoiding a Greek Tragedy, 30 July, 60.

63 *Handelsblatt*. 2011. [2 August]. Available at: http://www.handelsblatt.com/panorama/lifestyle/trotz-streik-griechenland-touristen-duerfen-gratis-taxi-fahren/4457216.html [accessed November 2011].

64 P. Beaumont. 2011. Greece's healthcare system is on the brink of catastrophe. *The Guardian* [11 August]. Available at: http://www.guardian.co.uk/world/2011/aug/05/greece-healthcare-brink-catastrophe [accessed December 2011].

65 P. Ronzheimer. 2011. Horr-Woche für Griechenland. *Bild* [17 October]. Available at: http://www.bild.de/politik/ausland/griechenland-krise/griechenland-krise-streikt-sich-das-land-diese-woche-selbst-kaputt-20497260.bild.html [accessed November 2011].

66 *Bild*. 2011. Athen stink zum Himmel [13 October]. Available at: http://www.bild.de/geld/wirtschaft/griechenland-krise/muellabfuhr-streikt-athen-stinkt-zum-himmel-20445650.bild.html [accessed November 2011].

*della Sera*⁶⁷ and *La Repubblica*⁶⁸ closely followed developments in the centre of the Greek capital in October 2011. Synthesising their work, foreign journalists were interested in covering two different dimensions. The first related to the use of violence and the second to the inability of the Greek Government to stop those responsible destroying public property.

The most painful experience for foreign journalists – especially correspondents based in Athens – was the coverage of the events of 5 May 2010 because of the death of three people in the centre of city. *Frankfurter Allgemeine Zeitung* went even further by commenting on the inability of the state to implement reforms:

> Thousands of demonstrators, arsons, the first dead people – Wednesday's incidents in Athens justify the view of those who put into question Papandreou's attempt to apply the austerity measures. Maybe the majority of Greeks is aware that their state cannot any longer continue on the same course and that it has to reinvent itself in order to make it in the 21st century and not to take its European partners with it to the abyss. However, extreme groups are not prepared to accept the fiscal reform plans as a collective goal.⁶⁹

Along with the death of 3 people on 5 May 2010, most reporters covered clashes between citizens and the police. Sharing their experience, they agreed that all demonstrations normally end with smoke and teargas.⁷⁰ An interesting example in the report included an incident in December 2010 when an ND MP, Costis Hatzidakis, was hurt by angry demonstrators. On that case, *Il Corriere della Sera* uploaded a

---

67 *Il Corriere della Sera*. 2011. Grecia, seconda giornata di scioperi [21 October]. Available at: http://www.corriere.it/esteri/11_ottobre_20/grecia-secondo-giorno-sciopero_3ea4b7b6-fb03-11e0-b6b2-0c72eeeb0c77.shtml [accessed January 2011].

68 *La Repubblica*. La protesta infiamma la Grecia in duecentomila contro l'austerity [19 October]. Available at: http://www.repubblica.it/economia/2011/10/19/news/sciopero_grecia-23478386/ [accessed January 2012].

69 K.D. Frankenberger. 2010. Brandsätze. *Frankfurter Allgemeine Zeitung* [5 May]. Available at: http://www.faz.net/aktuell/politik/griechenland-brandsaetze-1978325.html [accessed December 2011]. The original text is as such: 'Zehntausende Demonstranten, Brandsätze, die ersten Toten – das Geschehen in Athen am Mittwoch gibt denen recht, die bezweifeln, dass die Regierung Papandreou ihre Sparpolitik wird durchsetzen können. Vielleicht weiß die Mehrheit der Griechen, dass es wie bisher in ihrem Staat nicht weitergehen kann, dass das Land sich neu erfinden muss, um im 21. Jahrhundert bestehen zu können – und um die europäischen Partner nicht mit in den Abgrund zu ziehen. Aber die Militanten, die Radikalen sind nicht bereit, die Sanierung der Staatsfinanzen als kollektives Ziel zu akzeptieren'.

70 A. Salles. 2011. Violences lors de la première grève générale de l'année en Grèce. *Le Monde* [24 February]. See also: *La Repubblica*. 2011. Atene, esplode la protesta. Lacrimogeni contro dimostranti [28 June]. Available at: http://www.repubblica.it/esteri/2011/06/28/news/scontri_grecia_manifestanti_polizia-18344774/ [accessed November 2011].

video showing the attack and Mr Hatzidakis' face covered in blood.[71] For their part, *The New York Times*, in covering demonstrations in June 2011, published a picture on its website showing a policeman hitting a demonstrator in a cruel way.[72]

Breaking the Law

An Impunity Culture

The tendency of various Greek citizens to often break the law but remain unpunished could not but be an issue of interest for the media as well. A striking development in Hellenic society in the aftermath of the outbreak of the crisis related to the stance of various citizens to avoid paying for goods. As *The Washington Post* reports, 'thousands have joined an "I Won't Pay" movement, refusing to cover highway tolls, bus fares, even fees at public hospitals'.[73] The coverage by the American newspaper did not exaggerate the problem as the Greek Government was unable to provide an efficient solution and eliminate the activities of the above movement. Ironically, a few months later it would be the Greek Government itself leading a non-payment campaign by failing to pay back its creditors and impose an obligatory haircut to all bondholders.

The incidents in the town of Keratea, 40 kilometres south east of Athens, do constitute an additional example of the so-called impunity culture. For a period of approximately three months, residents of this small town were locked in a violent stand off with the police. They were strongly opposing the planned construction of a landfill aiming, in theory, at solving the capital's garbage problem. Commenting on the reaction of the citizens, *The New York Times* explained that 'the Keratea campaign [could be compared] to milder forms of civil disobedience appearing in a debt-stricken Greece'.[74] Likewise, for *Le Figaro*, the struggle of Keratea was 'a symbol of the fight against the government'.[75]

---

71   *Il Corriere della Sera*. 2010. Molotov e Auto in Fiamme, *Caos ad Atene* [15 December]. Available at: http://www.corriere.it/esteri/10_dicembre_15/grecia-sciopero-generale-scontri-atene_62c8abd4-0842-11e0-b759-00144f02aabc.shtml [accessed December 2011].

72   R. Donario. 2011. Greece approves tough measures on economy. Available at: http://www.nytimes.com/2011/06/30/world/europe/30greece.html?_r=1&scp=398&sq=greece&st=nyt, 29 June [accessed December 2011].

73   A. Faiola. 2011. In Greece, austerity kindles deep discontent. *The Washington Post* [14 May]. http://www.washingtonpost.com/world/in-greece-austerity-kindles-deep-discontent/2011/05/05/AFUQGy2G_story.html [accessed December 2011].

74   N. Kitsantonis. 2011. Greek town rises up against planned landfill. *The New York Times* [16 March]. Available at: http://www.nytimes.com/2011/03/17/world/europe/17greece.html?pagewanted=all [accessed April 2011].

75   A. Salles 2011. En Grèce, la lutte contre les décharges s'organise à Kératéa. *Le Monde*, 12 April, 5.

The inability of the Greek Government to impose the anti-smoking law is another bizarre example confirming the prevailing impunity culture. A correspondent for *The Guardian* in Athens, Helena Smith, published an article: 'Greece: Refusing to quit', in which she tested the application of the anti-smoking law in the country. Her conclusion was that: 'Sanctions came from neither staff nor any of the municipal police tasked with enforcing the ban'[76] As a result, one could ponder that a government which is not able to enact the anti-smoking law will also dramatically fail in doing so for complicated and more difficult cases. It comes as no surprise then that, according to the *Financial Times*, an estimated €3 billion per year are lost 'due to a pan-Balkan fuel smuggling operation'.[77]

An Unsafe Country

Within the framework of instability in a time of crisis, various newspapers also posed questions relating to security in the country. For *Le Figaro*, 'extremist groups' are always active in the country,[78] while for *Süddeutsche Zeitung*, they do belong to the left spectrum of politics.[79] Foreign journalists have, specifically, emphasised the activity of various terrorist organisations such as the so-called: 'Sect of Revolutionaries'. This terror group was responsible for the assassination of journalist Sokratis Gkiolias in July 2010.[80] In parallel with this, the international media also expressed their concern when parcel bombs originating from the Hellenic Republic were sent to various European countries in October, November and December 2010.[81] In this case, attention was mainly paid to the role of the 'Fire

---

76 H. Smith. 2010. Greece: Refusing to Quit. *The Guardian* [2 September]. Available at: http://www.guardian.co.uk/commentisfree/2010/sep/02/greece-smoking-ban?INTCMP=SRCH, [accessed December 2011].

77 M. Glenny. 2011. The Real Greek tragedy – its rapacious oligarchs. *Financial Times* [4 November]. Available at: http://www.ft.com/cms/s/0/618e57d6-0937-11e1-a20c-00144feabdc0.html#axzz1o8KgF71t [accessed February 2012].

78 T. Portes. 2011. En Bref. *Le Figaro*, 20 May, 9.

79 K. Strittmatter. 2011. Pure Lust an der Gewalt. *Süddeutsche Zeitung* [3 November]. Available at: http://www.sueddeutsche.de/politik/terror-in-griechenland-pure-lust-an-der-gewalt-1.1018986 [accessed April 2011].

80 See for example: *Le Monde*. 2010. Un journaliste grec abattu de dix balles à Athènes [18 July]. Available at: http://www.lemonde.fr/europe/article/2010/07/19/un-journaliste-grec-abattu-de-dix-balles-a-athenes_1389807_3214.html [accessed June 2011]. Also: *Frankfurter Allgemeine Zeitung*. 2010. Radiojournalist Erschossen, 19 July and *Il Corriere della Sera*. 2010. Giornalista Assassinato Sotto Casa. *Il Corriere della Sera* [19 July].

81 See for example: K. Hope. 2010. Papandreou raises stakes in local elections. *Financial Times* [3 November]. Available at: http://www.ft.com/intl/cms/s/0/9f3703ee-e787-11df-b5b4-00144feab49a.html#axzz1hpxgDAzz [accessed April 2011] and *Handelsblatt*. 2011. Paketbomben alarmieren EU-Spitze [3 November]. Available at: http://www.handelsblatt.com/politik/international/paketbomben-alarmieren-eu-spitze/3581434.

Nuclei' group. Writing in the *Wall Street Journal*, Alkman Granitsas commented in an ironic tone:

> If Europe's leaders didn't already have enough reasons to worry about Greece these days, they have just found another: the country's loony, left-wing extremists have discovered a new way to export their form of anarchy and terror abroad.[82]

A few titles went even further in their coverage and put into question the establishment of democracy in the Hellenic Republic. *The Observer* and *The Wall Street Journal* asserted that stability in the country could not be taken for granted and elaborated on the important role of the Greek military. The British newspaper did so for the first time in February 2010. Will Hutton, inter alia, argued:

> If Greece leaves, its new independent currency will collapse; its interest rates will soar; its public debts will become unfinanceable; it really will default on its debt as it has so frequently in the past. It will slide back into being a failed state – with a military coup one all too possible response to the crisis.[83]

As for the American economic newspaper, Allen Mattich recalled in September 2011 that generals in the Greek military had staged a coup in 1967 and did not exclude the possibility of a repetition of history in the aftermath of a possible sovereign default.[84] *The New York Times* followed a milder approach but reported that according to UBS, 'military coups and possible civil war that could afflict a departing country [from the eurozone]'.[85]

The aforementioned articles, mainly the comments of *The Observer* and *The Wall Street Journal*, are certainly the worst examples of journalistic work during the Hellenic crisis. If the tone of other commentaries – even ironic and offending

---

html?p3581434=all [accessed April 2011]. See also: A. Kefalas. 2010. La Grèce Frappéé par une Vague de Terrorisme Postale. *Le Figaro* [4 November]. Available at: http://www.lefigaro.fr/international/2010/11/03/01003-20101103ARTFIG00725-la-grece-frappee-par-une-vague-de-terrorisme-postal.php [accessed April 2011] and K. Strittmatter. 2010. Pure Lust an der Gewalt. *Süddeutsche Zeitung* [3 November]. Available at: http://www.sueddeutsche.de/politik/terror-in-griechenland-pure-lust-an-der-gewalt-1.1018986 [accessed April 2011].

82 A. Granitsas. 2010. Greece: Terror to Be Damned. *The Wall Street Journal* [3 November]. Available at http://blogs.wsj.com/source/2010/11/03/greece-terror-be-damned/ [accessed April 2011].

83 W. Hutton. 2010. Don't laugh at Europe's woes. The troubles facing Greece are also ours. *The Observer*, 14 February, 38.

84 A. Mattich. 2011. Greece: Don't miscount the role of the military. *The Wall Street Journal* [19 September]. Available at: http://blogs.wsj.com/source/2011/09/19/greece-dont-discount-role-of-military/ [accessed December 2011].

85 L. Thomas and N. Kitsantonis. 2011. Pondering a Dire Day: Leaving the euro. *The New York Times*, 13 December, Business Desk, 1.

ones – can be possibly justified, the ones synthesised around a possible military coup are not well placed, have not been confirmed by political developments and challenge the reliability of the sources in which they were published. In the final account, those kind of journalistic pieces only contribute to further instability in a country suffering from serious economic problems.

Is Everything Bad?

Foreign journalists and correspondents were keen to explore pathogenies of the Greek society, as in the ones already sketched out above. They became, in other words, particularly interested in preparing numerous negative stories. By contrast, they did not then do so with the positive developments which certainly exist in the Hellenic Republic. The excellent performance of the country in the area of shipping and maritime industry, for example, is certainly a crucial aspect the international media have almost ignored. Exceptions do exist, but they do not mirror general coverage.[86]

The tendency of journalists to prefer negative stories becomes clear even in the case of the coverage of Greek shipping. The *Financial Times*, for instance, published a piece on the theme when a wedding party on board the historical warship 'Averof' took place. This party shocked public opinion in the country as it was seen as a straightforward indication of indifference and a lack of respect for Hellenic history. Although the article refers to various shipping families in the country, the journalist, a freelance reporter, gave the impression of having searched for a striking pretext to put pressure on her editor to consider publication. Not only did she write the piece from a 'lifestyle' perspective, but she also commented that the images of the party had 'only added to the country's sense of dysfunction'.[87] At that time, the Hellenic Republic had already started to receive criticism internationally and the piece could be easily placed within this climate.

Positive or at least neutral articles on Greece have been published since October 2009. As it had happened, in the period before the national election, the country continued being a beautiful tourist destination, receiving hits with reference to classical times, while the presence of various figures in academia and in areas such as culture and sports was still active worldwide. Nevertheless, stories outlining the positive dimension of Greece have been marginalised by the critical economic problem of the country. In summary, Greece has been constructed as synonymous for a multi-faceted crisis in the media discourse in the aftermath of October 2009.

---

86 J. Miller. 2010. Greek shippers weather storms. *The Wall Street Journal* [13 May]. Available at: http://online.wsj.com/article/SB10001424052748704879704575236190728497962.html [accessed April 2011].

87 J. Kakissis. 2010. Greek shipping families in the spotlight. *Financial Times* [21 August]. Available at: http://www.ft.com/cms/s/2/4ee112a6-ab30-11df-9e6b-00144feabdc0.html#axzz1ALH67i3Q [accessed March 2011].

Better Not to Live Here...

Having the accessed newspapers as a source of information, Greece is not perceived as an ideal place for citizens to live, for businessmen to invest and for travellers to visit. By contrast, it has been regarded as a dangerous and problematic country where criminality, violence and unemployment are on the rise and corruption is flourishing. It has been also seen as a state where democracy is challenged and having a population which does not pay taxes, is often too lazy to work, does not respect the law and blames foreigners for the economic calamity. It has been, finally, illustrated as a country which has almost no future because it kicks out its charismatic young people, being unable to absorb them into its public and private sectors.

A few national differences have been observed in the coverage. Once again, the American, British and German newspapers have been more hostile and ironic towards the Greek society and its problems as opposed to French and Italian ones. At the same time, the Italian titles, namely *Il Corriere della Serra* and *La Repubblica*, have published less stories on the Hellenic Republic while all other sources have extensively dealt with the country in their comment and debate pages, either electronic or print versions. In spite of a few national differences, the general conclusion is not distorted. The country has been stigmatised in all international media with no end in sight as yet to improve its image. This said, it is important to remember that Greece has also been portrayed as a country with a parasitic economy and one that is governed by unreliable politicians.

Chapter 7
Greece as a Special Case: But Ideal for Journalists!

From October 2009 onwards Greece has been of particular interest for the international media. Coverage has been particularly negative for the country and often for its citizens too. Various pathogenies of the economy, the political system and the public administration have been highlighted while attention has been mainly paid to recurrent phenomena such as continuous strikes, demonstrations and violent actions. The Hellenic Republic has been criticised for its huge public debt and its government's inefficiency to meet fiscal targets, implement necessary reforms on the basis of international agreements, enact the law and keep its promises. In parallel with this, the tangible consequences of austerity measures have led journalists to prepare numerous stories – often moving ones – of Greek people experiencing the financial drama. Characteristic examples include the withdrawal of deposits from banks and the increase in suicide attempts.

It seems that the crisis acquired an additional dimension for the Hellenic Republic. Along with its economic, political and social aspects, the communication impact has been equally painful. The name 'Greece' has been internationally construed as synonymous with an almost failed state which not only violated the rules, submitting wrong data, but one that is allergic to change. Words such as 'zorbas and syrtaki', representing the beauty of the country, have been replaced by 'rousfeti' and 'fakelaki' in the media discourse. Looking at the general coverage there are two interconnected questions which arise: first, why have foreign journalists overstated the Greek cause? And second, why did they adapt a particularly critical stance towards the country? Attempting to answer these questions I will draw, on the one hand, on the rich literature of political communication, and on the other, on interviews I have conducted with journalists and bankers as well as on my own experience acting as an interviewee for news programmes in a time of a crisis.

Reporting the News

Different Criteria but Similar Results

The increased interest by the media in the Greek crisis can be attributed to its metastasis effect as well as to its potential impact on the euro. Ireland and Portugal have indeed asked for the activation of the bailout mechanism while strong market pressures have been exerted on Italy and Spain. At the same time, the stability of the common currency has been put into question and the eurozone into risk. The theory of communication studies confirms that 'the more an event concerns elite nations, the more probable is that it will become a news item'.[1] This is obviously the case with the Hellenic crisis. If Greece had not been a member of the common currency, the interest would have been much lower and the country would have hardly been on the agenda for such a long time.

From an orthodox point of view, the international media have certainly followed developments in their coverage of Greece. There is no question that the country has been on top of the European policy priorities for a period of more than two years. Several European summits, for instance, were called in a matter of urgency to provide solutions to the Hellenic problem. Furthermore, after October 2009, various European leaders such as German Chancellor Angela Merkel and former French President Nicolas Sarkozy often referred to the situation in the country in their discussions, statements and interviews. The same also happened with President of the European Commission, Jose Manuel Barroso, and President of the European Council, Herman van Rompuy. It has been, therefore, a logical consequence for foreign journalists to monitor closely what was occurring in Greece. At the same time, they could not ignore the flourishing debate not only in the political arena but also in the economic and academic circles as to whether the Hellenic Republic would be able to make it or not. We have seen, for example, that *Bloomberg* had conducted quarterly surveys of investors on the matter and that various think-tanks had extensively dealt with it. The Center for Economic Studies in Munich,[2] for example, does regularly elaborate on the need for a Greek return to its national currency.

The metastasis effects of the Hellenic crisis and its impact on the common currency provide the necessary basis for an understanding of the role of the media. Nevertheless, what has to be noted is that newspapers do normally follow different editorial lines on the grounds of the audience they attract. The economic newspapers, namely *Financial Times*, *Handelsblatt* and *The Wall Street Journal*, have informed their readers in detail on the status of the Hellenic economy in order to provide them with necessary information concerning its future. Elite opinion-making newspapers, as the eight analysed in the book, have attempted to offer an overview of the Hellenic crisis, concentrating on the economic as well as on the political and social dimensions of the problem. Finally, titles such as *The Sun* and mainly *Bild*[3] have covered the crisis by principally producing personal stories with ordinary citizens and using strong language which is typical of tabloids.

---

1 J. Galtung and M.H. Ruge. 1999. The Structure of Foreign News, in *News: A Reader*, edited by H. Tumber, Oxford and New York: Oxford University Press, 23.

2 This think-tank is better known as IFO institute. Its president is Professor Hans-Werner Sinn.

3 Otto Brenner Foundation (Otto Brenner Stiftung) has prepared an interesting study on how *Bild* perceived Greece and the European debt crisis in 2010. This report elaborates

In parallel with differences among editorial lines, national preferences are also significant. In British and American titles there is no particular interest for a potential fall of the euro, but only for its consequences on the world economy as both Britain and the USA do not belong to the euro area. British newspapers have even expressed their relief that the UK had not joined the common currency. This is not the case with the French, German and Italian media which do have a particular sensitivity for the sustainability of the euro. In addition, the German media have reflected disappointment if not anger for German people who have had to pay to rescue the Hellenic Republic. The German press may have also mirrored a frustration that the country had left the strong mark to join the euro, while the latter has been undermined by countries with high fiscal deficits such as Greece. For their part, the French media have naturally shared the concern of the banks of France for their exposure to the Greek debt. Finally, in France and especially in Italy it could be expected by some journalists to cover developments such as strikes and demonstrations in a more sympathetic way than Britain, Germany and the USA because of relevant experiences in their own countries.

There is, however, a common denominator in the coverage of all newspapers. This is the tendency of journalists to focus on negative stories. The narration of the Greek story under the current crisis has offered to foreign journalists the opportunity to explore and report various painful themes. This parameter had driven the coverage of the crisis in all newspapers, irrespective of their nationality or quality. A common discourse has, therefore, dominated media discourse. Greece has obviously offered a good opportunity for foreign journalists to explore issues such as corruption, bureaucracy, overspending, poverty and unemployment. It has also provided them with the chance to prepare stories synthesised around the fear and uncertainty of Greek citizens for the future of their personal assets and deposits.

Why Greece?

The insistence on the portrayal of the Greek drama does not mean that the coverage of other PIIGS has been marginalised. Portugal, Ireland, Italy and Spain also are on the media agenda of the European debt crisis. Economic and political developments in these four countries have been discussed. The main difference is that in their case no stereotypes for their societies have been largely produced, while original stories on the impact of austerity measures have been comparatively limited. At the same time, the Greek crisis has triggered an unprecedented clash

---

on the populist style of the German tabloid, criticises its journalistic practices and focuses on its emphasis on public relations. See: H.-J. Arlt and W. Storz. 2011. Drucksache Bild – Eine Marke und ihre Mägde. OBS-Arbeitsheft 67. Available at: http://www.otto-brenner-shop.de/uploads/tx_mplightshop/2011_04_06_Bildstudie_Otto_Brenner_Stiftung.pdf [accessed September 2011].

between the Hellenic Republic and Germany on both political and public opinion levels. Of all the national crises playing out within the eurozone, this is the only one to feature a degree of continuous hostility between two of its members on both political and public levels. In other problematic countries the phenomenon has not given the impression of a bilateral clash. The economic policy of Germany is certainly criticised there, but has not taken the extreme forms apparent in Greece.[4]

There is a plethora of examples highlighting the stance of Greek politicians towards their German partners. A striking one is the phrase used by President of Greece Karolos Papoulias on 15 February 2012. Referring to the German Minister of Finance, Mr Papoulias said: 'I don't accept that my country is vilified by Mr. Schäuble. I don't accept it as a Greek person. Who is Mr Schäuble who can humiliate Greece?'[5] As a natural consequence, a poll conducted in February 2012 revealed that 79 per cent of Greek people have a negative view of Germany, 32.4 per cent associate it with Nazism and the Third Reich and 77 per cent fear the creation of a Fourth Reich.[6] Further to this, some Greeks do not hesitate to burn German flags during demonstrations and parades. The Hellenic crisis has also generated an increased distrust in the EU. According to a May 2012 Eurobarometer, this sentiment was higher in Greece (79 per cent) compared to Spain (72 per cent), Portugal (63 per cent), Italy (62 per cent) and Ireland (56 per cent).[7]

Furthermore, Greece has unique features which often make its case seem a distinguished one in Europe. Analysing the crisis of my country for various international media outlets, I have often been asked to explain its distinguished dimension compared to other problematic countries. I always reply by emphasising the political parameter. I know that Greece continuously receives lower scores in most international surveys compared to Ireland, Italy, Spain and Portugal. I am also aware that this country is suffering a higher recession which negatively influences the real prospects for recovery and that its economy is the weakest one in the eurozone. Nonetheless, these are the results of the problem and not the causes. The main roots of the crisis are found in the modus operandi of the Greek political system. The Greek problem is principally a domestic one.

The Hellenic Republic entered the financial crisis suffering from a remarkable credibility deficit. This is not a new tendency in Greek politics. According to economist Kenneth Rogoff, 'loss of credibility, if it comes, can bite hard and fast. Indeed, the historical evidence slams you over the head with the fact that, whereas

---

4 G. Tzogopoulos. 2012. It's Germany stupid! The Greek German Misunderstanding. EPIN Paper, No. 33, June. Available at: http://www.ceps.be/book/germany-viewed-other-eu-member-states [accessed September 2012], 6.

5 Ibid., 7.

6 VPRC Poll. 2012. Greek angry with Germany [24 February]. Available at: www.epikaira.gr/epikairo.php?id=39059 [accessed March 2012].

7 Tables of Results – Public Opinion in the European Union. 2012. Standard Eurobarometer 77. Available at: http://ec.europa.eu/public_opinion/archives/eb/eb77/eb77_anx_en.pdf [accessed September 2012], T46.

government debt can drift upward inexorably for years, the end usually comes quite suddenly'.[8] This argument summarises the story of the Greek crisis. The falsified prosperity of the country in the years after its entrance to the eurozone suddenly collapsed when the world financial crisis broke out. Along with debt explosion in the pre-October 2009 era, the inability of the Hellenic Government to move from theory into action and to practically deliver on its promises has deteriorated its international position, even in the first critical years of the crisis. The decision of Mr Papandreou to call a referendum on Monday 31 October 2011 is a characteristic example. Although the EU and IMF were expecting Greece to work intensively and apply the decisions of the European summit of 26–27 October 2011, the former prime minister announced suddenly three days later that Greek citizens would have to vote and give a clear mandate for austerity measures.[9]

Journeying back to the first three years of the crisis, there are various examples which confirm the inconsistency between words and deeds in Greek politics. Table 7.1 highlights a few striking examples, partly justifying comments pointing out the unreliability of the political personnel of the country.

Table 7.1   Inconsistency between words and deeds in Greek politics (2010–12)

Theme	Initial Statement	Result
EU and IMF financial assistance	Mr Papandreou: 'Greece has not approached the international community nor the EU for economic assistance. Greece is committed to and capable of solving this problem on its own', 15 February 2010 in an interview with RIA Novosti	Mr Papandreou: 'We must, this is a national and imperative need, to officially ask our partners to activate the support mechanism', 24 April 2010
Return to the markets	Mr Papaconstantinou: 'Our intention is to return to the markets in 2012', 20 April 2011 talking to Greek journalists	It is uncertain if and when Greece will be able to re-access capital markets

---

8   K. Rogoff. 2010. Can Greece avoid the lion? [3 February]. Available at: http://www.project-syndicate.org/commentary/rogoff65/English [accessed February 2012].

9   In principle, the idea for a referendum is a good one and has to be endorsed. It gives the opportunity to citizens to democratically express their will. Nevertheless, the timing of Mr Papandreou to make this decision was not the correct one. Greek citizens should have been asked to vote before May 2010 when the country decided to activate the bailout mechanism and being supervised by unelected representatives of the European Commission, the European Central Bank and the International Monetary Fund. It was too late to do so after all critical decisions had been already made in Brussels.

Table 7.1   *Concluded*

Theme	Initial Statement	Result
The possibility of a default	Mr Papaconstantinou: 'Everyone who is betting on Greece's default will lose his/her shirt' (colloquial expression meaning losing everything), 26 April 2010, in a press conference	ISDA confirmed on 9 March 2012 that a credit event has occurred in Greece, triggering payment of CDS
Debt-restructuring	Mr Papandreou: 'A debt-restructuring would lead Greek banks to collapse', 23 March 2011 in his interview with *Stern*	A 21 per cent haircut was decided on 21 July 2011 and Mr Papandreou perceived it as a political success of his political party in the subsequent press conference. He also did so after the decision for the 50 per cent decided on 27 October
The September 2011 new property tax (paid through electricity bills)	Mr Venizelos: 'The electricity bills are not the proper instrument to collect taxes', in a press conference on 23 June 2011	Mr Venizelos: 'A new property tax will be applied and collected through electricity bills', in a statement, on 11 September 2011
Mr Papademos and the haircut	In article published in *Financial Times* and *To Vima* on 23 October 2011 Mr Papademos warned on the potential negative consequences of a large haircut	Mr Papademos' role as a prime minister from November 2011 was to negotiate and publicly defend the haircut he had strongly opposed a few weeks ago
Referendum	Mr Papandreou: 'We need to move on with a referendum. Greek people and every simple Greek citizen need to decide', in his speech in PASOK's parliamentary group on 31 October 2011	Mr Papandreou cancelled his decision three days later, on 3 November 2011
Bonds of small bondholders	Greek politicians were continuously encouraging Greek people to buy sovereign bonds and then assuring lenders for their normal payment	Mr Venizelos said that even natural persons would suffer from 53.5 per cent haircut in a press conference on 22 February 2012
The prospect for a renegotiation of the Memorandum	Mr Samaras: 'There are [ten] measures we will immediately renegotiate', in his speech on 31 May 2012	After becoming prime minister, Mr Samaras concentrated on the implementation of the Memorandum 'forgetting' his pre-election promises about renegotiating

Nonetheless, Greek authorities have not been the only ones who have failed to foresee future developments. European politicians such as Mr Barroso, Mr Van

Rompoy, Mr Rhen and other ones have also done so, mainly concerning debt-restructuring. Before July 2011 they emphatically rejected the possibility that creditors would have to write off part of their debt to the Hellenic Republic. On 18 June 2011, for instance, one month before the summit of 21 July, the EU Commissioner for internal markets, Michel Barnier, asserted: 'This question of a restructuring ... is not on the table [...] It would only postpone the problem and in the wake of a restructuring Greece would face exactly the same difficulties and would no longer have any credibility to borrow'.[10] Within this context, the label of unreliability can be attributed to European politicians along with Greek ones. Representatives of the so-called Troika can be arguably criticised for their wrong estimations and calculations in the course of the Hellenic economy, but they were certainly victims of the poor performance of the incompetent political personnel in the country.

Greece's credibility deficit was also worsened by the inability of Greek political parties to co-operate. Only in November 2011 was a unity government finally formed when three parties – PASOK, ND and the right-wing LAOS – decided to support Mr Lucas Papademos as a new prime minister. Before November 2011, Mr Papandreou and Mr Samaras had remarkably failed to reach a consensus. For his part, the leader of ND had aggressively opposed the Memorandum of Understanding until he realised Mr Papandreou would resign increasing his chances to come to power! This said, it had been a rather disappointing diagnosis for the international media to see that although the Hellenic Republic was on the brink of default, no single national economic policy had been adopted for a period of approximately two years.

The lack of political maturity of many Greek politicians was straightforward even after Mr Papandeou's decision to call a referendum. PASOK and ND could not agree on a technocrat they had been initially keen on appointing: old guard member of the socialist party and Speaker of the Hellenic Parliament, Philippos Petsalnikos.[11] Even after the formation of a coalition government cynicism was on the increase. The mission of this government under Mr Papademos was to vote for a new bailout agreement which would guarantee further financing for the country. Nevertheless, the right-wing party of Mr Karatzaferis decided to withdraw its participation in expressing strong opposition to the terms of the new bailout. It subsequently voted against a law, the approval of which had been the reason it had supported the unity government in November 2011. Another illustration of hypocrisy in Greek politics ...

---

10 *Irish Times*. 2011. Thousands march against Greece's austerity package [18 June]. Available at: www.irishtimes.com/newspaper/breaking/2011/0618/breaking15.html [accessed July 2011].

11 In a live TV interview for *France 24* in the afternoon of Wednesday 9 November 2011, I emphasised the lack of political maturity of Greek politicians and their passion to remain in power at any cost for the country and its citizens.

As opposed to political conditions in Greece, governments in other countries of the PIIGS have shown a much more creative stance. In Ireland, the Memorandum of Understanding has been supported by main political parties from the very beginning. This is also the case with Portugal. As far as Italy is concerned, a flexible government of technocrats under Mario Monti was almost immediately formed when premier Berlusconi realised he had no other option but to resign under pressure from international markets in November 2011. Things have been, finally, better in Spain. The new Prime Minister of Spain, Mariano Rajoy, has had a clear public mandate to apply austerity measures after he won the national election of 20 November 2011. This comparison sketches out once again why Greece preserves the attribute of the weakest link in the euroarea as it is the only country which is politically accustomed in such an inflexible way to new economic conditions.

All in all, the analysis by Philip Stephens in the *Financial Times* in February 2012 highlights why Greece can be considered as a special case for the EU. He sees it as a test case for the future of the eurozone, but also elaborates on disappointing domestic elements by arguing:

> On one level, Greece can be seen as an exception. It is small and it is different. To a greater or lesser degree, the other nations on the eurozone's periphery have taken the opportunity presented by EU membership to become modern European states. Ireland, for all its present troubles, has flowered as a self-confident nation free of a historic obsession with Britain. Spain has embraced modernity with enthusiasm. Greece's politicians have never really bothered. Seen from Athens, the EU has been a source of cash rather than political inspiration. Portugal has been slow to modernise. Its economy, like that of Greece is in a pretty fine mess. But its politicians show a demonstrable resolve to catch up. So they reservoir of trust has not been drained. Policymakers in Brussels and Berlin will tell you they put Greece and Portugal in very different categories.[12]

Although Mr Stephens did not refer to Italy by comparing Greece to other PIIGS, it can be argued that even this country is in a better position. In spite of its significant problems such as tax evasion and corruption, it has shown a remarkable inclination towards change and reform under Prime Minister Mario Monti, while its economy is generally much stronger.

The Paradox of Greek Democracy

Greece is correctly observed as the cradle of democracy. Although the linkage between the country and this type of government is unquestionable, it should rather

---

12   P. Stephens. 2012. Europe says goodbye to solidarity. *Financial Times* [23 February]. Available at: http://www.ft.com/intl/cms/s/0/4085f508-5d56-11el-869d-00144feabdc0.html [accessed February 2012].

refer to classical times. The modern version of Greek democracy has incorporated bizarre elements which often undermine the real meaning of the term itself. Although politicians are democratically elected every four years, their profession seems a closed one. It is particularly difficult for ordinary citizens to become actively involved in politics because they do not have the appropriate means to compete with traditionally powerful Greek families in the political arena. In an excellent analysis on this matter Robert Kaplan argues:

> Long into the 20th century, Greek political parties had a paternalistic, coffeehouse quality, centered on big personalities – chieftains in all but name – with little formal organisational support […] Political parties have been family businesses to a greater extent in Greece than in other Western democracies. The party in power not only dominated the highest echelons of the bureaucracy, as is normal and proper in a democracy, but the middle- and lower-echelons, too. State institutions from top to bottom were often overly politicised.[13]

Former Prime Ministers Karamanlis and Papandreou are the most characteristic examples of nepotism. These families add a dose of dynasty to Greek politics. They are not the only ones though. Table 7.2 suggests that various MPs of the Hellenic Parliament recently elected have a family tradition in politics.

Table 7.2 Recent and characteristic examples of nepotism in Greek politics for New Democracy and PASOK (not exhaustive list)

Name	Position	'Family qualifications'
Antonis Samaras	Prime Minister (ND)	Grandson of former MP Alexander Zabbas and nephew of former MP Georgios Samaras
Costas Karamanlis	Former Prime Minister	Nephew of former Prime Minister Constantinos Karamanlis
Dora Bakoyannis	ND MP, former Minister of Foreign Affairs	Daughter of former Prime Minister Constantinos Mitsotakis
Simos Kedikoglou	Minister of Communication, ND	Son of Vassilis Kedikoglou, former Minister
Olga Kefalogianni	Minister of Tourism (ND)	Daughter of former Minister Ioannis Kefalogiannis
Manolis Kefalogiannis	ND MP (former Minister of maritime affair)	Nephew of former Minister Ioannis Kefalogiannis
Michael Liapis	Former Minister of Culture (ND)	Nephew of former Prime Minister Constantinos Karamanlis

---

13 R. Kaplan. 2012. Is Greece European? [6 June]. Available at: http://www.stratfor.com/analysis/greece-european-robert-d-kaplan [accessed September 2012].

Table 7.2   *Continued*

Name	Position	'Family qualifications'
Vaggelis Meimarakis	Speaker of the Parliament (ND)	Son of former MP Ioannis Meimarakis
Kyriakos Mitsotakis	ND MP	Son of former Prime Minister Constantinos Mitsotakis
Miltiadis Varvitsiotis	ND MP	Son of former Minister Ioannis Varvitsiotis
George Voulgarakis	Former minister of culture	Nephew of former MP, Georgios Voulgarakis
George Papandreou	Former Prime Minister (PASOK)	Son of former Prime Minister Andreas Papandreou, grandson of PM Georgios Papandreou
Nasos Alevras	PASOK MP	Nephew of former Speaker of the Hellenic Parliament Ioannis Alevras
Fofi Gennimata	PASOK MP	Daughter of former Minister of Health, Georgios Gennimatas
Georgios Haralampopoulos	PASOK MP	Son of former Minister of Defence Giannis Haralampopoulos
Louka Katseli	Former Minister of Economics (PASOK)	Wife of former Minister of Defence and Education Gerasimos Arsenis
Theodoros Pangalos	Former Vice President (PASOK)	Grandson of dictator Theodoros Pangalos (1925–26)
George Papaconstantinou	Former Minister of Finance (PASOK)	Nephew of former Minister of Foreign Affairs, Michalis Papaconstatinou

Along with 'family qualifications', an active role in young groups of political parties has also been an asset for future politicians: former Minister of Public Order Christos Papoutsis, for example, was Deputy Secretary of PASOK's young people. Likewise, Minister of Development Costis Hatzidakis was president of a similar group supporting New Democracy. Also, Minister of Health Andreas Lykouretzos had been involved in the same group. Finally, a close friendship with important Greek politicians has guaranteed a successful political career. In the case of the former PASOK administration, for instance, Ms Tina Birbili and Mr Pavlos Geroulanos were appointed ministers of Energy and Culture respectively thanks to their personal acquaintance with Mr Papandreou as they had previously been almost unknown prior to 2009.

Greek MPs do not lack legitimacy. The paradox of democracy in the country is that an ill-established mechanism does often isolate or block healthy-thinking people from playing an active role. Individuals who do not have qualifications like the ones sketched out above have normally lower chances of pursuing a successful career in politics. As a result, the concept of 'virtue' is almost absent from the Hellenic political reality and a generation of 'professional politicians' is reproduced. Within this context, on the day of elections Greek citizens have no other choice but to select representatives from the ones who have posed their candidatures, even if they do not consider them capable or appropriate for the country.

The paradox of Greek democracy, however, goes even further. Politicians have rarely regarded their role as synonymous for putting political and personal interests above national ones. Their main priority in the decades before the outbreak of the crisis was to create the appropriate conditions for their political survival and re-election at any cost. In so doing, they were not sceptical of over-borrowing. In parallel with this, they have tolerated the stance of trade unions and powerful groups in spite of the lack of legitimacy of their actions. The Hellenic Republic continuously failed to enact laws against the interests of these oligarchies, gradually cultivating an impunity culture in the country. Minorities of oil-smugglers, tax-evaders, corrupt civil servants and media owners have benefited from the inability as well as from the deliberate indifference of the Greek state to block their activities at the expense of the majority of honest and sincere citizens.

At the same time, the dominating feeling in Hellenic society has been that a government which had systematically failed to enact the law could not but be particularly weak. On that basis, an organised public reaction based on demonstrations, use or threat of the use of violence, blockage of roads and occupation of public buildings has been considered a successful remedy to stop any reform plans. Bizarre phenomena such as the occupation of the monument of Acropolis could easily take place in Greece because the government is unable to control them and punish the conspirators. Would the Italian Government, for instance, allow demonstrators to regularly occupy the Colosseum once a month, kicking tourists out of it? It is a rhetorical question, but one which confirms that the Greek crisis is full of original elements.

After October 2009, Greek politicians naturally showed a weakness in modernising the country and to ignore small associations and interests, poisoning plans for change. At the same time, they continued to apply the logic of clientelism and promote their family interests. The hiring of their relatives in the public sector has been their common practice confirming cronyism. In the most striking example, after the elections of 6 May 2012, and although the country would take another round one month later, conservative MP Byron Polydoras used the only day he served as Speaker in the Parliament to give his daughter a permanent job in his office. This immoral move took place while unemployment of Greek young people was exceeding 50 per cent.

A Self-delusion Syndrome

The credibility deficit and the paradox of Greek democracy explain why Greece is a special case in the eurozone. The media attention on the country, however, can be attributed to additional factors. One of the most significant issues in the journalistic work is related to sources used. An investigation of those sources is a critical starting point for an understanding of the coverage. Surprisingly, in the case of the Hellenic crisis, foreign journalists could have quoted Greek authorities who often referred to various pathogenies of their country and talked to them. In the first stance, Greece's credibility deficit is not only related to the poor discontinuity between words and deeds. It can be also confirmed by statements by former Prime Minister George Papandreou. There is a plethora of examples which demonstrate this. On 27 January 2010, for instance, Mr Papandreou said to *Euronews*: 'There is a credibility gap. And we want to make sure that Greece is credible. It is I think our major, right now, problem'.[14] Likewise, Mr Papandreou said a few days later at a Davos conference that the credibility deficit had been Greece's more important one.[15]

Along with public acknowledgement of the credibility deficit, Greek authorities often emphasised corruption and the problematic status of the economy. Commenting on the poor modus operandi of the Greek state, Papandreou said in an interview for *Spiegel* magazine:

> Unfortunately, corruption is widespread in government agencies and public enterprises. Our political system promotes nepotism and wasting money. This has undermined our legal system and confidence in the functioning of the state. One of the consequences is that many citizens don't pay their taxes.[16]

As far as the economy is concerned, the most striking public comment comes from former Finance Minister George Papaconstantinou. In a press conference after a Eurogroup meeting of 15 February 2010, he parallelised it with the Titanic and said: 'We're trying to change the course of the Titanic, it cannot be done in a day'.[17] A few

---

14 *Euronews*. 2010. Interview with Prime Minister Papandreou by Christophe Midol-Monnet [27 January]. Available at: http://www.primeminister.gov.gr/english/2010/01/27/prime-ministers-george-a-papandreou-interview-on-euronews/[accessed November 2011].

15 J. Donovan. 2010. Papandreou says first deficit is Greece's credibility gap. *Bloomberg* website [28 January]. Available at: http://www.bloomberg.com/apps/news?pid=newsarchive&sid=aJcS98oA0zog [accessed November 2011].

16 *Spiegel*. 2010. It's a question of survival for Greece – Spiegel interview with Greek Prime Minister Papandreou [22 February]. Available at: http://www.spiegel.de/international/europe/0,1518,679415,00.html [accessed April 2011].

17 S. O'Grady. 2010. Greece faces tough measures in bid to save Titanic economy. *The Independent* [16 February]. Available at: http://www.independent.co.uk/news/business/news/greece-faces-tough-measures-in-bid-to-save-titanic-economy-1900731.html [accessed April 2011].

months later, in October 2010, he repeated the same comment and argued that his government had supposedly reversed indeed the course of the Titanic![18]

Both Mr Papandreou and Mr Papaconstantinou publicly used phrases such as the afore mentioned ones for political motives. They were seeking to disengage themselves from the policy of the previous conservative government to show their sincere and honest motivations and demonstrate their will and decisiveness to save Greece. Nevertheless, what they rather achieved was to entrap the country in a communication game, which finally worked at its expense in the world arena. From the moment the Greek prime minister and finance minister publicly concentrated on the pathogenies of the Hellenic Republic, it was a logical consequence for the foreign media to follow the same path.

The credibility deficit, the stagnated economy and corruption were not the only issues the international media could refer to through having Greek authorities as a source of information. Journalists also had the chance to quote them on two additional, particularly sensitive, issues and ones seeming once taboo for the Greek administration: the possibility of a sovereign default and that of an exit from the eurozone. Concerning the first one, a respectable figure who called on the need for a debt-restructuring was Costas Simitis, Prime Minister at the time the Hellenic Republic entered the euroarea. Although not actively involved in politics, his public intervention is certainly important because of his experience and knowledge on the matter. Mr Simitis gave an interview in the opinion-making Sunday newspaper *To Vima* on 17 April 2011. In this interview, he explained that a 'well-prepared debt-restructuring could boost the position' of Greece.[19]

The scenario of a return of Greece to its national currency was made public by another Greek politician, Maritime Affairs and Fishery European Commissioner Maria Damanakis. In particular, in a written statement on 25 May 2011, Ms Damanakis considered it an existing one and – inter alia – asserted: 'We have a historical responsibility to clearly see the dilemma: we either agree with our creditors on a programme of difficult sacrifices with tangible results, by taking responsibility for our past or we return to the drachma'.[20] Mr Simitis also took a clear position on this issue by publishing a comment in the Greek Sunday newspaper *Kathimerini* on 2 October 2011. In his piece, he argued that the

---

18 Ministry of Finance website. 2010. Press conference of Finance Minister on the margin of the annual IMF Meeting [9 October]. Available at: http://www.minfin.gr/portal/el/resource/contentObject/id/4a239bce-2a0d-4598-bcbf-284ad74cf929 [accessed April 2011].

19 C. Simitis. Personal website. 2011. Interview with *Vima tis Kyriakis* [17 April]. Available at: http://www.costas-simitis.gr/content/174 [accessed February 2012].

20 M. Damanaki. Personal website. 2011. Statement of Commissioner Maria Damanaki on the scenario of a Greek exit from the eurozone/Dilossi tis Epitropou Marias Damanaki gia to senario apomakrinsis tis Elladas apo to euro [25 May]. Available at: http://www.damanaki.gr/index.php?option=com_content&view=article&id=1362:2011-05-25-12-24-26&catid=48:2010-02-17-17-50-07&Itemid=57 [accessed February 2012].

Hellenic Republic was indeed affronting the danger of leaving the eurozone.[21] In the aftermath of Mr Papandreou's decision for a referendum and in view of the national elections of May and June 2012, the scenario of a Greek exit was largely discussed domestically. The current Prime Minister, Antonis Samaras, for instance, tends to portray the leftist SYRIZA party as representative of 'the drachma lobby', while the second does not consider the common currency as taboo.

To sum up, it is certainly surprising that Greek authorities blamed the international media, although their comments, interviews or statements could have been used as a source of information for the coverage of the country. From a critical perspective, this can be considered a hypocritical stance. In other words, a self-delusional tendency seems to have prevailed in Greek politics. In spite of public acknowledgment of hard realities, their reproduction by the international media has created frustration and annoyance.

The Inside Story

Foreign journalists who have covered developments in the Hellenic Republic have also used an additional domestic source for their information: the national media of the country. Even if they did not use Greek as a working language, they might access online dictionaries and easily translate electronic material from its original form. Likewise, they could have established contacts with colleagues in Greece and be informed about the content of the country's press. In this way, journalists working in international media were able to find a plethora of negative stories facilitating their attempt to cover the Hellenic crisis.

A systematic analysis of the main headlines in the first page of Greek newspapers can indeed give the impression that the Hellenic Republic was in dissolution, paralysed by corruption, overspending and tax evasion.[22] Two high-circulation Sunday newspapers, *Proto Thema* and *Real News*,[23] provided useful and interesting resources to international media. Both titles attempted to reveal corruption scandals in the Defence Ministry, especially during the years of former Minister Akis Tsochatzopoulos from 1996 until 2011. The main headline of the first paper on 11 February 2011, for instance, was: 'We paid for the new submarines 50 per cent more than the Turkish and everyone was asked to remain silent'.[24] In a similar case, the

---

21 C. Simitis. Personal website. 2011. Self-delusion syndrome [2 October]. Available at: http://www.costas-simitis.gr/content/177 [accessed January 2012].

22 Greece has a strong Sunday newspaper market. Daily editions sell much less. Therefore, examples used in this analysis derive from the Sunday market.

23 According to the company Argos S.A. which officially distributes newspapers in Greece, the first sold 146,053 copies and the second 89,657 ones per Sunday in 2010.

24 *Proto Thema*. 2011, 11 February.

second paper published a story two months later on its first page, entitled: 'centre of rake-off in Akis' office'.[25]

Another story *Proto Thema* and *Real News* focused on the overspending by Greek politicians. In this case, the two newspapers targeted former Minister of Tourism and Education, Aris Spiliotopoulos, for his luxurious life with public funds. *Proto Thema* wrote in its first page on 23 January 2011 that that Greek state owed €667,000 for official visits he had made to various world capitals.[26] According to the newspaper, his expenses included payment for presidential suites and limousines. For its part, *Real News* had warned of the high cost of Mr Spiliotopoulos' life, which was continuously being financed by public funds, from January 2009. At that time, it asserted on its front page that the former minister had even hired a personal chef.[27] Likewise, in May 2010, *Real News* revealed that the former minister had used €1.6 million 'in cruises, ties and neck-scarves'.[28]

Along with *Proto Thema* and *Real News*, other Greek newspapers also concentrated on the lack of transparency in politics, mainly dealing with procurements in the public sector. Examples include historical newspapers such as *Eleftherotypia*, *Kathimerini* and *To Vima*.[29] *To Vima*, for instance, elaborated on a corruption story in which former Interior and Transport Minister Tasos Mantelis had been involved. As the newspaper asserted on 30 May 2010, the procurements he had managed were worth €8.5 billion.[30] On the same day, *Kathimerini*'s main headline was: 'a detonating mix of insufficiency and corruption'.[31] In the health sector, another newspaper, *Eleftherotypia*,[32] wrote about a 'colpo grosso' (corruption scandal) of €5 billion with overpriced medicines.[33]

An additional newspaper, *Ethnos*,[34] concentrated on corruption and inefficiency by revealing various stories concerning irregular pensions granting. The paper wrote ironically on 7 August that 'a blindness epidemic' was spreading in various counties in Greece. The paper revealed that healthy people were receiving fake pensions on the island of Zakynthos; it also referred to people driving expensive jeeps and others having successfully undergone eye operations.[35] As far as tax

---

25 *Real News*. 2011, 3 April. 'Akis' is the first name of former Defence Minister Mr Tsochatzopoulos widely used in the Greek media discourse instead of his surname.

26 *Proto Thema*. 2011, 23 January.

27 *Real News*. 2009, 18 January.

28 *Real News*. 2010, 16 May.

29 According to the company Argos S.A, *Kathimerini* sold 135,870 copies, *Eleftherotypia* 112,581 copiesand *To Vima* 142,359 copies in their Sunday editions in 2010.

30 *To Vima*. 2010, 30 May.

31 *Kathimerini*. 2010, 30 May.

32 According to the company Argos S.A, *Eleftherotypia* sold 112,581 copies in its Sunday edition in 2010.

33 *Kyriakatiki Eleftherotypia*. 2010, 21 November.

34 According to the company Argos S.A, *Ethnos* sold 96,883 copies in its Sunday edition in 2010.

35 *Ethnos tis Kyriakis*. 2011, 7 August.

evasion is concerned, the same source asserted one week earlier in its front page: 'One billion euros on tax-evasion were found by the Financial and Economic Crime Unit (SDOE) The newspaper wrote that 3000 yachting boats were found in offshore [havens] while smuggling and money laundering was conducted by fake shipping companies'.[36] Within this context, *Eleftherotypia* newspaper concluded on the quality of life in the country and published a main headline on: '10 reasons for someone not to live in Greece'.[37] This front page concentrated on expensive prices for oil, on high taxes, unemployment, large deficits and inflation.

As far a default is concerned, the Greek media could be considered as a vehicle spreading fear among public opinion. It is striking that opinion-forming newspapers such as *To Vima* included special guides in their Sunday edition, suggesting ways Greek people could protect their money.[38] Concerning the exit from the eurozone, there is a particular Greek newspaper which considers this as the only choice: *Avriani*. This newspaper has very often urged the Greek Government to abandon the common currency area: 'The only way for Greece is to default and return to the drachma' was its main headline on 8 May 2011'.[39] The same headline was also featured in the edition on the following Sunday.[40]

Examples as the ones sketched out above demonstrated that it was not only international media which dealt with Greek pathogenies. By contrast, it was the national press of the country which, principally, elaborated on these issues. Therefore, a discussion on the coverage of the Hellenic crisis by international media should have the Greek media as an important point of reference. The content of some of the front pages of Hellenic newspapers complemented one of the statements by one of the authorities of the country, thus confirming Greek politicians and the media as a news source for foreign journalists.

Media War

Our German 'Friends'

The Greek media have also played a significant role in cultivating the misunderstanding between Athens and Berlin. Although they did mean to play this game, they actively participated. In particular, the first source clearly insulting Greek society was *Focus* magazine when it depicted, in its cover page, Goddess Aphrodite of Melos[41] asking for money and was entitled: 'cheaters in the eurofamily'. The subsequent reaction from the other side was similarly populist.

---

36 *Ethnos tis Kyriakis*. 2010, 1 August.
37 *Kyriakatiki Eleftherotypia*. 2010, 21 November.
38 *To Vima tis Kyriakis*. 2011, 5 June.
39 *Kyriakatiki Avriani*. 2011, 8 May.
40 *Kyriakatiki Avriani*. 2011, 15 May.
41 Focus. 2010, 22 February.

The conservative *Eleftheros Typos* decided to provide its own answer to *Focus*. The newspaper portrayed the Berlin's Victory column holding a swastika and asserted that 'economic occupation of the Fourth Reich was expanding in Europe'.[42]

In the Greek media discourse Germany was highly demonised. It was perceived as a country which continuously sought to economically dominate the Hellenic Republic, although it failed to pay World War II reparations. *Eleftherotypia* newspaper, for instance, selected as its main headline after the European Summit of 26–27 October 2011: 'The new Memorandum brings German tanks'. Likewise, its sub-deadline was: 'Merkel Doctrine: new hard measures and permanent supervision'.[43] The anti-German feeling was so strong in the media coverage that even sport media placed football games in the context of politics. When Olympiacos FC played against Borussia Dortmund FC for the group stage of the Champions League in October 2011, a sport newspaper published a picture of Chancellor Merkel with a Nazi uniform, encouraging the players of Olympiacos to win for Greece.[44]

Greek media criticism against Germany was also on the rise in February 2012. In this month almost all newspapers showed an aggressive stance vis-à-vis Berlin as a reaction to Mr Schäuble's proposal for the appointment of a European Commissioner in the Hellenic Republic. On this occasion, the main headline in the front page of *Eleftheros Typos* was that the Hellenic Republic was under 'Schäuble's junta'.[45] Commentaries in various newspapers also blamed Germany for its economic policy. In indicative cases a columnist for *Ethnos* regularly used terms such as 'Gauleiter'[46] and 'Gestapo'[47] while the managing director of *To Vima* portrayed Mr Schäuble as a 'Taliban'.[48] In the most striking case, a fine of €25,000 was imposed on a Greek journalist as he publicly vilified Chancellor Merkel and Germany.[49]

Foreign journalists might easily have found various negative comments on Germany when reading national newspapers of the country. German journalists, in particular, were keen to investigate stereotypes against their country in the Greek media discourse. *Bild*, for instance, was a characteristic example. Its articles often

---

42   *Eleftheros Typos*. 2010, 23 February.
43   *Eleftherotypia*. 2011, 27 October.
44   *Gavros*. 2011, 17 and 18 October.
45   *Typos tis Kyriakis*. 2012, 16 February.
46   G. Delastik. 2012. O gauleiter echase to dromo (The gauleiter lost his way) *Ethnos* [31 January]. Available at: http://www.ethnos.gr/article.asp?catid=22792&subid=2&pubid=63609750 [accessed February 2012].
47   G. Delastik. 2012. Vouleftes sta nichia tis Gestapo (MPs in Gestapo's hands) *Ethnos*. [1 February]. Available at: http://www.ethnos.gr/article.asp?catid=22792&subid=2&pubid=63610455 [accessed February 2012].
48   A. Karakoussis. 2012. O Taliban kyrios Schäuble (Mr Schäuble as a Taliban) *To Vima* [16 February]. http://www.tovima.gr/opinions/article/?aid=443921 [accessed February 2012].
49   In particular, Greek journalist George Tragas repeatedly used obscene phrases in portraying Chancellor Merkel and her economic policy towards Greece.

drew on material highlighting the anti-German rhetoric of the Hellenic press. On that basis, the media clash between the countries has not been appeased. Responsibility for this misunderstanding has to be equally distributed among journalists from both sides as they have shown a tendency to reproduce negative stereotypes and cultivate a climate of hostility.

Journalists as 'Enemies'

A close examination of the work of foreign journalists covering the Greek crisis often reflects their disappointment and frustration about the way authorities in the country treated them. The most characteristic example is the incident involving *BBC* correspondent Malcolm Brabant in Thessaloniki in September 2010. Mr Brabant filmed a scene with an angry protester throwing a shoe at George Papandreou and uploaded it on the website of his corporation. The Greek Government, however, complained about the originality of the video, leading the *BBC* to take it down, initially. After allegations were proved to be unfounded it re-uploaded the footage.[50]

The tonality of Greek politicians in their communication with foreign journalists has also reflected their problematic professional relationship. In a press conference of 2 May 2010, for instance, Mr Barnaby Philipps from *Al-Jazeera* asked Mr George Papaconstantinou a question, expressing his uncertainty that the new economic programme would succeed and taking the discontinuity between his words and deeds into account. The former Finance Minister started his answer by ironically commenting: 'I would expect this question from a Greek journalist, mirroring the fear of Greek citizens'.[51] In this case it is connoted that the question by Mr Philipps was not welcome although the journalist had correctly focused in his question on the aspect of the credibility deficit.

Greek communication strategy vis-à-vis foreign correspondents could hardly be based on the so-called spin industry. With the exception of a few cases of personal sympathy between officials and journalists, political public relations did not play an important role. This contrasts the tendency of Greek authorities to closely co-operate with some journalists working in media organisations within the country. A letter by former US ambassador in Athens, Mr Charles Ries, which was revealed by WikiLeaks, mirrors this tactic:

---

50 T. Conlan. 2010. *BBC* under fire after removing video of Greek shoe protest from its website. *The Guardian* [21 September]. Available at: http://www.guardian.co.uk/media/2010/sep/21/bbc-under-fire-video-shoe-protest [accessed April 2011].

51 Greek Ministry of Finance website. 2010. Press conference transcript [2 May]. Available at: http://www.minfin.gr/portal/el/resource/contentObject/id/c674b46b-951a-431e-9403-3337e512e40d [accessed January 2011].

> It's not unusual for a journalist to work in a ministry press office, even while covering the beat that includes that ministry. They're very conscious of their multiple masters [...] It's also acceptable for journalists to take gifts or even money from those on whom they report.[52]

At the same time, Greek communication strategy mainly focused on expanding the presence of government members in international media. Important as it was for the promotion of national positions abroad, this method was not sufficient. Greek authorities did not efficiently manage to provide foreign correspondents with the necessary information they needed in order to prepare their stories. Background meetings and telephone conversations, for instance, were not organised as often as journalists would prefer. The availability of Greek authorities was rather limited for correspondents who continuously sought clarification on the economy and the progress of the government in implementing the international agreements. In parallel with this, the material provided by the official website of the Hellenic Finance Ministry, especially its electronic archive, was not always translated from Greek into English.

As a whole, the main problem with the communication method of the Hellenic Republic was that it realised how quickly markets operated. Within this context, Greek officials did not manage to efficiently appease anxieties and concerns by providing accurate and on-time information to international media. Their communication strategy seemed rather to have been based on personal relations with journalists and to have lacked professionalism and co-ordination. Even press offices of the Hellenic Republic in foreign countries mainly operated on the basis of their personnel's experience and not on guidelines provided by the Greek Government.

Speculation Games?

The negative coverage of Greece by the media and especially the insistence by several titles that the Hellenic Republic would be unable to deliver raised concerns over speculation games played. We have seen that former Prime Minister Papandreou was straightforward in supporting this claim. Attention here was principally – but not only – turned towards economic newspapers because their target group was composed of bankers, traders and people working in the finance sector. Can it thus be confirmed that the international media were involved in rogue-trading games at the expense of the Hellenic Republic? This is certainly a particularly delicate issue in the analysis of the coverage.

In March 2010, Mr Papandreou along with Mr Juncker, Ms Merkel and Mr Sarkozy explored the possibility of the EU boosting transparency and blocking

---

52 WikiLeaks letter from the US Embassy of Athens. 2006. [13 July]. ID: 71198, 4.

speculative practices.⁵³ They principally concentrated on credit default swaps (CDS) and proposed that that the European Commission would initiate an inquiry into their role and impact.⁵⁴ One month later, while an investigation was indeed being conducted in Brussels this issue was discussed in the US House of Representatives. During a hearing on 29 April, Professor of Finance at Stanford University Darrell Duffie was the main speaker. What he argued was that there had been no evidence that speculation with credit default swaps had been responsible for raising the borrowing costs of Greece. As Professor Duffie explained in his testimony:

> The net amounts of default swaps referencing these issuers is a small fraction of the amounts of their debt outstanding. Even if all of the CDS trading is purely speculative, there is just not enough of it to move the needle very much.⁵⁵

In summary, the work of Professor Duffie in co-operation with Professor Zhipeng Zhang of Boston College suggests there was no statistically significant relationship between weekly changes in net CDS positions and weekly changes in the CDS rates of Greece, Italy, Ireland, Portugal and Spain.

In December 2010, the European Commission published its own report on the functioning of the sovereign CDS market, the findings of which were rather similar. The main conclusion was: 'The empirical investigation [...] provides no conclusive evidence that developments in the CDS market cause higher borrowing costs for member states'.⁵⁶ Making particular reference to Greece, the report asserted that the 'trigger for the widening of yield and CDS spreads was the announcement of

---

53 G. Papandreou, J.C. Juncker, A. Merkel and N. Sarkozy. 2010. Letter to José Manuel Barroso and José Luis Rodríguez Zapatero [10 March]. Available at: http://www.primeminister.gov.gr/english/2010/03/10/letter-to-jose-manuel-barroso-and-jose-luis-rodriguez-zapatero/ [accessed April 2011].

54 Professor of Finance at Stanford University Darell Duffie explains the meaning of CDS: 'A credit default swap, or "CDS" is a derivative security. The buyer of protection pays an annual fee to the seller of protection, referencing a particular borrower such as Greece, and an amount of the borrower's debt. For example, if the agreed CDS rate is 5% and the amount of the referenced debt is 100 million US dollars, then the annual protection fee is 5 million US dollars. In the event that the named borrower, say Greece, defaults on its debt, the seller of protection then gives the buyer of protection the difference between the referenced amount of debt and the market value of the defaulted debt'. Duffie, D. 2010. Credit Default Swaps on Government Debt: Potential Implications of the Greek Debt Crisis – Statement at the Unites States House of Representatives [29 April].

55 D. Duffie. 2010. Credit Default Swaps on Government Debt: Potential Implications of the Greek Debt Crisis – Statement at the Unites States House of Representatives [29 April].

56 Report on Sovereign CDS. 2010 [8 December]. Available at: http://online.wsj.com/article/SB10001424052748703296604576005551530863030.html [accessed March 2011].

the draft budget with a deficit of 12.7 per cent of GDP twice as much as previously expected'. In other words, it mainly transferred the responsibility to the Greek Government itself and the unreliability of national statistics in the country.

The research conducted by Professor Duffie as well as by the European Commission is certainly important. Nevertheless, its results are not necessarily sufficient to prove that no speculation was made on the occasion of a potential default of the Hellenic Republic. The report of the European Commission itself acknowledged the limitation of data provided by the Depository Trust & Clearing Corporation (DTCC) on a weekly basis. Their completeness, for instance, is not verified. Along with this, the analysis was based on a weekly basis and daily transactions which possibly mirrored speculation were not taken into account. Noting that markets operate particularly quickly and are often shaped by information reported by the media, even transactions per hour would have been interesting to investigate. Finally, no research study has been conducted for the year of 2011 and the beginning of 2012 which could complete the conclusions of the aforementioned ones. This is a critical period during which the European decision to write off the Greek debt was made and the haircut percentage vacillated from 21 per cent to 53.5 per cent.

The possibility of speculation in the framework of the Greek debt crisis cannot be excluded. There are various media reports which discuss the role of funds which were involved. The *Financial Times* reported that at the end of January 2010 bankers, asset managers and hedge fund analysts had gathered in Athens to discuss the Greek economy and 'how to make money from it'.[57] Furthermore, according to a *New York Times* article of 24 February 2010, 'bets by some of the same banks that helped Greece shroud its mounting debts may actually now be pushing the nation closer to the brink of financial ruin'. The same article also referred to specific numbers and asserted:

> Trading in Markit's sovereign credit derivative index soared this year [in 2010]. The cost of insuring 10 million dollars of Greek bonds rose to more than 400.000 in February, up from 282.000 in early January.[58]

The role of CDS only constitutes an aspect of the story. Speculation may have also included bond transactions as well as currency exchanges. We know, for instance, from the current alternate Minister for Finance, Christos Staikouras, that from the end of December 2009 until the beginning of the PSI, international banks limited their investment in Greek sovereign bonds from €141.5 billion to €45.9 billion on

---

57 S. Jones. 2010. Athens dinner that led to political indigestion. *Financial Times* [4 March] Available at: http://www.ft.com/intl/cms/s/0/56cde15a-27bf-11df-863d-00144feabdc0.html#axzz1n7MJDINl [accessed April 2011].

58 N. Schwarz, N. and E. Dash. 2010. Banks bet Greece defaults on debt they helped hide. *The New York Times* [24 February] Available at: http://www.nytimes.com/2010/02/25/business/global/25swaps.html?ref=global-business [accessed April 2011].

31 December 2010 and €35 billion on 31 December 2011. The opposite happened for Greek banks which expanded their investment in Greek bonds by 51.2 per cent from the end of 2010 until the end of 2011.[59] Concerning currency exchanges, *The Wall Street Journal*, for example, asserted in February 2010 that 'hedge funds titans such as SAC Capital Advisors LP and Soros Fund Management LLC' were launching large 'bearish bets against the euro'.[60] Likewise, almost two years later *The Guardian* echoed the view that a Greek departure from the eurozone 'would continue to top the list of the 10 biggest risks investors should look out for'.[61]

Along with various media reports, the internet and blogosphere are full of similar content as far as speculation is concerned. An unorthodox theory similar to a conspiracy one has flourished that the Greek crisis and the subsequent expansion of it on other PIIGS was caused by an orchestrated attack of markets. In the view of its supporters, the Hellenic Republic has been arguably lured into a trap by banks first prepared to lend to the country at low interest rates but then starting to demand extremely high ones. In particular, the role of Goldman Sachs received particular attention as it had allegedly masked the Greek debt to facilitate its adhesion in the eurozone in return for high compensation. Along with Goldman Sachs, rating agencies such as Fitch, Moody's and Standard & Poors have been criticised for their central role in the assessment of Greece's borrowing capacity.

The discussion on possible rogue-trading games certainly creates scepticism. Whether speculation was driving various transactions and investments during the Greek crisis, however, will remain an unanswered question as long as available evidence cannot prove it. In any case, the media themselves cannot be easily considered as servants of funds and traders. We know from the rich literature of political communication that news production can be linked to the economic interests of their owners. This theoretical linkage lacks a practical dimension though because the influence of hedge funds or rating agencies on international media and journalists during the Greek crisis can hardly be confirmed. The coverage, by contrast, has been rather accurate as it was synthesised around the weakness of the Greek Government to deliver from the very beginning.

Greek politicians have frequently blamed markets for the crisis and have criticised the media for playing the game of speculator and allegedly manipulating stories pushing the Hellenic Republic towards default. This view is rather a populist one. It has been used by Greek political elites as a smart communication technique which could possibly justify their poor performance or explain their failure. In

---

59 Mr Staikouras provided these data in the Hellenic Parliament on 7 September 2012.

60 S. Pulliam, K. Kellyand and C. Mollenkamp. 2011. *The Wall Street Journal* [26 February] Available at: http://online.wsj.com/article/SB10001424052748703795004575087741848074392.html [accessed November 2011]

61 H. Smith. 2011. Greece's euro future: the speculation goes on. *The Guardian* [11 December] Available at: http://www.guardian.co.uk/business/2011/dec/11/greece-euro-future-speculation [accessed February 2012].

the final account, politicians who are theoretically marionettes of markets and cannot control their operation are not appropriate to govern a country during a crucial economic war. But Greek politicians have been experts in transferring the responsibility of their faults and economical in acknowledging the truth.

Approaching the Work of Journalists

A close look at the work of journalists covering developments in Greece leads to additional observations. That is because their mission seems to have been different from their routine practices and has been certainly an original one. At a first glance, journalists have had to prepare and deliver their stories under particularly tight deadlines. Although this rule is a typical one in media culture, the main difference with the coverage of the Greek crisis is that events have been unprecedented. They could thus easily affect markets and create terror for Greek and European citizens who were concerned for the future of their deposits and bonds.

In parallel with the lack of experience in covering a financial war, correspondents of international newspapers might not necessarily have been experts in economics. Irrespective of their studies or specific knowledge, the requirements of their job would be to immediately familiarise themselves with terms such as CDS, haircut, debt-restructuring and spreads and then subsequently clearly explain them to their readers. Could anyone even imagine before the beginning of the Greek crisis that the sustainability of the eurozone would become a political hot potato? Journalists, however, have had no alternative but to get quickly accustomed to new developments and to cover them in a simple and straightforward way.

An additional parameter which can also explain the task of journalists is related to their personal reaction on seeing domestic developments. Greece is certainly not the only civilised country in Europe which suffers from strikes and demonstrations. Examples can be found not only in other PIIGS but also in states like Great Britain which saw riots spreading in its capital in August 2011. The main difference is that in the case of the Hellenic Republic, strikes and demonstrations are not exceptions but almost part of everyday life, while perpetrators of violence are rarely arrested and brought to justice. Foreign journalists covering public reaction in the main square of Athens have been regularly caught by surprise to discover that similar catastrophes take place quite regularly but the police lack an efficient strategy by extensively using tear-gas.

The reportage of Greece has also offered the opportunity for journalists to explore the practical dimension of pathogenies such as bureaucracy and corruption. Although other countries of the PIIGS, mainly the Mediterranean ones Italy and Spain, are experiencing similar problems, a careful study of the Hellenic Republic can provide further details. These are not only related to important and widely known issues such as the inability of the Greek state to absorb EU funds and the Siemens scandal, but also to simple issues affecting everyday life. A story on the 'fakelaki' logic in Greek hospitals, for example, could be of interest to readers and provides a tangible taste of the problematic public sector in the country. It goes thus far beyond reports and scores by international bodies.

The tendency of foreign journalists to concentrate on the Greek crisis and sketch out numerous negative stories is not surprising. They are themselves aware that even if they plan to cover positive ones, the chance of publication is rather limited. My personal experience acting as a commentator for international media can also confirm the trend of reporting the news within a negative framework. On only one occasion in January 2012, a journalist from Danish national television asked me to discuss a positive development. This was related to the success story of a small Greek village, Anavra, a model of small-scale sustainable development. I can hardly recall another time I could escape from analysing the existing pathogenies of the Hellenic Republic.

In the case of correspondents based in Greece, the crisis has been a great opportunity for their career. Although their work had received relatively limited attention by their media organisations before October 2009, this dramatically changed after the Greek bubble blew up. Their contributions started to be almost necessary for their editors who carefully looked at domestic developments in the most problematic eurozone state. From the perspective of correspondents based in Athens, a possible continuation of this crisis might strengthen their presence in media outlets and then lead to salary increases and promotion. At the same time, freelance journalists working in Greece could have the chance to secure a permanent job position and sign an open-ended contract with their outlets. It has been thus in their personal interest not only to carefully deal with political and economic news of the country but also to frequently explore additional aspects of its crisis and contribute to news-making.

Practical elements of day-to-day journalistic work, as the ones sketched out above, can also explain why sometimes the coverage showed signs of inaccuracy or overgeneralisation. The emphasis on a small country like Greece and the attack on its society as a whole has been a convenient tool for the media. The work under pressure does not often allow the journalist to cross-check information and sources. The production and reproduction of stereotypes that Greek people are lazy or corrupt can be sometimes regarded as easy alternatives. In the final account, it not surprising for reporters to attempt to show their audience that they know almost everything on any topical issue: this tendency mainly affects the quality of work of journalists who prefer to report or comment on the news from their desks instead of immersing themselves in different cultures by travelling to other countries and closely monitoring developments.

The 'Greek Effect'

The originality in the coverage of the Greek crisis is that it was synthesised around economics, politics and social affairs all at the same time. The work of journalists has required a combination of information from all three areas, making their mission even more difficult in a time of economic war. In spite of a few inaccuracies and overgeneralisations, foreign journalists have, as a whole, reported developments in the Hellenic Republic in a clear, comprehensive and fair way. The Greek crisis is an existing one and its importance is particularly high. Therefore, any argument attributing a supposed exaggeration of its dimension to media coverage seems rather problematic.

Usage of populist rhetoric and production of stereotypes have certainly been located in the media discourse. They do not, however, mirror general coverage. As a whole, foreign journalists did not distort the image of Greece after the crisis broke out. By contrast they contributed to its internationalisation. They did so by revealing the social dimension of the crisis which was often excluded from negotiations taking place in Brussels and other world capitals and cities. The beginning of 2012 saw many European citizens demonstrating in favour of the Hellenic Republic, showing solidarity and chanting slogans like: 'We are all Greeks'!

A few years ago, scholar Piers Robinson invented the '*CNN* effect', exploring the impact of this network on the conduct of the state's foreign policy. In the case of the coverage of the Greek crisis, the seeds of a similar model – even broader one – can be found. This can be called the: 'Greek effect'. The pain felt by people in the Hellenic Republic might equally be experienced soon by other European citizens, not only in the PIIGS but also in states of the eurozone core such as Belgium and France. EU leaders have to seriously consider whether harsh austerity is the only appropriate remedy as an economic strategy as, for the moment, politicians show no progress in carrying out structural reforms, beating tax evasion and implementing privatisations. Here, the media role can possibly direct their attention from European and world leadership towards the real problems of ordinary citizens just as *CNN* did with its coverage of Somalia at the beginning of the 1990s.

The majority of Greek citizens are not responsible for the current crisis they are experiencing. Young people who cannot find a job, their parents who lose theirs and their grandparents who see their pensions continuously reduced are paying a heavy price for the irresponsibility and the unreliability of their politicians in the last three decades. They now have only one vision: to isolate the ones responsible for the crisis and work together with their European partners on the road to prosperity. Greek people are no cheaters, nor are they lazy and corrupted. They belong to the European family and respect its values. They thus expect the international media to disassociate them from their leadership as well as from oligarchies co-operating with it in the country and to consider them capable of transforming the country from within.

Is it Europe's business to become more actively involved in the Hellenic Republic and contribute more efficiently to its future change? The answer is positive. From the moment the EU financially supports it and frequently monitors the course of its national economy, Brussels' mission should not be myopic in focusing only on fiscal targets. This insistence only leads to rising euroscepticism.

Europe has to push actively and efficiently for institutional reforms such as the improvement of the justice system. It should not consider the application of more and more taxes and cuts in salaries and pensions as an antidote for the incompetence of Greek politicians. Such a policy leads to recession, thus killing the patient. Greek citizens are human beings. Not numbers.

Chapter 8
Post Scriptum:
From Drama into Tragedy?

The administration of George Papandreou represents the first stage of the modern Greek drama, while the unity government of Lucas Papademos and the coalition one of Antonis Samaras represent its natural continuation. Whether this drama will end in tragedy remains to be seen. In the first months of 2012 the Greek society – hit by depression – was suffering from austerity measures while authorities were still unable to implement the necessary reforms, tackle tax evasion, beat corruption and save the country. In parallel with this, continuing recession and rising unemployment almost eliminate hopes for a recovery. Predictions for the future are disappointing and pessimistic. According to a study of the National Confederation of Hellenic Commerce released in February 2012, the Hellenic Republic will soon experience 'conditions of absolute poverty'.[1] The Greek economy, the state and its citizens are imprisoned in a vicious circle with no light at the end of the tunnel. Indeed, at the beginning of 2013 conditions for the middle class are rather dramatic as I highlighted in a interview for Bloomberg.

The successful bond exchange, which was completed on 8 March 2012 in the framework of the so-called private sector involvement (PSI), releases Greece from its obligation to pay back a significant part of its private debt. This development, nevertheless, officially means that the Hellenic Republic is the first Western country for approximately 60 years to have failed to cover its financial obligations, triggering payment of CDS.[2] The label of being a bankrupt state is not a particularly honorary one even if chaotic default was prevented. In parallel with this, the real danger for the country is that it will hardly regain confidence from national and international creditors who feel betrayed as well as deceived by the unreliability of its political personnel. Hence, it remains unclear if and when it will be able to borrow again from markets, being a hostage of the will of the EU and the IMF to provide financial assistance imposing unbearable terms. Under these circumstances and taking the uncertainty for the future into account, the attention of foreign journalists towards Greece could hardly return to its pre-October 2009 normal state.

---

1 Press Release of the National Confederation of Hellenic Commerce. 2012 [1 February] Available at: http://www.esee.gr/page.asp?id=3893 [accessed March 2012].
2 Press Release of ISDA. 2012. ISDA EMEA Determinations Committee: Restructuring credit event has occurred with respect to the Hellenic Republic. [9 March].

Greece Still on the Agenda

International media welcomed – as a whole – the formation of the unity government in Greece in November 2011. The appointment of Mr Papademos as new prime minister was endorsed because he was generally perceived a serious technocrat who could theoretically restore the credibility of the country at the international level and play a pivotal role in the negotiations with its creditors. These negotiations were mainly synthesised around the finding of a mutually accepted formula for the procedure of bonds swap after the EU agreement of 27 October 2011. The additional mission of the unity government was to vote in favour of the new bailout package in the Hellenic Parliament, accepting thus new austerity measures and further flexibility in the labour market.

It is interesting, however, that some foreign journalists were hesitant in trusting Mr Papademos from the very beginning. That is because they remembered that this public figure had been Governor of the Bank of Greece at the time the Hellenic Government had submitted wrong data in order to enter the eurozone. I recall one of the most difficult themes I needed to deal with commenting in international media was their distrust for a person who had been allegedly involved in cooking the books.[3] At the same time, it was certainly not promising for the potential success of the new government that its cabinet would be composed of 49 members the majority of which had been the same as during the PASOK term.

The main difference in the coverage of the Greek crisis after the formation of the unity government is the insistence of foreign journalists on the potential exit of the country from the eurozone. Although this element had been displayed in the discourse of American, British and German newspapers even in the previous two years, it started then to dominate their agenda, including now titles of France and Italy. This was the logical consequence after the decision of former Prime Minister George Papandreou to call a referendum. On 7 February 2012, for instance, *La Repubblica* explained that time was running out for Greece.[4] All in all, a reader of the international newspapers after November 2011 might be well-prepared for a potential expulsion of the country from the common currency.

From November 2011 onwards various newspapers also showed an interest in the rise of new parties in the Greek political arena. The new government was supported not only by PASOK and New Democracy, but also by the right-wing LAOS. Foreign journalists were particularly concerned whether this development might possibly lead to the expansion of the extreme right. *Le Figaro*, for example,

---

3 In this case, my answer was that it was mainly the responsibility of Greek politicians, and in particular of the Simitis government to provide the data for Greece's entrance to the eurosystem and not of the Bank of Greece. Nevertheless, I explained I could understand their cautious stance.

4 A. Bonanni. 2012. Bruxelles: Tempo scaduto per la Grecia. *La Repubblica* [7 February] Available at: http://ricerca.repubblica.it/repubblica/archivio/repubblica/2012/02/07/bruxelles-tempo-scaduto-per-la-grecia.html [accessed March 2012].

argued that it was the first time after the fall of the junta that such a party was joining the government.⁵ For its part, *Bild* attempted to investigate the stance of LAOS leader Mr Karatzaferis in relation to Israel and Jews.⁶ Along with LAOS, the international media were particularly alarmed by various Greek polls suggesting that an additional neo-Nazi party, the Golden Dawn, might pass the 3 per cent threshold to enter the Hellenic Parliament in the next national election, as finally happened a few months later.⁷

In the months after November the media attention was mainly directed towards the so-called PSI negotiations process. Within this framework important news items published included meetings between Greek authorities and representatives of the Institute of International Finance (IIF) and their disagreement on the interest rates coupon of the new bonds. They also included coverage of the Eurogroup meeting of 13 February 2012 which decided on a new haircut amounting to 53.5 per cent of the face value of Greek bonds. It was certainly dramatic for the Hellenic Republic that even after an announcement of a credit event on 9 March 2011 various international media still distrusted it had escaped danger, and expected a second default in due course which would affect not only the private but also the public sector. On that day, for instance, *The New York Times* asserted that 'many analysts do expect that [it] will eventually ask need to ask its public sector creditors to renegotiate its debt'.⁸

The coverage of political and economic affairs does not mean media foreign journalists ignored the social dimension of the Greek crisis in the months of Mr Papademos' administration. With the crisis continuing to unfold, their work after mid-November 2011 continuously revealed aspects of poverty and distress in Athens. The Italian *Il Corriere della Sera*, for instance, covered the way Greek citizens passed their Christmas holidays in December 2011. Its main conclusion was that no celebrations were taking place.⁹ The Italian correspondent who travelled to Athens to explore this theme explained – inter alia – that almost 40 per cent of young people in the country were affected by unemployment. Finally, the

---

5   *Le Figaro*. 2011. Grèce: l'extrême droite participe à l'union nationale. [11 November] Available at: http://www.lefigaro.fr/international/2011/11/11/01003-20111111ARTFIG00439-grece-l-extreme-droite-participe-a-l-union-nationale.php [accessed February 2012].

6   P. Ronzheimer. 2011. Bringt er diesen Juden-Hasser an die Macht? *Bild* [7 November] Available at:http://www.bild.de/politik/ausland/georgios-papandreou/juden-hasser-in-regierung-20857796.bild.html [accessed February 2012].

7   See for example: *The Wall Street Journal*. 2012. Greek poll shows fragmented political landscape. [4 March] Available at: http://online.wsj.com/article/BT-CO-20120304-701023.html [accessed March 2012].

8   L. Thomas. 2012. Next time, Greece may need new tactics. *The New York Times* [9 March] Available at: http://www.nytimes.com/2012/03/10/business/global/greece-debt-restructuring-deal-private-lenders.html?_r=1&pagewanted=all [accessed March 2012].

9   Argentieri, B. 2011. Grecia 2011, il Natale senza festa. *Il Corriere della Sera* [20 December] Available at: http://www.corriere.it/esteri/11_dicembre_20/natale-grecia-crisi_89bb53e6-2ae6-11e1-b7ec-2e901a360d49.shtml [accessed February 2012].

international media concentrated on the riots of 12 February 2012 which resulted in many buildings being burnt in the centre of Athens, further distorting the already negative image of Greece.[10]

The Unknown Adventure

The period of political uncertainty from the beginning of April 2012 until the formation of a coalition government in June was one of the most interesting times in terms of media coverage. The spectacular success of the leftist SYRIZA party in the national election of 6 May led to an increased anxiety – if not fear – for its potential win on 17 June. Almost all surveys conducted between the twin elections could hardly anticipate the new winner. The gifted leader of SYRIZA, Alexis Tsipras, did publicly condemn the bailout terms, promising Greece would stay in the eurozone without the Memorandum. As I commented on the day after the election of 6 May for *Associated Press*: 'Yesterday's elections mark the beginning of the second stage of the Greek drama. And whether this drama will lead into a tragedy remains to be seen in the next weeks'.[11] It is not surprising that foreign journalists criticised again the inability of Greek politicians to co-operate and form a government after the 6 May result. Commenting on the matter for the 'Hub' news programme at *BBC* World News TV on 10 May, I can recall I was put in an awkward position by the journalist's insistence. Mr Nik Gowing directly asked me whether Greek politicians put political interests above national ones. A question which can be easily answered but not publicly!

The possibility of an exit by Greece from the common currency was largely discussed in the view of a possible SYRIZA win. Even elite opinion-making newspapers such as *The Times* did not hesitate to speculate on this. This title, for instance, reported on 18 May 2012 that British company De la Rue, which prints sterling and euro, was preparing for a potential reintroduction of the drachma.[12] Likewise, *Bild* published a story exploring whether euro-banknotes circulated in Greece were different from the ones used in other eurozone countries. This article in the German tabloid also asserted that Greek banknotes have the letter 'Y' as a

---

10 See for example: D. Blanchflower. 2012. Greece and the return of the economic death spiral. *The Guardian* [13 February] Available at: http://www.guardian.co.uk/commentisfree/cifamerica/2012/feb/13/greece-return-economic-death-spiral [accessed March 2012] and *Handelsblatt*. 2012. Strassenschlachten in Griechenland [12 February] Available at: http://www.handelsblatt.com/politik/international/proteste-gegen-das-sparpaket-strassenschlachten-in-griechenland/6201338.html [accessed March 2012].

11 P. Williams. 2012. Greeks punish government over crisis. Available at: *ABC* website [7 May] Available at: http://www.abc.net.au/lateline/content/2012/s3497518.htm [accessed September 2012].

12 N. Fildes. 2012. British banknote printers dust off drachma. *The Times* [18 May] Available at: http://www.thetimes.co.uk/tto/news/world/europe/article3418503.ece [accessed September 2012].

specific country code.¹³ All in all, scenarios about a potential dramatic exit of the Hellenic Republic from the eurosystem widely appeared in the media discourse and the term 'Grexit' almost became a colloquial expression. The *Financial Times*, for example, started a debate about the pros and cons of such a development in Europe and a discussion emerged as to what extent Europe was prepared to tackle its immediate repercussions.¹⁴

The alarming period ended on the night of 17 June when the conservative New Democracy party won the election. The formation of a coalition government three days later in co-operation with PASOK and Democratic Left led to a return of calm sentiment in the media coverage. At the same time, the decisiveness of the new Prime Minister Antonis Samaras to apply the bailout terms was the springboard for positive comments. *Handelsblatt*, for instance, emphasised his 'spectacular transformation' in his effort to make difficult decisions and keep Greece in the euro.¹⁵ In my view, however, Mr Samaras changed stance – compared to his previous intransigence because he had no alternative as a premier. While in opposition he invented populism in order to hit the then government party of PASOK and achieve his political objectives. Therefore, his transformation should only be attributed to his adjustment to hard reality, which he had deliberately ignored from 2009 until 2011.

Mr Samaras attempted in his first months in office to improve the international image of the country. He decided to expand his presence in foreign newspapers by granting interviews to titles such as *Bild*,¹⁶ *Le Monde*,¹⁷ and *Süddeutsche Zeitung*¹⁸ and sharing his determination to guarantee the European orientation of the Hellenic

---

13   K Breuer and J.W. Schäfer. 2012. Was wird aus den Griechen-Euros in meinem Portemonnaie? *Bild* [29 May] Available at: http://www.bild.de/geld/wirtschaft/griechenland-krise/was-wird-aus-den-griechen-euros-24370334.bild.html [accessed September 2012].

14   See for example: R. Atkins. 2012. Greek exit from eurozone 'possible'. *Financial Times* [13 May] Available at: http://www.ft.com/intl/cms/s/0/55d4f61c-9cd9-11e1-9327-00144feabdc0.html#axzz25sgmSoWp [accessed September 2012].

15   R. Berschens and D. Riedel. 2012. Die wundersame Wandlung des Hernn Samaras. *Handelsblatt* [29 August] Available at: http://www.handelsblatt.com/politik/international/vom-blockierer-zum-reformer-die-wundersame-wandlung-des-herrn-samaras/7067624.html [accessed September 2012].

16   P. Ronzheimer. 2012. Die Drachme wäre eine Katastrophe für uns. *Bild* [22 August] Available at: http://www.bild.de/politik/ausland/antonis-samaras/griechenlands-premier-ueber-schulden-sparen-und-euroausstieg-25779000.bild.html [accessed September 2012].

17   A. Salles. 2012. Samaras: Si nous faisons notre travail, la Grèce peut être sauvée. *Le Monde* [23 August] Available at: http://www.lemonde.fr/economie/article/2012/08/23/si-nous-faisons-notre-travail-la-grece-peut-etre-sauvee_1748749_3234.html   [accessed September 2012].

18   A. Hagelüken and C. Schlötzer. 2012. Die Deutschen bekommen ihr Geld zurück. *Süddeutsche Zeitung* [22 August] Available: http://www.sueddeutsche.de/politik/griechenlands-premier-samaras-die-deutschen-bekommen-ihr-geld-zurueck-1.1447818 [accessed September 2012].

Repubblic. At the same time, however, Greece staying in the euro continues to be considered as uncertain by foreign journalists. In a characteristic article published on 2 September 2012, *The New York Times* elaborated on preparation by American companies for a potential Greek return to its national currency.[19]

To Complete the Puzzle

The European debt crisis which started in Greece and has expanded to other countries of the EU, mainly Ireland, Portugal, Spain, Italy and also Cyprus, is far from over. The continuity of the interest shown by the media in the Hellenic case confirms that the problem has not yet been solved. Pessimistic scenarios foresee not only its deterioration but also the dissolution of the common currency area. The current crisis is certainly the worst one to hit the Western world since the Great Depression. The evolution of the debt crisis influences not only the sustainability of sovereign debts but also life conditions of ordinary citizens who suffer through austerity measures and see no end to their economic adventure.

The role of journalists will be even more important in the next years. They have to be particularly careful and accurate in transmitting information regarding critical themes such as the possibility of a sovereign default or the potential exit of a eurozone country from the common currency area. The media are similar to a battleground upon which the financial war is taking place. Economic prosperity is no longer taken for granted and markets seem to be the real adversary. Mistakes and omissions in journalistic work, as the ones observed here, can be avoided. With the crisis entering its third year, journalists are now able to get accustomed to the new reality, learning lessons from the past. As opposed to the beginning of the crisis, they are now able to benefit from their invaluable experience. This experience is mainly related to their better understanding of Greek politics and their understanding of the real pain of Greek citizens.

The coverage of the Hellenic crisis by international media has contributed to its internationalisation. The 'Greek effect' might possibly drive the attention of world policymakers towards the tangible aspects of the problem, mainly human dignity, poverty and unemployment. The coverage has indeed been comprehensive, giving potential readers the opportunity to familiarise themselves with the main elements of an unprecedented, multi-facet crisis at the economic, political and social level. A significant deficiency, however, has been the tendency of journalists to overgeneralise. They have often dealt with the Greek society as a whole without distinguishing between policymakers and ordinary citizens. They

---

19 N. Schwartz. 2012. US companies brace for an exit from the euro by Greece. *The New York Times* [2 September] Available at: http://www.nytimes.com/2012/09/03/business/economy/us-companies-prepare-in-case-greece-exits-euro.html?_r=2&hp [accessed September 2012].

have also considered bizarre elements of the Greek crisis as representative of the whole population and not only a small part of it.

In a democratic country like Greece the role of citizens is certainly catalytic. They have the right to vote and elect politicians of their choice. This said, they should also take some responsibility for being imprisoned in a system of clientelism and statism. From 1980 onwards, they many times democratically voted in their majority for a dynasty of politicians – belonging either to the conservative or the socialist party – who finally led the country to economic and social catastrophe. Here, the popular quote of philosopher Joseph Marie de Maistre that 'every country has the government it deserves' seems applicable.

The criticism of Greek citizens for their political choices in a historical perspective is of high significance but has also limits. People should not be judged for decisions made by their leaders over the years which led to overspending in a corrupt and untransparent way. They should not be judged for being ill-informed by politicians and bankers on the danger of over-borrowing, often having limited access to political debates behind closed doors. The Hellenic society nowadays struggles to survive, paying an unfair price for the crisis. The main people responsible are politicians and domestic oligarchies ravaging the country, not Greek citizens and especially not the young generation who have not yet voted. This specific distinction has been largely absent from the media coverage of the country since October 2009.

Can Greece Change?

International media have developed various theories on the economic future of Greece. Some of them advocate the need for debt-restructuring – a second one in the official sector after the haircut of private bondholders – and an exit of the country from the eurozone. Others insist on the necessity of the implementation of reforms, acceleration of privatisations, reduction of tax evasion and eradication of corruption within the eurosystem along with a relaxation of terms of the bailout, possibly with more time for Greece.[20] Ironic suggestions encouraging the government of the country to sell its ancient sites and a few islands also represent

---

20   In an appeal sent to European leaders in June 2012, 50 signatories, including important personalities across the Continent, argued: 'Policymakers must find a compromise in which Greece brings its public finances in order in exchange for more time to reduce its deficit and to pay back bilateral and multilateral loans. The interest rates Greece pays to its European partners should be cut. This could potentially be linked to progress on clearly defined reforms. This would give the Greek people hope that they will be able to return to economic growth while underlining their own responsibility to deliver on necessary reform'. In their view, 'a Greek exit could trigger a break-up of the Eurozone, which would in turn lead to a deep recession and a new global financial crisis'. It would also 'destroy Europe's soft power and irreversibly damage its standing in the world'. See: An Appeal to European leaders for compromise and flexibility. 2012. Available at: http://savetheeuro.wordpress.com/ [accessed August 2012].

part of the coverage. Comments urging for a stronger European leadership and a common vision for Europe aiming at creation of a political union are, additionally, a recurrent feature. These include proposals for the mutualisation of the European debt, an expanding role of the ECB[21] and the creation of a eurozone banking union.

The Hellenic Republic can certainly benefit from an improvement in the climate of the eurosystem and from decisions enforcing stronger European economic governance. Nevertheless, the main problem of the country is that is has been imprisoned in a vicious circle of recession. 2012 was the fifth consecutive year of contraction and the country has cumulatively lost approximately one fifth of its 2008 GDP. Although it has managed to significantly reduce its budget deficit since the crisis broke out in October 2009, this decline is mainly based on cuts in salaries and pensions, as well as on tax rises. By contrast, progress in beating tax evasion and corruption[22] is rather low while the real economy is suffering from the frozen credit[23] due to uncertainty, fear and speculation of a potential exit of the country from the eurozone. On 26 July 2012, for instance, Citigroup expressed the view that there was a 90 per cent possibility that Greece would leave the common currency in the next 12–18 months.[24] Under these circumstances, an investor or an investing company can hardly come into play and action. They prefer to keep a wait-and-see stance.

Moreover, Greece lacks so-far a growth-oriented policy which can possibly kick-off the economy. No national strategy has been set up which can constitute the basis for a systematic recovery.[25] In one of his pre-election speeches on 31 May 2012, for example, the current Prime Minister, Antonis Samaras, elaborated on the strategy of his party to lead Greece out of the crisis without specifying and explaining how

---

21 On 6 September 2012, Mario Draghi, President of the ECB, unveiled details of his bond-buying plan aimed at easing the Eurozone debt crisis. He, inter alia, announced the decision for the ECB to undertake Outright Monetary Transactions (OMT) in secondary markets for sovereign bonds in the Eurozone.

22 According to data announced by the Greek Ministry of Finance in September 2012, six out of ten self-employed people declared income below the tax-free threshold of €12,000 in 2010. In the same month, the Council of Europe Group of States against Corruption (GRECO) expressed its concern for the inability of the Hellenic Republic to follow its recommendations on the matter.

23 Many suppliers of Greek companies demand cash a priori while liquidity has become an almost unknown word in the market.

24 K. Mackenzie. 2012. Buinzer now predicting Grexit probability of 90 per cent. [26 July] Available at: http://ftalphaville.ft.com/blog/2012/07/26/1096631/ [accessed August 2012].

25 McKinsey & Company has published a comprehensive report on possibilities for growth in Greece. See: McKinsey & Company. 2012. Greece 10 years ahead: Defining Greece's new growth model and strategy. 2012. Available at: http://www.mckinsey.com/locations/athens/GreeceExecutiveSummary_new/pdfs/Executive_summary_English_new.pdf [accessed September 2012].

growth could be boosted.[26] Nonetheless, the country has the potential to recuperate. The areas of energy, tourism, trade and transportation, for example, should have the lion's share in future governmental policy. Actions such as the exploration of domestic oil and gas reserves, the exportation of solar energy, the upgrade of cruise embarkation ports, the development of new marinas, the expansion of major ports for cargo gateway and the construction of a high-speed cargo train line can possibly pave the way for a return to growth.[27] In parallel with this, the country can lay the foundations in key economic sectors including manufacturing of generic pharmaceuticals, aquaculture, medical tourism, elderly care, waste management and promotion of Greek specialty foods in international markets.[28] It can also improve the standards of higher education offered domestically in order not only to limit the number of Greeks who prefer foreign institutions, but also to attract students from the Balkan Peninsula and the Mediterranean Basin. Furthermore, the country can also rely on shipping, a record which is impressive at the world stage.

Last, but not least, the Greek crisis is interwoven into a critical sociological dimension. A new social contract is required, linking politicians to citizens. The current political personnel of the country – with only a few exceptions – are naturally stigmatised. Their responsibility is not only related to over-borrowing and overspending for many years before October 2009, but also to their mistakes and omissions from this month onwards. In my view, Greek politicians are now the main cause of the vilification of the Hellenic Republic and often of its citizens at the world stage. They have associated the policy of reform with a required process imposed from abroad without assuming ownership of this movement of change for the country. Being unable to offer their own solutions to the crisis, they have not hesitated to blame their European partners for setting up a necessary plan to modernise the Greek economy. They have thus failed to benefit from their advice and experience which would be critical for recovery in Greece.

Those who have the fate of the country in their own hands are the Greek people themselves. Greek people obviously suffer from austerity measures but the main reason they react and demonstrate is not because they are not prepared to make more sacrifices. The main reason is that they have the conviction that the burden of the crisis is not shared in an equal and fair way and that the ones responsible for the Greek drama have not been brought to justice. As long as

---

26 On 31 May 2012, Mr Antonis Samaras named 18 priority measures for Greece such as the increase of the tax-free threshold from €5,000 to €8,000, the compensation of small bondholders, the acceleration of privatisation, the demarcation of Greece's exclusive economic zone, the fair counterbalance of debts from and to the state, the recapitalisation of banks and the economic settlement for loan-takers. His speech, however, did not name specific areas for growth in the country. See: Speech of Antonis Samaras on the national plan to overcome the crisis. 2012 [31 May] Available at: http://www.nd.gr/web/12001/press/-/journal_content/56_INSTANCE_Rb5c/36615/998337 [accessed September 2012].

27 McKinsey & Company. 2012. Greece 10 years ahead, 36.

28 McKinsey & Company. 2012. Greece 10 years ahead, 64 and 65.

this feeling of injustice dominates Hellenic society, the country will not be able to reboot, suffering as it is from a serious confidence crisis. In its most cynical dimension this confidence crisis is highlighted by the haircut imposed on small Greek bondholders who had kept their savings in the Hellenic Republic by buying sovereign bonds – responding to encouragement by various national politicians – instead of transferring their deposits in foreign countries. Ironically, the money transfer abroad has proved to be the correct choice.

The new generation of Greek people is one which will need to play a pivotal role in the coming years. Time has now come for honest, sincere and well-educated young people to postpone their emigration to foreign countries and stay in the Hellenic Republic. They have to be prepared to put up a difficult fight to oust the status quo of old-guard politicians by becoming actively involved in politics and protect its European orientation. Their battle will be a democratic one though. It will be organised via conferences, debates with ordinary citizens, media exposure and increased participation in civil society. Greece has lacked inspired leadership for many years. But if young people attempt to take the lead, they will receive overwhelming support by a society which needs hope for the future. The wind of change will only come internally with a democratic revolution led by young, open-minded, promising and pro-European leaders.

Appendix: Interviews–discussions

Prof. Dimitri Papadimitriou	Levy Institute	12 August 2010, by phone
Dr Stavros Panageas	Chicago Booth School	17 September 2010, face-to-face, London
Prof. Dimitri Vayanos	LSE	17 September 2010, face-to-face, London
Ms Kerin Hope	*Financial Times*	27 September 2010, face-to-face, Athens
Mr Vassilis Papadimitriou	Personal counsellor of Mr Papandreou on communication affairs	4 October 2010, face-to-face, Athens
Dr Michael Masourakis	*Alpha Bank*	6 October 2010, face-to-face, Athens
Ms Dina Kyriakidou	*Reuters*	13 October 2010, face-to-face, Athens
Ms Irini Anastasopoulou	*Deutsche Welle*	18 October 2010, face-to-face, Athens
Ms Catherine Boitard	*AFP*	20 October 2010, face-to-face, Athens
Mr Gerd Höhler	*Handelsblatt*	25 October 2010, by email
Ms Angelique Kourounis	*L'Express*	31 October 2010, by email
Ms Maria Petrakis	*Bloomberg*	4 November 2010, face-to-face, Athens
Dr Nikos Skrekas	Journalist, former reporter for *Wall Street Journal, Dow Jones Newswires*	4 November 2010, by email
Dr Costas Mavroidis	Hellenic Association for Press Attachés	1 December 2011, face-to-face, Athens
Mr Achilleas Paparsenos	Press Office of the Hellenic Republic, Geneva	3 December 2010, by email
Mr Nikolaus Blome	*Bild*	7 December 2010, face-to-face, Athens
Mr Quentin Peel	*Financial Times*	7 December 2010, by email
Dr Dimitri Tsomocos	University of Oxford	5 January 2011, face-to-face, Athens
Ms Filio Lanara	Press Office, Greek Ministry of Finance during the Papandreou government	17 January 2011, face-to-face, London
Ms Maria Choukli	*Antenna TV*	1 March 2011, face-to-face, Athens
Mr Vassilis Chiotis	*Vima Fm*	8 March 2011, face-to-face, Athens
Mr Yannis Pretenteris	*Mega Channel*	16 March 2011, face-to-face, Athens

Mr Takis Kampylis	Athens 9.84 radio	18 March 2011, face-to-face, Athens
Mr Pantelis Kapsis	Journalist, Greek Minister of Communication during the Papademos government	21 March 2011, face-to-face, Athens
Mr Vassilis Korkidis	Hellenic Confederation of Commerce	30 March 2011, face-to-face, Athens
Mr Panos Amiras	Eleftheros Typos	13 April 2011, face-to-face, Athens
Ms Alexia Kefalas	Le Figaro	31 May 2011, face-to-face, Athens
Mr Paul Ronzheimer	Bild	16 June 2011, face-to-face, Athens
Mr Paul Taylor	Reuters	8 July 2011, face-to-face, Poros
Prof. Yannis Stournaras	Greek Minister of Finance	25 July 2011, face-to-face, Athens
Mr Babis Papadimitriou	Hi Kathimerini	18 July 2011, face-to-face, Athens
Ms Natalie Savaricas	Associated Press and France 24	21 July 2011, face-to-face, Athens
Mr Costas Kallitsis	National Bank of Greece	26 July 2011, face-to-face, Athens
Mr Michael Martens	Frankfurter Allgemeine Zeitung	10 November 2011, face-to-face, Athens
Ms Deborah Kyvrikosaios	Reuters	27 December 2011, face-to-face, Athens
Ms Beneddeta Bergentieri	Il Corriere della Sera	12 January 2012, by phone
Mr Patrick Cockborn	The Independent	19 February 2012, face-to-face, Athens
Dr Jeroen Kremers	Royal Bank of Scotland	24 April 2012, face-to-face, Athens
Mr Mark Lowen	BBC	1 May 2012, face-to-face, Athens
Dr Jens Bastian	EU Taskforce	7 July 2012, München
Mr Allain Salles	Le Monde	25 July 2012, face-to-face, Athens
Mr Markus Bernath	Financial Times Deutschland	30 July 2012, face-to-face, Athens
Ms Julia-Amalia Heyer	Der Spiegel	16 October 2012, face-to-face, Athens

Sources Accessed

Alco Poll. 2010. *Proto Thema*, newspaper, 9 May, 4.
Alco Poll. 2011. *Proto Thema*, 4 September, 1.
Alpha Bank weekly report on Economic Developments. 2011, 27 January.
Ahrens, A. and Faiola, A. 2010. Greece moves closer to default situation. *The Washington Post*, 23 April, A01.
Amann, M. 2011. Postdemokratisch? *Frankfurter Allgemeine Zeitung* [6 November]. Available at: http://www.faz.net/aktuell/wirtschaft/europas-schuldenkrise/griechenland-postdemokratisch-11519476.html [accessed February 2011].
Amato, R. 2011. La crisi ha distrutto il welfare e i diritti Società disgregata, disuguaglianze record. *La Repubblica* [7 June]. Available at: http://www.repubblica.it/economia/2011/06/07/news/rapporto_sui_diritti_globali_2011-17353030/ [accessed November 2011].
An Appeal to European leaders for compromise and flexibility. 2012. Available at: http://savetheeuro.wordpress.com/ [accessed August 2012].
Announcement of George A. Papandreou. 2010. [2 February] Available at: http://www.primeminister.gov.gr/2010/02/02/816, 2 February [accessed September 2011].
Annual Report of the General Inspector of Public Administration. 2009. Available at: http://www.gedd.gr/article_data/Linked_files/79/Ekthesh2009GEDDfinal.pdf, p. 12. [accessed August 2011].
Applebaum, A. 2010. America's Greek tragedy. *The Washington Post*, A13.
Applebaum, A. 2010. Germany's tug-of-war with Greece. *The Washington Post* [9 March 2010]. Available at: http://www.washingtonpost.com/wp-dyn/content/story/2010/03/08/ST2010030803490.html?sid=ST2010030803490 [accessed January 2012].
Argentieri, B. 2011. Grecia 2011, il Natale senza festa. *Il Corriere della Sera* [20 December]. Available at: http://www.corriere.it/esteri/11_dicembre_20/natale-grecia-crisi_89bb53e6-2ae6-11e1-b7ec-2e901a360d49.shtml [accessed Febriary 2012].
Arlt, H.-J. and Storz, W. 2011. Drucksache Bild – Eine Marke und ihre Mägde. OBS-Arbeitsheft 67. Available at: http://www.otto-brenner-shop.de/uploads/tx_mplightshop/2011_04_06_Bildstudie_Otto_Brenner_Stiftung.pdf [accessed September 2011].
Artavanis, N., Morse, A. and Tsoutsoura, M. 2012. Tax evasion across industries: soft credit evidence from Greece. Chicago Booth Paper No. 12–25 [25 June]. Available at: http://greekeconomistsforreform.com/uncategorized/tax-evasion-across-industries-soft-credit-evidence-from-greece/ [September 2012].

Atkins, R. 2012. Greek exit from eurozone 'possible'. *Financial Times* [13 May]. Available at: http://www.ft.com/intl/cms/s/0/55d4f61c-9cd9-11e1-9327-00144feabdc0.html#axzz25sgmSoWp [accessed September 2012].

Atkins, R. 2011. Frankfurt's dilemma. *Financial Times*, 25 May, 9.

Atkins, R. and Peel, Q. 2010. Germans oppose Greek aid, poll shows. *Financial Times* [21 March]. Available at: http://www.ft.com/cms/s/0/ee055e82-3529-11df-9cfb-00144feabdc0.html#axzz1EIkc3yii [accessed November 2011].

Aurélien, V. 2010. Grèce: aide-toi, l'Europe t'aidera. *Le Monde* [5 March]. Available at: http://www.lemonde.fr/idees/article/2010/03/05/grece-aide-toi-l-europe-t-aidera-par-aurelien-veron_1314802_3232.html [accessed April 2011].

Ayadi, R. 2011. A three pillar firepower to solve the European sovereign crisis: a last chance. [19 October] CEPS Commentary.

Baldwin, R. and Gros, D. 2010. Introduction: the Euro crisis – What to do? in *Completing the Eurozone Rescue: What More Needs to Be Done*, edited by Baldwin, R. et al. London: voxEU.org. Available at: http://www.voxeu.org/reports/EZ_Rescue.pdf [accessed February 2012].

Bank of Greece Annual Report. 2008. Available at: http://www.bankofgreece.gr/BogEkdoseis/Annrep2008.pdf [accessed August 2011].

Bank of Greece Summary of the Annual Report. 2010. Available at: http://www.bankofgreece.gr/BogEkdoseis/Summary_Annrep2010.pdf [accessed September 2011].

Barber, T. 2010. Saving the Euro: tall ambition, flawed foundations [11 October]. Available at: http://www.ft.com/intl/cms/s/0/643daffa-d57a-11df-8e86-00144feabdc0.html#axzz1YJWFlqMo [accessed August 2010].

Beaumont, P. 2011. Athens is plastered with one message: enoikiazetai. To let. *The Guardian* [4 August]. Available at: http://www.guardian.co.uk/world/2011/aug/04/athens-to-let-signs-are-everywhere [accessed December 2011].

Beaumont, P. 2011. Greece's healthcare system is on the brink of catastrophe. *The Guardian* [11 August]. Available at: http://www.guardian.co.uk/world/2011/aug/05/greece-healthcare-brink-catastrophe [accessed December 2011].

Bernau, P. 2011. Ich rette die Griechen nicht! *Frankfurter Allgemeine Zeitung*. [29 October]. Available at: http://www.faz.net/aktuell/finanzen/staatsanleihen-ich-rette-die-griechen-nicht-11510478.html [accessed November 2011].

Berschens, R., Ludwig, T. and Kurm-Engels, M. 2010. IWF-Hilfe für Griechenland spaltet EU und EZB [24 March]. Available at: http://www.handelsblatt.com/politik/international/iwf-hilfe-fuer-griechenland-spaltet-eu-und-ezb/3397592.html [accessed January 2011].

Berschens, R. and Riedel, D. 2012. Die wundersame Wandlung des Hernn Samaras. *Handelsblatt* [29 August]. Available at: http://www.handelsblatt.com/politik/international/vom-blockierer-zum-reformer-die-wundersame-wandlung-des-herrn-samaras/7067624.html [accessed September 2012].

Bild. 2011. 14.000 Griechen schulden dem Staat 36 Mr. Euro [14 July]. Available at: http://www.bild.de/politik/ausland/griechenland-krise/griechenland-krise-papandreou-14000-griechen-schulden-staat-36-milliarden-euro-steuern-18857554.bild.html [accessed February 2012].

Bild. 2011. Athen stink zum Himmel [13 October]. Available at: http://www.bild.de/geld/wirtschaft/griechenland-krise/muellabfuhr-streikt-athen-stinkt-zum-himmel-20445650.bild.html [accessed November 2011].

Bild. 2011. Dramatischer Appeal an Merkel. [24 August]. Available at: http://www.lemonde.fr/europe/article/2011/07/18/angela-merkel-destabilisee-par-le-dossier-de-la-dette-grecque_1550210_3214.html [accessed November 2011].

Bild. 2010. Haben wir jetzt ruhe vor den Pleiten-Griechen? [26 March]. Available at: http://www.bild.de/politik/2010/gipfel/eu-gipfel-bruessel-aufatmen-in-athen-11986622.bild.html [accessed January 2011]

Bild. 2011 Ich zahle keinen Cent für Pleite-Griechen Griechen! [22 September]. Available at: http://www.bild.de/politik/inland/euro-krise/steuerrebell-kein-cent-fuer-griechenland-20090790.bild.html [accessed November 2011].

Bild. 2010. Ihr griecht nix von uns [5 March]. Available at: http://www.bild.de/BILD/politik/wirtschaft/2010/03/05/griechenland-bild-schreibt-pleite-premier/keine-hilfe-fuer-griechen.html [accessed April 2011].

Bild. 2010. Keine Finanzhilfe f'ür Griechenland. [11 February]. Available at: http://www.bild.de/politik/wirtschaft/griechenland/was-kostet-die-rettung-der-pleite-griechen-11433914.bild.html [accessed November 2010].

Bild. 2011. Muss Griechenland die Akropolis verkaufen? [17 May]. Available at: http://www.bild.de/politik/ausland/griechenland-krise/muss-griechenland-die-akropolis-verkaufen-17937616.bild.html [accessed November 2011].

Bild. 2011. Pleite-Griechen wollen die Sonne anzapfen [5 September]. Available at: http://www.bild.de/politik/ausland/griechenland-krise/griechenland-krise-jetzt-pumpen-sie-auch-die-sonne-an-19777402.bild.html [accessed November 2011].

Bild. 2010.Verkauft doch eure Inseln, ihr Pleite-Griechen. [27 October]. Available at: http://www.bild.de/politik/wirtschaft/griechenland-krise/regierung-athen-sparen-verkauft-inseln-pleite-akropolis-11692338.bild.html [accessed April 2011].

Bilefsky, D. and Kitsantonis, N. 2010. Statistician rejects blame for Greece's financial turmoil. Available at: http://query.nytimes.com/gst/fullpage.html?res=9C02E1D91F30F930A25751C0A9669D8B63&scp=2&sq=greek+statistics+%2B+lies&st=nyt, 13 February [accessed December 2011].

Blog of 'non-payment campaign' at: http://denplirono.wordpress.com/about/ [accessed January 2011].

Bones, J. 2011. Austerity in birthplace of Olympic forces athletes to choose between work and play. *The Times* [15 October]. Available at: http://www.thetimes.co.uk/tto/news/world/europe/article3195235.ece [accessed December 2011].

Bones, J. 2011. Crime shows dark side of ancient capital, *The Times* [15 October]. Available at: http://www.thetimes.co.uk/tto/news/world/europe/article3195239.ece, [accessed December 2011].

Bones, J. 2011. Jobs crisis forces thousands to seek a better life abroad. *The Times* [14 October] http://www.thetimes.co.uk/tto/news/world/europe/article3193945.ece [accessed December 2011].

Bouilhet, A. 2010. La France n'est pas la Grèce ou l'Irlande. *Le Figaro Magazine*, 29 November, 25.

Boutelet, C. 2011. Angela Merkel déstabilisée par le dossier de la dette grecque. *Le Monde* [19 July]. Available at: http://www.lemonde.fr/europe/article/2011/07/18/angela-merkel-destabilisee-par-le-dossier-de-la-dette-grecque_1550210_3214.html [accessed November 2011].

Bouzou, N. La crise grecque est aussi française. *Le Figaro* [30 April]. Available at: http://www.lefigaro.fr/editos/2010/04/29/01031-20100429ARTFIG00629-la-crise-grecque-est-aussi-francaise-.php [accessed January 2011].

Boyes, R. 2011. Greeks line up for lunch as new man sets terms. *The Times*, 8 November, 6–7.

Braunberger, G. 2010. Krückstock für den kranken Mann? *Frankfurter Allgemeine Zeitung* [29 April]. Available at: http://www.faz.net/aktuell/wirtschaft/europas-schuldenkrise/griechenlands-schuldenkrise-krueckstock-fuer-den-kranken-mann-1575521.html [accessed March 2012].

Bremmer, I. 2011. Greece escapes collapse, but is true problems are only just beginning. *Financial Times* [29 June]. Available at: http://blogs.ft.com/the-a-list/2011/06/29/greece-has-escaped-collapse-but-its-problems-are-only-beginning/#axzz1i3LQYFXm [accessed September 2011].

Bremmer, C. 2011. In Athens some whisper it: revolution. *The Times* [18 June]. Available at: http://www.thetimes.co.uk/tto/news/world/europe/article3066434.ece [accessed December 2011].

Breuer, K. and Schäfer, J.W. 2012. Was wird aus den Griechen-Euros in meinem Portemonnaie? *Bild* [29 May]. Available at: http://www.bild.de/geld/wirtschaft/griechenland-krise/was-wird-aus-den-griechen-euros-24370334.bild.html [accessed September 2012].

Briançon, P. 2010. L'Europe n'a pas le choix: le drame grec ne finira pas en tragédie. *Le Monde*, 1 February.

Briançon, P. 2010. Le point de vue des chroniqueurs de l'agence économique Reuters Breakingviews. *Le Monde*, 13 July, 13.

Brown, G. 2010. *Beyond the Crash: Overcoming the First Crisis of Globalization*. New York, London, Toronto, Sydney: Free Press.

Brown, M. 2010. Moody's: Greece, Portugal risk slow death. Available at: http://online.wsj.com/article/SB10001424052748704362004575000800814712706.html, 13 January [accessed July 2011].

Brüggman, M. 2011. Junge Griechen-Elite verlässt ihr Land. *Handelsblatt* [29 October]. Available at: http://www.handelsblatt.com/politik/international/exodus-der-akademiker-junge-griechen-elite-verlaesst-ihr-land/5765892.html [accessed December 2011].

Bryant, C. 2011. German banks can stomach Greek debt. *Financial Times* [29 September]. Available at: http://www.ft.com/intl/cms/s/0/7cbdc3f4-e9f0-11e0-b997-00144feab49a.html#axzz1oEERGUZP [accessed December 2011].

Bryman, A. 2004. *Social Research Methods*. Oxford: Oxford University Press.

Bulmer, S. and Paterson, W.E. 2010 Germany and the European Union: from tamed power to normalized power. *International Affairs*, 86(5), 1051–73.

Bundesregierung website. 2010. Merkel: Tarifabschluss im öffentlichen Dienst beispielhaft. [28 February]. Available at: http://www.bundesregierung.de/nn_1272/Content/DE/Artikel/2010/02/2010-02-28-merkel-ard-bericht-aus-berlin.html [accessed September 2011].

Calla, C. 2010. L'aide à la Grèce anime le débat politique en Allemagne. *Le Monde*, 14 March, 8.

Campbell, M. 2009 Party's over for Greek gaspers. *The Sunday Times* [20 December]. Available at: http://www.thesundaytimes.co.uk/sto/news/world_news/article193206.ece [accessed December 2011].

Castle, S. 2010. IMF is more likely to lead efforts for aid to Greece. *The New York Times*, 30 March, Business/Financial Desk, 2.

Cathy, T.B. 2002. Called to account. Available at: http://www.time.com/time/business/article/0,8599,263006,00.html. [accessed September 2010].

Census Report Results. 2010 [30 July]. Available at: http://apografi.gov.gr/2010/07/379 [accessed August 2011].

Cheyvialle, A. 2010. Athènes lance sa réforme fiscale. *Le Figaro*, 15 April, 21.

Cheyvialle, A. 2010. Un plan douloureux et à risques pour l'"économie grecque. *Le Figaro*, 4 May, 22.

Clogg, R. 2002. *A Concise History of Greece*. Cambridge: Cambridge University Press.

Conlan, T. 2010. BBC under fire after removing video of Greek shoe protest from its website. *The Guardian* [21 September]. Available at: http://www.guardian.co.uk/media/2010/sep/21/bbc-under-fire-video-shoe-protest [accessed April 2011].

Connolly, K. 2010. Ordinary Germans balk at second euro bailout. *The Guardian* [16 November] http://www.guardian.co.uk/business/2010/nov/16/germany-balks-at-ireland-bailout [accessed December 2011].

Cramme, O. 2011. In Search of leadership, in *The Delphic Oracle on Europe: Is There a Future for the European Union*, edited by L. Tsoukalis and Y.A. Emmanouilidis. Oxford and New York: Oxford University Press.

Curran, J. 2002. *Media and Power*. London and New York: Routledge.

Curran, J. 2005. Mediations of democracy, in *Mass Media and Society*, edited by J. Curran and M. Gurevitch. London: Arnold.

Daley, S. 2011. Bureaucracy in Greece defies efforts to cut it. *The New York Times* [17 October] http://www.nytimes.com/2011/10/18/world/europe/greeces-bloated-bureaucracy-defies-efforts-to-cut-it.html?pagewanted=all [accessed January 2012].

Daley, S. 2010. Greek wealth is everywhere but tax forms. *The New York Times* [1 May]. Available at: http://www.nytimes.com/2010/05/02/world/europe/02evasion.html?pagewanted=all [accessed November 2011].

Damanaki, M. personal website. 2011. Statement of Commissioner Maria Damanaki on the scenario of a Greek exit from the eurozone/Dilossi tis Epitropou Marias Damanaki gia to senario apomakrinsis tis Elladas apo to euro [25 May]. Available at: http://www.damanaki.gr/index.php?option=com_content&view=article&id=1362:2011-05-25-12-24-26&catid=48:2010-02-17-17-50-07&Itemid=57 [accessed February 2012].

Davis, B. 2010. Who is on the hook for the IMF's Greek bailout? *The Wall Street Journal* [5 May]. Available at: http://online.wsj.com/article/SB10001424052748704866204575224421086866944.html [accessed November 2010].

De Capèle, 2011. Le dangereux poker grec. *Le Figaro*, 2 November, 2.

Déclaration du Président de la République à l'issue de l'entretien avec Monsieur Antonis Samaras, PremierMinistre de la République Hellenique. 2012 [25 August] Available at: http://www.elysee.fr/president/lesactualites/declarations/2012/declaration-du-president-de-la-republique-a.13801.html?search=SAMARAS&xtmc=samaras&xcr=1 [accessed September 2012].

Declaration of French President Nikolas Sarkozy after his meeting with Greek Prime Minister, George Papandreou. 2011 [30 September]. Available at: http://www.elysee.fr/president/les-actualites/declarations/2011/declaration-du-president-de-la-republique-a.12130.html [accessed October 2011].

De Foucaud, I. 2010. La Grèce pourrait vendre des îles pour renflouer sa dette: *Le Figaro* [25 June]. Available at: http://www.lefigaro.fr/conjoncture/2010/06/25/04016-20100625ARTFIG00388-la-grece-pourrait-vendre-des-iles-pour-renflouer-sa-dette.php [accessed April 2011].

De Malet, C. 2010. Pour une agence européenne de la dette. *Le Figaro*, 11 February, 14.

Delastik, G. 2012. O gauleiter echase to dromo (The gauleiter lost his way) *Ethnos* [31 January]. Available at: http://www.ethnos.gr/article.asp?catid=22792&subid=2&pubid=63609750 [accessed February 2012].

Delastik, G. 2012. Vouleftes sta nichia tis Gestapo (MPs in Gestapo's hands) *Ethnos* [1 February]. Available at: http://www.ethnos.gr/article.asp?catid=22792&subid=2&pubid=63610455 [accessed February 2012].

De Tricornot, A. and Dumoulin, S. 2010. Grèce: Le danger, c'est la contagion à l'ensemble de la zone euro. *Le Monde*. Available at: http://www.lemonde.fr/economie/article/2010/02/08/grece-le-danger-c-est-la-contagion-a-l-ensemble-de-la-zone-euro_1302840_3234.html [accessed November 2010].

De Vergès, M. 2010. La restructuration de la dette, un scénario envisagé mais tabou. *Le Monde*, 28 April.

De Vergès, M. 2011. Les trois options envisagées. *Le Monde* [27 May], p. 15 and Kansas, D. 2011. Greek bond yield spreads widen, restructuring chatter grows. *The Wall Street Journal* [27 April]. Available at: http://blogs.wsj.com/marketbeat/2011/04/27/greek-bond-yield-spreads-widen-restructuring-chatter-grows/?KEYWORDS=greece+++haircut [accessed November 2011].

Dizard, J. 2010. Eurozone crisis averted for now. *Financial Times* [16 May]. Available at: http://www.ft.com/cms/s/0/718569b8-5f83-11df-a670-00144feab49a.html#axzz1Dqko0ArR [accessed January 2011].

Dizard, J. 2010. It's no secret: Greece is restructuring debt. *Financial Times* [4 July]. Available at: http://www.ft.com/cms/s/0/2ac462f6-8600-11df-bc22-00144feabdc0.html#axzz1Dqko0ArR [accessed January 2011].

Dennis, N. 2010. Greek debt woes spread to Portugal and Spain. *Financial Times* [4 February]. Available at: http://www.ft.com/intl/cms/s/0/953bfda8-117d-11df-9195-00144feab49a.html#axzz1k6mVMEQu [accessed November 2010].

Donario, R. 2011. Greece approves tough measures on economy. http://www.nytimes.com/2011/06/30/world/europe/30greece.html?_r=1&scp=398&sq=greece&st=nyt 29 June [accessed December 2011].

Donovan, J. 2010. Papandreou says first deficit is Greece's credibility gap. *Bloomberg*, website [28 January]. Available at: http://www.bloomberg.com/apps/news?pid=newsarchive&sid=aJcS98oA0zog [accessed November 2011].

Dorning, M. and Dodge, C. 2010. China losing to US among investments of choice. Available at: http://www.bloomberg.com/apps/news?pid=newsarchive&sid=asETTCYSxjfA, 21 January [accessed July 2011].

Duffie, D. 2010. Credit default swaps on government debt: potential implications of the Greek debt crisis – statement at the United States House of Representatives [29 April].

Dunn, T.N. and Hawkes, S. 2011. I owe Youzo; Euro debt crisis: things can only get feta. *The Sun*, 22 July, 8–9.

Ecoiffier, P. and Conthargis, T. La Grèce nous donnera toujours des leçons essentielles *Le Monde* [17 May]. Available at: http://www.lemonde.fr/idees/article/2011/05/17/la-grece-nous-donnera-toujours-des-lecons-essentielles_1523220_3232.html [accessed January 2011].

Elafros, G. 2009. Energeiaki spatali 450,000 euro to hrono/Energy loss 450,000 euros per year. [22 March]. Available at: http://news.kathimerini.gr/4Dcgi/4Dcgi/_w_articles_civ_11_22/03/2009_308353 [accessed September 2011].

Eleftheros Typos. 2010, 23 February.

Eleftherotypia. 2010, 27 October.

Enrich, D. and Gauthier-Villars. 2011. Struggling French banks fought to avoid oversight. *The Wall Street Journal* [21 October]. Available at: http://online.wsj.com/article/SB10001424052970204485304576641561540266494.html [accessed November 2011].

Entman, R. 1993. Framing: toward clarification of a fractured paradigm. *Journal of Communication*, 43(4), 51–8.

Errard, G. 2010. Les banques françaises très Exposées à la dette grecque, *Le Figaro* [11 May] Available at: http://www.lefigaro.fr/societes/2010/05/06/04015-20100506ARTFIG00561-l-exposition-des-banques-francaises-a-la-dette-grecque.php.

Ethnos tis Kyriakis. 2011. 7 August.

Ethnos tis Kyriakis. 2010. 1 August.

EU website. 2010. Commission assesses stability programme of Greece; makes recommendations to correct the excessive budget deficit, improve competitiveness through structural reforms and provide reliable statistics [3 February] Available at: http://europa.eu/rapid/pressReleasesAction.do?reference=IP/10/116 [accessed August 2011].

Eurogroup Statement. 2012. [21 February]. Available at: http://consilium.europa.eu/uedocs/cms_data/docs/pressdata/en/ecofin/128075.pdf [accessed February 2012].

Euronews. 2010. Interview of Prime Minister Papandreou with Christophe Midol-Monnet [27 January]. Available at: http://www.primeminister.gov.gr/english/2010/01/27/prime-ministers-george-a-papandreou-interview-on-euronews/ [accessed November 2011].

European Commission. 2010. Report on Greek government deficit and debt statistics [8 January]. Available at: http://eurlex.europa.eu/LexUriServ/LexUriServ.do?uri=SPLIT_COM:2010:0001(01):FIN:EN:PDF [accessed April 2011].

European Parliament (EP) website. 2009. Results of the 2009 European elections, Greece. Available at: http://www.europarl.europa.eu/parliament/archive/elections2009/en/greece_en_txt.html [accessed July 2011).

Euro Summit Statement. 2011. [26 October]. Available at: http://www.consilium.europa.eu/uedocs/cms_Data/docs/pressdata/en/ec/125644.pdf [accessed November 2011].

Eurostat information note on Greek fiscal data. 2010. [15 November]. Available at: http://epp.eurostat.ec.europa.eu/portal/page/portal/government_finance_statistics/documents/Report_EDP%20GR%20-%20final.pdf [accessed August 2011].

Eurostat newsrelease. 2010. [22 April]. Available at: http://epp.eurostat.ec.europa.eu/cache/ITY_PUBLIC/2-22042010-BP/EN/2-22042010-BP-EN.PDF [accessed August 2011].

Excerpts from the speech of Costas Karamanlis at the Athens Chamber of Commerce & Industry. 2008 [8 July]. Available at: http://www.axiaplus.gr/Default.aspx?id=42431&nt=108&lang=1 [accessed April 2011].

Faiola, A. 2011. Amid crisis, Italy confronts a culture of tax evasion. *The Washington Post* [24 November]. Available at: http://www.washingtonpost.com/world/amid-crisis-italy-confronts-a-culture-of-tax-evasion/2011/11/22/gIQAef4JtN_story.html [accessed February 2012].

Faiola, A. 2011. In Greece, austerity kindles deep discontent. *The Washington Post* [14 May]. Available at: http://www.washingtonpost.com/world/in-greece-austerity-kindles-deep-discontent/2011/05/05/AFUQGy2G_story.html [accessed December 2011].

Featherstone, K. and Papadimitriou, D. 2008. *The Limits of Europeanization: Reform Capacity and Policy Conflict in Greece*. New York: Palgrave Macmillan.

Featherstone, K. 2011. The Greek sovereign debt crisis and the EMU: a failing state in a skewed regime. *Journal of Common Market Studies*, 49(2).

Feldstein, M. 2012. The failure of the Euro: little currency that couldn't. *Foreign Affairs*, January/February, 91(1), 105–16.

Ferreira-Marques, C. 2010. WRAPUP 1- EU's Almunia says no chance Greece default [29 January]. Available at: http://www.reuters.com/article/2010/01/29/greece-idUSLDE60S0XN20100129 [accessed July 2011].

Fildes, N. 2012. British banknote printers dust off drachma. *The Times online edition* [18 May]. Available at: http://www.thetimes.co.uk/tto/news/world/europe/article3418503.ece [accessed September 2012].

Finch, J. 2010. Greece to sell off islands and artworks. *The Guardian* [4 March]. Available at: http://www.guardian.co.uk/world/2010/mar/04/greece-greek-islands-auction [accessed April 2011].

Finance Ministry list. 2011. [8 September]. Available at: http://www.gsis.gr/debtors/kerdoskopika-np.html [accessed September 2011].

Financial Times/Harris Poll. 2012. [August]. Available at: http://www.ft.com/intl/cms/eb1b2004-f542-11e1-b120-00144feabdc0.pdf [accessed September 2012].

Forelle, C. and Blackstone, B. 2011. Europe divided over Greek crisis. *The Wall Street Journal*, 25 May, 7.

Frankenberger, K-D. 2010. Brandsätze. *Frankfurter Allgemeine Zeitung* [5 May]. Available at: http://www.faz.net/aktuell/politik/griechenland-brandsaetze-1978325.html [accessed December 2011].

Frankfurter Allgemeine Zeitung. 2010. Höhe der Griechenland für Griechenland noch offen, 29 April.

Frankfurter Allgemeine Zeitung. 2011. Kein Brot, kein Benzin [19 October] Available at: http://www.faz.net/aktuell/wirtschaft/europas-schuldenkrise/generalstreik-in-griechenland-kein-brot-kein-benzin-11498150.html [accessed November 2011].

Frankfurter Allgemeine Zeitung. 2010. Kein Euro den Griechen. [4 March]. Available at: http://www.faz.net/s/Rub28EF38B483C94193A70B58D41ADA26A4/Doc~E85989C21022F42FFA52F92A3F33A22E0~ATpl~Ecommon~SMed.html [accessed January 2011].

Frankfurter Allgemeine Zeitung. 2010. Radiojournalist Erschossen, 19 July.

Frankfurter Allgemeine Zeitung. 2011. Sollen die Griechen raus aus dem Euro? [8 October]. Available at: http://m.faz.net/aktuell/wirtschaft/europas-schuldenkrise/schaeuble-und-issing-im-streitgespraech-sollen-die-griechen-raus-aus-dem-euro-11486535.html [accessed December 2012].

Focus. 2010, 22 February.

French Presidency website. 2010. Conférence de presse conjointe – M. Georges Papandreou, Premier Ministre de la République Héllénique [10 March] Available at: http://www.elysee.fr/president/les-actualites/conferences-de-presse/2010/conference-de-presse-conjointe-m-georges.8035.html?search=mars&xtmc=&xcr= [accessed September 2011].

Fuest, C. 2010. EU braucht ein Insolvenzverfahren für Staaten. *Handelsblatt* [10 January] http://www.handelsblatt.com/meinung/gastbeitraege/fuest-eu-braucht-ein-insolvenzverfahren-fuer-staaten; 2510303 [accessed January 2010].

Fuhrmans, V. and Moffet, S. 2010. Exposure to Greece weighs on French, German banks. *The Wall Street Journal* [17 February]. Available at: http://online.wsj.com/article/SB10001424052748703798904575069712153415820.html [accessed December 2010].

Galtung, J. and Ruge, M.H. 1999. The structure of foreign news, in *News: A Reader*, edited by H. Tumber. Oxford and New York: Oxford University Press.

Gammelin. C., Hulverscheidt, C. and Kornelius, S. 2010. Hilfe? Bloss nicht. *Süddeutsche Zeitung* [22 March]. Available at: http://www.sueddeutsche.de/geld/streit-um-griechland-hilfe-bloss-nicht-1.9595 [accessed January 2011].

Gavros, 2011, 17 and 18 October.

GENOP DEI Decision. 2011. [11 June] Available at: http://www.genop.gr/index.php?option=com_content&view=article&id=985:2011-06-11-18-48-52&catid=1:2009-08-08-10-27-00&Itemid=2, 11 June [accessed August 2011].

Giavazzi, F. 2010. Non scherzate con la Grecia. *Corriere della Sera* [18 February]. Available at: http://www.corriere.it/editoriali/10_febbraio_18/scherzare_grecia_01508468-1c56-11df-beab-00144f02aabe.shtml [accessed January 2011].

Girard, R. 2011.Grèce : la spirale infernale, économique et politique. *Le Figaro* [7 November].Available at: http://www.lefigaro.fr/international/2011/11/07/01003-20111107ARTFIG00696-grece-la-spirale-infernale-economique-et-politique.php [accessed February 2011].

Glenny, M. 2011. The Real Greek tragedy – its rapacious oligarchs. *Financial Times,* 4 November. Available at: http://www.ft.com/cms/s/0/618e57d6-0937-11e1-a20c-00144feabdc0.html#axzz1o8KgF71t [accessed February 2012].

Global Competitiveness Report. 2010 – 2011. Available at: http://www3.weforum.org/docs/WEF_GlobalCompetitivenessReport_2010-11.pdf [accessed August 2011].

Golding, P. and Murdock, G. 1991. Culture, communications, and political economy, in *Mass Media and Society*, edited by J. Curran and M. Gurevitch. London and New York – Melbourne – Auckland: Arnold.

Goodhart, C. and Tsomocos, D. 2010. The California solution for the club Med. *Financial Times* [24 January].Available at: http://www.ft.com/cms/s/0/5ef30d32-0925-11df-ba88-00144feabdc0.html#axzz1EOlF63dE [accessed January 2011].

GPO Poll. 2009. [7 September]. Available at: http://www.eklogika.gr/uploads/files/Dimoskopiseis/MEGA-GPO.pdf, 7 September 2009 [accessed August 2011].

GPO Poll. 2010. [8 March]. Available at: http://www.eklogika.gr/uploads/files/Dimoskopiseis/GPO-Mega8-3.pdf [accessed August 2011].

GPO Poll. 2010 [26 April]. Available at: http://www.eklogika.gr/uploads/files/Dimoskopiseis/GPO-Mega26-4-2010.pdf [accessed August 2011].

GPO Poll. 2011 [21 June]. Available at: http://www.eklogika.gr/uploads/files/Dimoskopiseis/Mega-GPO-22-6-2011.pdf [accessed August 2011].

Granitsas, A. 2009. Attacking Greece's bureaucratic beast. *The Wall Street Journal* [20 October]. Available at: http://online.wsj.com/article/SB100014240527487045006045744849726857560 20.html [accessed December 2010].

Granitsas. A. 2010. Greece: Terror to be damned. *The Wall Street Journal* [3 November]. Available at http://blogs.wsj.com/source/2010/11/03/greece-terror-be-damned/ [accessed April 2011].

Granitsas, A. Walker, M. and Paris, C. 2011.Greek vote threatens bailout. *The Wall Street Journal* [1 November]. Available at: http://online.wsj.com/article/SB10001424052970204394804577010091283798750.html [accessed December 2011].

Grant, C. 2011. Greece doesn't belong in the euro. It must go. *The Times* [20 June]. Available at: http://www.thetimes.co.uk/tto/opinion/columnists/article3067279.ece [accessed December 2011].

Greece at a glance: policies for a sustainable recovery. Available at: http://www.oecd.org/dataoecd/6/39/44785912.pdf.

Greek Ministry of Finance website. 2010. Press conference transcript. [2 May]. Available at: http://www.minfin.gr/portal/el/resource/contentObject/id/c674b46b-951a-431e-9403-3337e512e40d [accessed January 2011].

Greek Ministry of Finance website. 2010. Stability and growth programme [15 January]. Available at: http://www.minfin.gr/portal/en/resource/contentObject/id/4b0500ea-0f9f-4a58-858f-c43f5f38753e [accessed August 2011].

Guérot, U. and Leonard, M. 2011. The new German question: how Europe can get the Germany it needs [April] ECFR policy brief. Available at: http://www.ecfr.eu/page/-/ECFR30_GERMANY_AW.pdf [accessed November 2011].

Hackhausen, J. 2010. Griechenland muss pleitegehen. *Handelsblatt*. [15 April]. Available at: http://www.handelsblatt.com/finanzen/anlagestrategie/bert-flossbach-im-interview-griechenland-muss-pleitegehen; 2562021 [accessed January 2011].

Hagelüken, A. 2010. Liebe Griechen, so geht's. *Süddeutsche Zeitung* [30 December] http://www.sueddeutsche.de/geld/euro-zone-estland-tritt-bei-liebe-griechen-so-gehts-1.1041245.

Hagelüken, A. and Schlötzer, C. 2012. Die Deutschen bekommen ihr Geld zurück. *Süddeutsche Zeitung* [22 August]. Available at: http://www.sueddeutsche.de/politik/griechenlands-premier-samaras-die-deutschen-bekommen-ihr-geld-zurueck-1.1447818 [accessed September 2012].

Handelsblatt. 2011. [2 August]. Available at: http://www.handelsblatt.com/panorama/lifestyle/trotz-streik-griechenland-touristen-duerfen-gratis-taxi-fahren/4457216.html [accessed November 2011].

Handelsblatt. 2010. Experte fürchten Domino-Effekt. [20 February]. Available at: http://www.handelsblatt.com/politik/international/experten-fuerchten-domino-effekt/3373726.html?p3373726=all [accessed November 2010].

Handelsblatt. 2011. Griechenland braucht neuen Mut. [27 October]. Available at: http://www.handelsblatt.com/politik/international/griechenland-braucht-neuen-mut/5752022.html?p5752022=all [accessed November 2011].

Handelsblatt. 2010. Griechenland braucht schnelle Hilfe. [10 April]. Available at: http://www.handelsblatt.com/politik/international/griechenland-braucht-schnelle-hilfe/3408568.html?p3408568=1 [accessed January 2011].

Handelsblatt. 2010. Griechenland muss aus dem Euro raus. [27 April]. Available at: http://www.handelsblatt.com/finanzen/boerse-maerkte/anleihen/anleihen-unter-druck-griechenland-muss-aus-dem-euro-raus/3421902.html [accessed November 2010].

Handelsblatt. 2011. Griechenland riskiert seine Euro-Mitgliedschaft. [1 November] Available at: http://www.handelsblatt.com/politik/international/geplantes-referendum-griechenland-riskiert-seine-euro-mitgliedschaft/5784286.html [accessed December 2011].

Handelsblat. 2011. Griechenland: Verfallende Olympiastadien [25 October]. Available at: http://videokatalog.handelsblatt.com/Sport/video-Griechenland-Verfallende-Olympiastadien-Video-News-Sportst%C3%A4tten-Spiele-132587.html [accessed November 2011].

Handelsblatt. 2011. Paketbomben alarmieren EU-Spitze. [3 November]. Available at: http://www.handelsblatt.com/politik/international/paketbomben-alarmieren-eu-spitze/3581434.html?p3581434=all [accessed April 2011].

Hankel, W., Nolling W., Albrecht, K. and Starbatty, J. 2010. A euro exit is the only way out for Greece. *Financial Times* [25 March]. Available at: http://www.ft.com/cms/s/0/6a618b7a-3847-11df-8420-00144feabdc0.html#axzz1AuRXYVYq [accessed January 2010].

Harvey, O. 2011. Greece play 4–4–2 *The Sun* [18 May] http://www.thesun.co.uk/sol/homepage/features/2976628/Cost-of-corruption-in-Greece.html [accessed December 2011].

Hawkes, S. 2011. Acropolis now. *The Sun*, 28 June, 46.

Hawkes, S. 2011. The UK never joined the euro. You're in control. It's fantastic. *The Sun*, 2 July, 18, 19.

Hawkes, S. and Parker, N. 2011. Greece loses its marbles. Available at: http://www.thesun.co.uk/sol/homepage/news/politics/3909249/Greece-loses-its-marbles.html, 2 November [accessed January 2012]

Health Expenditure and Financing. 2009. Available at: http://www.oecd-ilibrary.org/docserver/download/fulltext/8109111ec071.pdf?expires=1330370023&id=id&accname=guest&checksum=EE85D8BD4ED3EF0B61DD98E7BE164313 [accessed April 2011].

Henley, J. 2011. In Greece corruption pervades every corner of life. *The Guardian* [20 October]. Available at: http://www.guardian.co.uk/world/blog/2011/oct/20/europe-breadline-corrution-pervades-corner [accessed December 2011].

Herman, R. 2011. Die Griechen geben weniger Geld aus. *Frankfurter Allgemeine Zeitung*. [1 August]. Available at: http://www.faz.net/aktuell/wirtschaft/europas-schuldenkrise/schuldenkrise-die-griechen-geben-weniger-geld-aus-11106443.html [accessed November 2011].

Herman, R. 2011. Griechen kaufen weniger deutsch.] *Frankfurter Allgemeine Zeitung*. [23 April]. Available at: http://www.faz.net/aktuell/wirtschaft/europas-schuldenkrise/konsum-in-der-krise-griechen-kaufen-weniger-deutsch-1970654.html [accessed April 2011].

Herman, E. and Chomsky, N. 1988. *Manufacturing consent: The Political Economy of the Mass Media*. New York: Pantheon.

Hoagland, J. 2011. We are all Greeks now – hiding from tax truths. *The Washington Post* [10 November]. Available at: http://www.washingtonpost.com/opinions/we-are-all-greeks-now--hiding-from-tax-truths/2011/11/09/gIQADepS6M_story.html [accessed January 2012].

Hoeren, D. and Santen, O. 2010.Warum Zahlen wir den Griechen ihre Luxus-Renten? *Bild* [27 April]. Available at: http://www.bild.de/politik/wirtschaft/griechenland/wir-zahlen-luxus-rente-mit-milliarden-hilfe-12338430.bild.html [accessed January 2011].

Höhler, G. 2010. Steuer-Ablasshandel in Athen. *Handelsblatt* [23 September]. Available at: http://www.handelsblatt.com/politik/international/zahlungsmoral-der-griechen-steuer-ablasshandel-in-athen/3546168.html [accessed April 2011].

Hope, K. 2010. Greece makes strong start on reforms. *Financial Times* [18 July]. Available at: http://www.ft.com/intl/cms/s/0/a5478676-927f-11df-9142-00144feab49a.html#axzz1pYLeDy1r [accessed November 2010].

Hope, K. 2011. Greek savers rush for gold. *Financial Times* [21 June] http://www.ft.com/cms/s/0/c986823e-9bf8-11e0-bef9-00144feabdc0.html#axzz1o8KgF71t [accessed November 2011].

Hope, K. 2010. Papandreou raises stakes in local elections. *Financial Times* [3 November]. Available at: http://www.ft.com/intl/cms/s/0/9f3703ee-e787-11df-b5b4-00144feab49a.html#axzz1hpxgDAzz [accessed April 2011].

Hutton, W. 2010. Don't laugh at Europe's woes. The troubles facing Greece are also ours. *The Observer*, 14 February, 38.

Hulverscheidt, C. 2010. Der Richtige Muss Helfen. *Süddeutsche Zeitung* [2 March]. Available at: http://archiv.sueddeutsche.de/sueddz/index.php?id=A46818504_EGTPOGWPOPPEPWGRAHOHSPR [accessed January 2011].

IFOP Poll. 2011. Europeans and the Euro crisis. [29 June]. Available at: http://www.ifop.com/media/poll/1562-2-study_file.pdf [September 2012].

Il Corriere della Sera. 2010. Crisi, Merkel: Troppe speculazioni. La CSU Bavarese: Via la Grecia dall' euro. [24 April]. Available at: http://www.corriere.it/economia/10_aprile_24/grecia-merkel-germania-euro_190c0c4a-4f9a-11df-9c4e-00144f02aabe.shtml [accessed January 2011].

Il Corriere della Sera. 2011. Grecia, è allarme suicidi per la crisi. [20 September]. Available at: http://www.corriere.it/salute/11_settembre_20/grecia-crisi-suicidi-aumento_e91e128e-e391-11e0-bc23-ba86791f572a.shtml_[accessed November 2011].

Il Corriere della Sera. 2011. Grecia: referendum sul piano degli aiuti fa scattare un vertice d'emergenza Ue [1 November]. Available at: http://www.corriere.it/economia/11_novembre_01/grecia-referendum-piano-aiuti_338fdca2-0468-11e1-89f9-a7d4dc298cd1.shtml [accessed December 2011].

Il Corriere della Sera. 2011. Grecia, seconda giornata di scioperi. [21 October]. Available at: http://www.corriere.it/esteri/11_ottobre_20/grecia-secondo-giorno-sciopero_3ea4b7b6-fb03-11e0-b6b2-0c72eeeb0c77.shtml [accessed January 2011].

Il Corriere Della Sera. 2010. Grecia: si dimette ministro il cui marito era accusato di evasione fiscale. [17 May]. Available at: http://www.corriere.it/notizie-ultima-ora/Esteri/Grecia-dimette-ministro-cui-marito-era-accusato-evasione-fiscale/17-05-2010/1-A_000105138.shtml [accessed April 2011].

Il Corriere della Sera. 2010. Grecia: Trichet, tema default non si pone. [8 April]. Available at: http://www.corriere.it/notizie-ultima-ora/Economia/Grecia-Trichet-Tema-default-non-pone/08-04-2010/1-A_000095812.shtml [accessed January 2011].

Il Corriere della Sera. 2010. Giornalista Assassinato Sotto Casa, 19 July.

Il Corriere della Sera. 2010. Molotov e Auto in Fiamme, Caos ad Atene [15 December]. Available at: http://www.corriere.it/esteri/10_dicembre_15/grecia-sciopero-generale-scontri-atene_62c8abd4-0842-11e0-b759-00144f02aabc.shtml [accessed December 2011].

IFOP Research Report. 2010. Europeans and the Greek crisis. [20 March]. Available at: http://www.ifop.fr/media/poll/1118-2-study_file.pdf [accessed April 2011].

IIF Press Release. 2011. [21 July]. Available at: http://www.iif.com/press/press+198.php [accessed July 2011].

IIF Press Release. 2012. [28 February]. Available at: http://www.iif.com/press/press+231.php [accessed March 2012].

IMF Country No 117/175. 2011. Greece: fourth review under the stand-by arrangement and request for modification and waiver of applicability of performance criteria [July]. Available at: http://www.imf.org/external/pubs/ft/scr/2011/cr11175.pdf [accessed September 2011].

IMF website. 2010. [2 May] Europe and IMF agree 110 billion euros financing plan with Greece. Available at: http://www.imf.org/external/pubs/ft/survey/so/2010/CAR050210A.htm [accessed July 2011].

Inman, P. and Smith, H. 2010. Greece should sell islands to keep bankruptcy at a bay, say German MPs. *The Guardian* [4 March]. Available at: http://www.guardian.co.uk/business/2010/mar/04/greece-sell-islands-german-mps [accessed April 2011].

Inspection Report. 2011. [April]. Available at: http://www.gedd.gr/article_data/Linked_files/83/PorismaGENOP.pdf [accessed August 2011.

International Transparency Corruption Perception's Index. 2009. Available at: http://www.transparency.org/policy_research/surveys_indices/cpi/2009/cpi_2009_table [accessed August 2011].

International Transparency Corruption Perception's Index. 2010. http://www.transparency.org/policy_research/surveys_indices/cpi/2010/results [accessed August 2011].

Intervention of Ms. Vasso Papandreou. 2011. [7 June]. Available at: http://www.tovima.gr/politics/article/?aid=405168 [accessed August 2011].

Interview of Dr. Wolfgang Schäuble with *Wirtschaftwoche*. 2011. Available at: http://www.wolfgang-schaeuble.de/index.php?id=37&textid=1476&page=1, 24 September [accessed September 2011].

Interview of Theodoros Pangalos with *BBC* journalist Malcolm Brabant. 2010 [25 February]. Available at: http://www.pangalos.gr/portal/?p=647 [accessed September 2011].

IOBE Quarterly Bulletin. 2009. The Greek economy. Available at: http://www.iobe.gr/media/engoik/IOBE_econ_04_09_eng.pdf, 58 (4/09) [accessed September 2011].

IOBE Quarterly Bulletin. 2011. The Greek economy [March]. Available at: http://www.iobe.gr/media/engoik/IOBE_Greek_econ_02_11_en.pdf 63 (02/11) [accessed September 2011].

Irish Times. 2011. Thousands march against Greece's austerity package [18 June]. Available at: www.irishtimes.com/newspaper/breaking/2011/0618/breaking15.html [accessed July 2011].

Issing, O. 2010. Die Europäische Union Währungsunion am Scheidenweg. *Frankfurter Allgemeine Zeitung*, 29 January.

Jelloun Ben, T. 2010. Peurs. *Le Monde*, 6 June, 28.

Johnson, S. and Boone, P. 2010. The Greek tragedy that changed Europe. *The Wall Street Journal* [13 February]. Available at: http://online.wsj.com/article/SB10001424052748703525704575061172926967984.html [accessed November 2010].

Joint Statement on Greece by Finance Ministers of Korea, Canada, the United States, the United Kingdom and France. 2010 [3 May]. Available at: http://www.treasury.gov/press-center/press-releases/Pages/tg684.aspx, 3 May [accessed September 2011].

Jones, S. 2010. Athens dinner that led to political indigestion. *Financial Times* [4 March] Available at: http://www.ft.com/intl/cms/s/0/56cde15a-27bf-11df-863d-00144feabdc0.html#axzz1n7MJDINl [accessed April 2011].

Kakissis, J. 2007. 36 hours in Athens, Greece. *The New York Times* [4 May]. Available at: http://travel.nytimes.com/2008/05/04/travel/04hours.html [accessed September 2012].

Kakissis, J. 2010. Greek shipping families in the spotlight. *Financial Times* [21 August]. Available at: http://www.ft.com/cms/s/2/4ee112a6-ab30-11df-9e6b-00144feabdc0.html#axzz1ALH67i3Q [accessed March 2011].

Kapalschinski, C. 2011. Griechenland Braucht Neuen Mut. [27 October]. Available at: http://www.handelsblatt.com/politik/international/griechenland-braucht-neuen-mut/5752022.html?p5752022=all [accessed January 2012].

Kapa Research Poll. 2010. [7 February]. Available at: http://www.tovima.gr/politics/article/?aid=313921 [accessed August 2011].

Kapa Research Poll. 2011. *To Vima tis Kyriakis*, 4 September, A10-A11.

Kapa Research Poll. 2011. [30 October]. Available at: http://www.eklogika.gr/uploads/files/Dimoskopiseis/KapaResearch-Vima27-10-11.pdf [accessed September 2012].

Kaplan, R. 2012. Is Greece European? [6 June]. Available at: http://www.stratfor.com/analysis/greece-european-robert-d-kaplan [accessed September 2012].

Karakoussis, A. 2012. O Taliban kyrios Schäuble (Mr Schäuble as a Taliban) *To Vima* [16 February] Available at: http://www.tovima.gr/opinions/article/?aid=443921 [accessed February 2012].

Kathimerini. 2010, 30 May.

Kathimerini website. 2010. Provopoulos: Eixame enhmerwssei thn politikh hgesia/We had informed political leadership. Available at: http://news.kathimerini.gr/%20%3Chttp://news.kathimerini.gr/4dcgi/_w_articles_politics_1_04/05/2010_399715 [4 May] [accessed August 2011].

Kefalas, A. 2011. Georges Papandréou joue son va-tout. *Le Figaro*. 17 June, 8.

Kefalas, A. 2010. Grèce: La restructuration de la dette est hors de question. *Le Figaro*. 16 November. Available at: http://www.lefigaro.fr/conjoncture/2010/11/15/04016-20101115ARTFIG00702-grece-la-restructuration-de-la-dette-est-hors-de-question.php [accessed January 2011].

Kefalas, A. 2010. La Grèce Frappéé par une Vague de Terrorisme Postale. *Le Figaro* [4 November]. Available at: http://www.lefigaro.fr/international/2010/11/03/01003-20101103ARTFIG00725-la-grece-frappee-par-une-vague-de-terrorisme-postal.php [accessed April 2011].

Kennedy, S. 2011. Greece default with Ireland breaks euro by 2016 in global poll [26 January]. Available at: http://www.bloomberg.com/news/2011-01-25/greece-default-with-ireland-breaks-euro-by-2016-in-global-poll.html [accessed August 2011].

Kennedy, S. 2011. Greece defaulting on debts anticipated by 85% in global poll of investors [13 May] http://www.bloomberg.com/news/2011-05-13/greece-defaulting-on-debts-anticipated-by-85-in-global-poll-of-investors.html, 13 May [accessed September 2011].

Kirkegaard, K.F. 2011. The Euro area crisis: origin, current status, and European and US responses [27 October]. Testimony before the US House Committee on Foreign Affairs Subcommittee on Europe and Eurasia. Available at: http://www.iie.com/publications/testimony/kirkegaard20111027.pdf [accessed February 2012].

Kitsantonis, N. 2011. Greek town rises up against planned landfill. *The New York Times* [16 March]. Available at: http://www.nytimes.com/2011/03/17/world/europe/17greece.html?pagewanted=all [accessed April 2011].

Kitsantonis, N. 2012. In Greece's sour economy, some shops are thriving. *The New York Times* [2 January]. Available at: http://www.nytimes.com/2012/01/03/world/europe/as-greece-struggles-pawnbrokers-prosper.html?_r=1 [accessed February 2012].

Klau, T. and Godement Fr. with Torreblanca J.I. 2010. Beyond Maastricht: a new deal for the Eurozone. Available at: http://www.ecfr.eu/page/-/ECFR26_BEYOND_MAASTRICHT_AW(2).pdf, December [accessed July 2011].

Krugman, P. 2011. The conscience of a liberal. *The New York Times* [10 May] Available at: http://krugman.blogs.nytimes.com/2011/05/10/greek-out/ [accessed December 2011].

Kyriakatiki Avriani. 2011, 8 May.

Kyriakatiki Avriani. 2011, 15 May.

Kyriakatiki Eleftherotypia. 2010, 21 November.

Kyriakatiki Eleftherotypia. 2010, 21 November.

Kyriakidou, D. 2009. Greek PM calls snap election, blames economic crisis [2 September]. Available at: http://www.reuters.com/article/2009/09/02/us-greece-election-idUSTRE5815ZZ20090902 [accessed July 2011].

Lachman, D. 2010. Greece looks set to go the way of Argentina. *Financial Times* [12 January]. Available at: http://www.ft.com/intl/cms/s/0/5ffb0694-ff1b-11de-a677-00144feab49a.html [accessed January 2011].

Lachman, D. 2010. Greece long road to default. *The Wall Street Journal* [1 February]. Available at: http://online.wsj.com/article/SB40001424052748704 1072045750387818229306O8.html [accessed January 2011].
Lacombe, C. 2010. Athènes s'attaque à l'évasion fiscale, sport national. *Le Figaro*. Economie – Enterprises, 12.
Lacombe, C. 2010. Entretien; La Grèce est obligée de diminuer ses dépenses militaries. *Le Figaro*, 15 May, 5.
Lamassoure, A. 2011. M. Papandréou joue avec le feu! Available at : http://www.lemonde.fr/idees/article/2011/11/03/m-papandreou-joue-avec-le-feu_1598287_3232.html, 3 November [accessed January 2011].
Landon, T. Jr. 2011. A Greek political scion undone by economics. *The New York Times*. 7 November. Available at: http://www.nytimes.com/2011/11/08/world/europe/prime-minister-george-papandreou-of-greece-undone-by-economics.html?_r=1 [accessed February 2012].
La Repubblica. 2011. Atene, esplode la protesta. Lacrimogeni contro dimostranti. [28 June]. Available at: http://www.repubblica.it/esteri/2011/06/28/news/scontri_grecia_manifestanti_polizia-18344774/ [accessed November 2011].
La Repubblica. 2011. La protesta infiamma la Grecia in duecentomila contro l'austerity. [19 October]. Available at: http://www.repubblica.it/economia/2011/10/19/news/sciopero_grecia-23478386/ [accessed January 2012].
La Repubblica. 2010. Sciopero in Grecia: bloccati I tragheti dei touristi [23 June]. Available at: http://video.repubblica.it/dossier/grecia-crisi-economica/sciopero-in-grecia-bloccati-i-tragheti-dei-turisti/49443/48952.
La Repubblica. 2011. S&P taglia ancora la Grecia [13 June]. Available at: http://www.repubblica.it/economia/2011/06/13/news/s_p_taglia_grecia_default_vicino-17648848/ [accessed November 2011].
Le Figaro. 2011. Grèce: l'extrême droite participe à l'union nationale. [11 November]. Available at: http://www.lefigaro.fr/international/2011/11/11/01003-20111111ARTFIG00439-grece-l-extreme-droite-participe-a-l-union-nationale.php [accessed February 2012].
Le Figaro. 2010. Troisième matinée de grève à l'Acropole. [15 October] http://www.lefigaro.fr/conjoncture/2010/10/13/04016-20101013ARTFIG00366-l-acropole-bloque-par-des-fonctionnaires.php [accessed April 2011].
Le Monde. 2011. Crise grecque: Il ne nous reste que 300 euros par mois pour vivre [28 June]. Available at: http://www.lemonde.fr/europe/article/2011/06/28/crise-grecque-il-ne-nous-reste-que-300-euros-par-mois-pour-vivre_1542203_3214.html [accessed September 2011].
Le Monde. 2010. Italie: la fin du berlusconisme se joue sur fond de corruption, 4 August. 15.
Le Monde. 2010. Euro et FMI, 27 March.
Le Monde. 2011. Editorial; La Grèce dans l'euro : la question se pose, 2 November, 1.
Le Monde. 2010. La Grèce dément les rumeurs sur la sortie de l'euro. [9 June] Available at: http://www.lemonde.fr/europe/article/2010/06/09/la-grece-dement-les-rumeurs-sur-sa-sortie-de-l-euro_1370194_3214.html [accessed January 2011].

Le Monde. 2010. L' exposition des banques françaises à la Grèce ne susciterait pas d' inquiétude particulière' [9 April]. Available at: http://www.lemonde.fr/economie/article/2010/04/09/l-exposition-des-banques-francaises-a-la-grece-ne-susciterait-pas-d-inquietude-particuliere_1331170_3234.html [accessed November 2010].

Le Monde. 2009. Les jeunes Grecs ou la génération des '700 euros'. [8 December]. Available at: http://www.lemonde.fr/europe/video/2009/12/08/les-jeunes-grecs-ou-la-generation-des-700-euros_1277507_3214.html [accessed April 2011].

Le Monde. 2010. Un journalist grec abattu de dix balles à Athènes [18 July]. Available: http://www.lemonde.fr/europe/article/2010/07/19/un-journaliste-grec-abattu-de-dix-balles-a-athenes_1389807_3214.html [accessed June 2011].

Letter of Prime Minister George Papandreou to the President of the Eurogroup and Prime Minister of Luxemburg Jean Claude Juncker. 2011. Availabe at: http://www.primeminister.gov.gr/english/2011/07/11/letter-to-the-president-of-the-eurogroup-and-prime-minister-of-luxembourg-jean-claude-juncker/, 11 July [accessed July 2011].

Lewis, M. 2010. Beware of Greeks bearing bonds. [1 October]. Available at: http://www.vanityfair.com/business/features/2010/10/greeks-bearing-bonds-201010 [accessed April 2011].

Lewis, D. 2010. One possible outcome of Greece crisis: only splitting the Euro will save it. *The Wall Street Journal* [17 February]. Available at: http://online.wsj.com/article/SB10001424052748704804204575069570005834614.html?KEYWORDS=Greece+++default [accessed January 2010].

Little, A. 2012. How magic made Greek debt disappear before it joined the Euro. *BBC* website [3 February]. Available at: http://www.bbc.co.uk/news/world-europe-16834815 [accessed February 2012].

Lynch D. 2010 Ireland default predicted by majority in global investor poll [12 November]. Available at: http://www.bloomberg.com/news/2010-11-12/ireland-s-debt-default-predicted-by-majority-of-investors-in-global-poll.html [accessed July 2011].

K. Mackenzie, 2012. Buinzer now predicting Grexit probability of 90% [26 July]. Available at: http://ftalphaville.ft.com/blog/2012/07/26/1096631/ [accessed August 2012].

Maddox, B. 2010. A Greek crisis may well become Germany's problem [18 January]. Available at: http://www.thetimes.co.uk/tto/opinion/columnists/bronwenmaddox/article2052937.ece [November 2010].

Maddox, B. 2010. Parasite economy lies behind Greek financial tragedy. *The Times* [6 January]. Available at: http://www.thetimes.co.uk/tto/opinion/columnists/bronwenmaddox/article2052930.ece [accessed January 2012].

Maisch, M. 2010. Griechenland Braucht ernsthafte Hilfe. *Handelsblatt* [15 April]. Available at: http://www.handelsblatt.com/finanzen/boerse-maerkte/boerse-inside/griechenland-braucht-ernsthafte-hilfe/3412106.html [accessed January 2011].

Mangan. L. 2010. Saturday: this week: people: no halting the defaulting: Greece. *The Guardian* [1 May], Comment pages, 46.

Marc Poll. 2011. [27 June]. Available at: http://www.eklogika.gr/uploads/files/ Dimoskopiseis/MarcEthnos26-6-11.pdf, 27 June [accessed September 2011].
Marc Poll. 2012. [24 March]. Available at: http://www.eklogika.gr/uploads/files/ Dimoskopiseis/Marc-Ethnos_24-3-12.pdf [accessed September 2012].
Marcus, J.S. In Lisbon writers dies but art lives on. *The Wall Street Journal* [13 December]. Available at: http://online.wsj.com/article/SB10001424052748704278 404576037881506425842.html?KEYWORDS=Greece [accessed April 2011].
Marsh, B. 2011. It's all connected: an overview of the Euro crisis. *The New York Times* [22 October]. Available at: http://www.nytimes.com/interactive/2011/10/23/sunday-review/an-overview-of-the-euro-crisis.html [accessed November 2011].
Martens, N. 2010. Am Pranger im Dienste der Zahlungsmoral. *Frankfurter Allgemeine Zeitung* [29 July]. Available at: http://www.faz.net/aktuell/politik/ausland/steuerhinterziehung-in-griechenland-am-pranger-im-dienste-der-zahlungsmoral-11007640.html [accessed April 2011].
Martens, M. 2011. Neue Griechen braucht das Land. *Frankfurter Allgemeine Zeitung* [6 November]. Available at: http://www.faz.net/aktuell/politik/ausland/koalitionsverhandlungen-in-athen-neue-griechen-braucht-das-land-11519713.html [accessed January 2012].
Masciaga, M. 2011. Linea dura della Merkel sulla Grecia. *La Repubblica* [12 September]. Available at: http://www.repubblica.it/economia/2011/09/12/news/linea_dura_della_merkel_sulla_grecia_borse_in_calo_a_picco_i_titoli_bancari-21568560/index.html?ref=search [accessed November 2011].
Massourakis, M. 2010. Privatisations offer Greece the best way to avoid a bailout, *Financial Times* [11 February]. Available at: http://cachef.ft.com/cms/s/0/816b0f86-173a-11df-94f6-00144feab49a.html#axzz1EUujJ2Dn [accessed January 2011].
Mattich, A. 2011. Greece: don't miscount the role of the military. *The Wall Street Journal* [19 September]. Available at: http://blogs.wsj.com/source/2011/09/19/greece-dont-discount-role-of-military/ [accessed December 2011].
Mattich, A. 2010. Trust Greece ... to default. *The Wall Street Journal* [17 September]. Available at: http://blogs.wsj.com/source/2010/09/17/trust-greeceto-default/ [January 2011].
Matsaganis, M. and Leventi, Ch. 2011. The distributional impact of the crisis in Greece, in *The Greek Crisis in Focus: Austerity, Recession and Paths to Recovery: Special Issue*, edited by V. Monastiriotis. Available at: http://www2.lse.ac.uk/europeanInstitute/research/hellenicObservatory/pdf/GreeSE/GreeSE%20Special%20Issue.pdf [accessed July 2011].
Maurisse, M. 2011. Avec la crise, la fuite de capitaux grecs vers la Suisse s'accélère. *Le Figaro*, 4 June. 20.
Marzinotto, B. 2011. A European fund for economic revival in crisis countries [February]. Available at: http://www.bruegel.org/fileadmin/bruegel_files/Publications/Policy_Contributions/2011/PC_A_European_fund_for_economic_revival_in_crisis_countries_BM.pdf [accessed February 2012].
McCombs, M. 2004. *Setting the Agenda: The Mass Media and Public Opinion*. Cambridge: Polity Press.

McCrum, D. and Jenkins, P. 2011. Money market funds cut Euro bank exposure. *Financial Times* [24 July]. Available at: http://www.ft.com/intl/cms/s/0/1cda4056-b495-11e0-a21d-00144feabdc0.html#axzz1oEERGUZP [accessed August 2011].

McKinsey & Company. 2012. Greece 10 years ahead: defining Greece's new growth model and strategy. 2012. Available at: http://www.mckinsey.com/locations/athens/GreeceExecutiveSummary_new/pdfs/Executive_summary_English_new.pdf [accessed September 2012].

McManus, J. 1999. Market driven journalism: let the citizens beware, in *News: A Reader*, edited by T. Howard. Oxford – New York: Oxford University Press.

Meghir, C., Vayanos, D. and Vettas, N. 2010. Greek reforms can yet stave off default. *Financial Times* [23 August]. Available at: http://www.ft.com/intl/cms/s/0/a39c6a50-aee8-11df-8e45-00144feabdc0.html#axzz1k0Won1bd [accessed April 2011].

Meghir, C., Vayanos, D. and Vettas, N. 2010. The Economic crisis in Greece: a time for reform and opportunity [5 August]. Available at: http://greekeconomistsforreform.com/wp-content/uploads/Reform.pdf [accessed July 2011].

Memo/11/393. 2011. President Barroso's meeting with Mr Antonis Samaras, leader of the main Greek opposition party [8 June]. Available at: http://europa.eu/rapid/pressReleasesAction.do?reference=MEMO/11/393&type=HTML[accessed September 2011].

Memo/11/599. 2011. Questions and answers on the task force for Greece [13 September]. Available at: http://europa.eu/rapid/pressReleasesAction.do?reference=MEMO/11/599&type=HTML [accessed September 2011].

Metron Analysis Poll. 2011. [21 July]. Available at: http://www.eklogika.gr/uploads/files/Dimoskopiseis/MetronAnalysis-Etypos21-7-11.pdf [accessed September 2011].

Mevel, J.-J. 2010. LEurope accouche d'un accord sur la Grèce. *Le Figaro* [26 March]. Available at: http://www.lefigaro.fr/conjoncture/2010/03/25/04016-20100325ARTFIG00734-grece-l-allemagne-impose-son-plan-.php [accessed January 2011].

Milas, K. 2011. Greek default, an 84 per cent probability. Available at: http://www.publicserviceeurope.com/article/583/greek-default-an-84-per-cent-probability, 8 July [accessed July 2011].

Miller, R. 2010. Greek default seen by almost 75% in poll doubtful about Trichet [8 June]. Available at: http://www.bloomberg.com/news/2010-06-08/greek-default-seen-by-almost-75-in-poll-of-investors-doubtful-on-trichet.html [accessed July 2011].

Miller, J. 2010. Greek shippers weather storms. *The Wall Street Journal*. [13 May]. Available at: http://online.wsj.com/article/SB10001424052748704879704575236190728497962.html [accessed April 2011].

Ministry of Defence website. Cost of Olympic Games. 2011. [28 June]. Available at: http://www.mod.gr/el/enimerosi/konovouleytiki-drastiriotita/erwtiseis/4528-kostos-olympakon-agwnwn.html [accessed November 2011].

Ministry of Finance website. 2010. Press conference of Finance Minister on the margin of the annual IMF Meeting [9 October]. Available at: http://www.minfin.gr/portal/el/resource/contentObject/id/4a239bce-2a0d-4598-bcbf-284ad74cf929 [accessed April 2011].

Ministry of the Interior Website. 2009. Ethnikes Ekloges 2009 (2009 National Elections). Available at: http://ekloges-prev.singularlogic.eu/v2009/pages/index.html [accessed August 2011].

Monastiriotis, V. 2011. (ed.) *The Greek Crisis in Focus: Austerity, Recession and Paths to Recovery: Special Issue.* Available at: http://www2.lse.ac.uk/europeanInstitute/research/hellenicObservatory/pdf/GreeSE/GreeSE%20Special%20Issue.pdf [accessed July 2011].

Moya, E. 2010. Greece starts putting island land up for sale to save economy. *The Guardian* [24 June] http://www.guardian.co.uk/world/2010/jun/24/greece-islands-sale-save-economy [accessed April 2011].

MRB Poll. 2012. [19 February]. Available at: http://www.eklogika.gr/uploads/files/Dimoskopiseis/realnews-mrb_19-2-12.pdf [accessed September 2012].

Mucchetti, M. 2011. Banche, il conto della crisi è di 13 miliardi. *Il Corriere della Sera.* [26 September]. Available at: http://www.corriere.it/economia/corriereconomia/11_settembre_26/mucchetti-banche-conto-crisi-miliardi_1ca7b5d2-e83e-11e0-9000-0da152a6f157.shtml [accessed November 2011].

Muccheti, M. 2010. La Grecia e l'Europa a tre velocità. *Il Corriere Della Sera.* [28 Apil]. Available at: http://www.corriere.it/economia/10_aprile_28/grecia-europa-velocita-mucchetti_f08835c4-528b-11df-82ed-00144f02aabe.shtml [accessed November 2010].

Münchau, W. 2010. Greece's bailout only delays the inevitable. *Financial Times* [18 April]. Available at: http://www.ft.com/cms/s/0/da5b9516-4b1f-11df-a7ff-00144feab49a,s01=1.html [accessed January 2011].

Münchau, W. 2010. Greece will default but not this year. *Financial Times* [4 April]. Available at: http://www.ft.com/cms/s/0/372886dc-400d-11df-8d23-00144feabdc0.html#axzz1EOlF63dE [accessed January 2011].

Müller, R. 2011. Die Krisenflüchtlinge. *Frankfurter Allgemeine Zeitung.* Available at: http://www.faz.net/sonntagszeitung/gesellschaft/arbeitsziel-deutschland-die-krisenfluechtlinge-11542594.html [accessed: December 2011].

Mussler, W. 2010. Griechenland muss sich selbst retten. *Frankfurter Allgemeine Zeitung* [11 December]. Available at: http://www.faz.net/s/Rub3ADB8A210E754E748F42960CC7349BDF/Doc~E7254A19463C54B7D895B9990C5046777~ATpl~Ecommon~Scontent.htm [accessed January 2011].

Mussler, W. 2010. Schwere Fehler in der griechischen Statistik. *Frankfurter Allgemeine Zeitung* [12 January]. Available at: http://www.faz.net/aktuell/wirtschaft/europasschuldenkrise/staatsdefizit-schwere-fehler-in-der-griechischen-statistik1908399.html [accessed November 2010].

Mussler, W., Frühauf, M. and Hermann, R. 2011. Griechen ziehen ihr Geld von Bankkonten ab. *Frankfurter Allgemeine Zeitung* [25 May] Available at: http://www.faz.net/aktuell/wirtschaft/europas-schuldenkrise/furcht-vor-

staatsbankrott-griechen-ziehen-ihr-geld-von-bankkonten-ab-1642173.html [accessed November 2011].
National Bank of Greece Monthly Economic Outlook. 2009 [November/ December]. Available at: http://www.nbg.gr/wps/wcm/connect/5f789b8040b 0f66ebb31bfdd20353c80/Monthly_November09_3.pdf?MOD=AJPERES&C ACHEID=5f789b8040b0f66ebb31bfdd20353c80 [accessed August 2011].
ND website. 2010. Hi Historia mas (Our History). Available at: http://www.nd.gr/ our-history;jsessionid=C070071834C87A178FEA43781463075F [accessed August 2011].
Nelson, R., Belkin, P. and Mix, D. 2011. Greece debt crisis: overview, policy responses, and implications. Available at: http://www.fas.org/sgp/crs/row/R41167.pdf, 18 August, Congressional Research Service [accessed September 2011].
Niri, R. 2011. Economia, una tragedia greca, la crisi has cambiato il mondo. *La Repubblica*. [11 December]. Available at: http://ricerca.repubblica.it/ repubblica/archivio/repubblica/2011/12/11/economia-una-tragedia-greca-la-crisi-ha.html [accessed January 2012].
Nye, J.S. 2011. Angela Merkel's vision thing. [7 November]. Available at: http://www. project-syndicate.org/commentary/nye100/English [accessed February 2012].
OECD Report. 2010. Greece at a Glance: Policies for a Sustainable Recovery.
Offeddu, L. 2010. La Crisi di Atene Scuota l'Euro. *Corriere della Sera* [19 March]. Available at: http://archiviostorico.corriere.it/2010/marzo/19/crisi_ Atene_scuote_euro_co_9_100319076.shtml [accessed January 2011].
O'Grady, S. 2010. Greece faces tough measures in bid to save titanic economy. *The Independent* [16 February]. Available at: http://www.independent.co.uk/ news/business/news/greece-faces-tough-measures-in-bid-to-save-titanic-economy-1900731.html [accessed April 2011].
Ott, K. and Telloglou, T. 2011. Schöner wohnen mit deutschem Schmiergeld? *Süddeutsche*
Zeitung [20 June]. Available at: http://www.sueddeutsche.de/wirtschaft/korruption-in-griechenland-schoenerwohnenmitdeutschem-schmiergeld-1.1110217 [accessed November 2011].
Pagoulatos, G. 2003. *Greece's New Political Economy: State, Finance and Growth from Postwar to EMU*. Basingstoke and New York. Palgrave Macmillan.
Padoa-Schioppa, T. 2010. Europe cannot leave Athens on its own. *Financial Times* [18 February]. Available at: http://www.ft.com/intl/cms/s/0/f1eef94a-1cc9-11df-8d8e-00144feab49a.html#axzz1kH8dnNP2 [accessed January 2011].
PAME press release. 2011. [7 September]. Available at: http://www.pamehellas. gr/fullstory.php?lang=1&wid=1915 [accessed September 2011].
Pangalos, P. 2011. Families battle to survive rising bills and falling incomes. *The Times* [17 June]. Available at: http://www.thetimes.co.uk/tto/news/world/europe/ article3065121.ece [accessed January 2011].
Pangalos, P. 2011. Young talent flees stricken Greece. *The Sunday Times* [3 July]. Available at: http://www.thesundaytimes.co.uk/sto/news/world_news/Europe/ article661584.ece [accessed January 2012].

Papaconstantinou, G. 2009. The Greek Problem [30 November]. Available at: http://www.minfin.gr/portal/en/resource/contentObject/id/d4ab026b-a1cd-4024-b634-12b2b385e116 [accesses August 2011].

Papandreou, G., Juncker, J-C., Merkel, A. and Sarkozy, N. 2010. Letter to José Manuel Barroso and José Luis Rodríguez Zapatero10 March. Available at: http://www.primeminister.gov.gr/english/2010/03/10/letter-to-jose-manuel-barroso-and-jose-luis-rodriguez-zapatero/ [accessed April 2011].

Parliamentary Proceedings. 2010. [6 May]. Available at: http://www.hellenicparliament.gr/UserFiles/a08fc2dd-61a9-4a83-b09a-09f4c564609d/es20100506_1.pdf [accessed September 2011].

Parliamentary Proceedings. 2011 [29 June] Available at: http://www.hellenicparliament.gr/UserFiles/a08fc2dd-61a9-4a83-b09a-09f4c564609d/es20110629-30.pdf.

PA.SO.K's website. 2009. Omilia Giwrgou Papandreou sthn 74h Diethnh Ekthesh Thessalonikis (Speech of George Papandreou in the 74th International Exhibition of Thessaloniki). Available: http://www.pasok.gr/portal/resource/contentObject/id/88010eb4-9503-4dd7-8301-ed9bab0d1fdd [accessed August 2011].

PA.SO.K website. 2009. Synenteyksh Giwrgou Papandreou sthn efhmerida Real News (Interview of George Papandreou with *Real News* [2 August]. Available at: http://www.pasok.gr/portal/resource/contentObject/id/79fea74d-1cdc-48bc-9879-3b1cdc25ad82 [accessed July 2011].

Patton, M. 1990. *Qualitative Evaluation and Research Methods*. Newbury Park, London, New Delhi: Sage.

Pensions at a Glance: Retirement-Income Systems in OECD and G20 countries. 2011. Available at: http://www.dgaep.gov.pt/upload//RIareas/Pensions_at_a_glance_2011.pdf [accessed February 2012].

Pisany-Ferry, J. 2010. Eurozone governace: what went wrong and how to repair it, in *Completing the Eurozone Rescue: What More Needs to Be Done*, edited by R. Baldwin et al. London: voxEU.org Publication. Available at: http://www.voxeu.org/reports/EZ_Rescue.pdf [accessed February 2012].

Pisani-Ferry, J. and Sapir, A. 2010. The best bourse for Greece is to call in the fund. *Financial Times* [1 February 2010]. Available at: http://www.ft.com/cms/s/0/01554c86-0f69-11df-a450-00144feabdc0.html#axzz1CoNW2LYD [accessed April 2011].

Polemarchakis, H. 2011. Credit and crocodile hearts. Available at: http://www2.warwick.ac.uk/fac/soc/economics/research/centres/eri/bulletin/special_edition_final_revised.pdf, Bulletin of the Economics Research Institute – The University of Warwick [accessed February 2012].

Pop, V. 2011. Greece to face restricted default as bailout details emerge. Available at: http://euobserver.com/9/32653 [accessed August 2011].

Portes, T. 2011. En Bref. *Le Figaro*, 20 May, 9.

Press release on the meeting of the Speaker of the Hellenic Parliament with the German Ambassador. 2010 [25 February]. Available at: http://www.petsalnikos.gr/frontend/article.php?aid=377&cid=69, 25 February [accessed September 2011].

Press Release No. 10/168. 2010. [23 April]. Available at: http://www.imf.org/external/np/sec/pr/2010/pr10168.htm [accessed September 2011].
Press Release No. 10/246. 2010. Statement by the EC, ECB and IMF on the interim review mission to Greece [17 June]. Available at: http://www.imf.org/external/np/sec/pr/2010/pr10246.htm [accessed September 2011].
Press Release No. 10/308. 2010. Statement by the EC, ECB and IMF on the first review mission to Greece [5 August]. Available at: http://www.imf.org/external/np/sec/pr/2010/pr10308.htm [accessed September 2011].
Press Release No. 10/454. 2010. Statement by the EC, ECB and IMF on the second review Mission to Greece. [23 November]. Available at: http://www.imf.org/external/np/sec/pr/2010/pr10454.htm [accessed September 2011].
Press Release No. 11/37. 2011. Statement by the EC, ECB and IMF on the third review Mission to Greece. [11 February]. Available at: http://www.imf.org/external/np/sec/pr/2011/pr1137.htm [accessed September 2011].
Press Release No. 11/212. 2011. Statement by the EC, ECB and IMF on the fourth review mission to Greece [3 June]. Available at: http://www.imf.org/external/np/sec/pr/2011/pr11212.htm [accessed September 2011].
Press Release of the IIF. 2011. Greece Financing Offer: Statement by the IIF Board of Directors [21 July]. Available at: http://www.iif.com/press/press+198.php [accessed July 2011].
Press Release of ISDA. 2012. ISDA EMEA Determinations Committee: Restructuring credit event has occurred with respect to the Hellenic Republic. [9 March].
Press Release of the National Confederation of Hellenic Commerce. 2012. [1 February]. Available at: http://www.esee.gr/page.asp?id=3893 [accessed March 2012].
Prodi, R. 2010. A Europe under fire can still make its voice heard. *Financial Times* [12 December]. Available at: http://www.ft.com/intl/cms/s/0/a69c9eae-061e-11e0-976b-00144feabdc0.html#axzz1pbKEiWRH [accessed March 2011].
Proto Thema. 2011, 23 January.
Proto Thema. 2011, 11 February.
Provopoulos, G. 2010. Greece will fix itself, from inside the eurozone. *Financial Times*, [21 January]. Available at: http://www.ft.com/cms/s/0/018d0a1e-06cb-11df-b058-00144feabdc0.html#axzz1CoNW2LYD [accessed January 2011].
Public Issue Poll. 2011. [19 May]. Available at: http://www.publicissue.gr/wp-content/uploads/2011/05/mnimonio-debt-a-year-after-may-2011-all-survey-final.pdf [accessed August 2011].
Pulliam, S., Kellyand, K. and Mollenkamp, C. 2011. *The Wall Street Journal* [26 February] http://online.wsj.com/article/SB10001424052748703795004575087741848074392.html [accessed November 2011].
Rampini, F. 2010. Wall Street ha aiutato Atene a truccare i conti pubblici. *La Repubblica* [15 February]. Available at: http://www.repubblica.it/economia/2010/02/15/news/rampini_grecia-2302829/ [accessed November 2010].
Rampoldi, G. 2010. La sfida di Papandreou nella Grecia dei corrotti. *La Repubblica* [6 February]. Available at: http://www.repubblica.it/economia/2010/02/06/news/dossier-grecia-2204292/ [accessed April 2011].

Rapanos. V. 2009. Megethos kai evros drastiriotiton tou dhmosiou tomea/Size and activities breadth of the public sector. Available at: http://www.iobe.gr/media/delttyp/keimerg1.pdf [accessed August 2011].

Rass Poll. 2012. [1 June]. Available at: http://www.eklogika.gr/uploads/files/Dimoskopiseis/Rass-eltypos_1-6-12.pdf [accessed September 2012].

Real News. 2009, 18 January.

Real News. 2010, 16 May.

Real News. 2011, 3 April.

Reinhart, C. and Rogoff, K. 2009. *This Time is Different: Eight Centuries of Financial Folly.* Princeton: Princeton University Press.

Remarks by President Obama and Chancellor Merkel in a Joint Press Conference. 2011. [7 June]. Available at: http://www.whitehouse.gov/the-press-office/2011/06/07/remarks-president-obama-and-chancellor-merkel-joint-press-conference [accessed September 2011].

Renaud, G. 2011. Papandréou, un capitaine sans charisme. *Le Figaro*, 3 November, 16.

Report of the Association of Press Attachés. 2010. Available at: http://icp-forum.gr/wp/wp-content/uploads//2010/11/EUROPEAN-MEDIA_GREECE_A.doc [accessed October 2011].

Report on Sovereign CDS. 2010 [8 December]. Available at: http://online.wsj.com/article/SB10001424052748703296604576005551530863030.html [accessed March 2011].

Ricard, P. 2011. Le marasme grec illustre la défaillance du leadership européen. *Le Figaro*, 22 June, 14.

Rice, T. 2011. *Athenian Democracy.* Available at: http://www.thetimes.co.uk/tto/opinion/leaders/article3213531.ece [2 November] [accessed January 2012].

Rogoff, K. 2010. *Can Greece Avoid the Lion?* 2010. 3 February. Available at: http://www.project-syndicate.org/commentary/rogoff65/English [accessed February 2012].

Romano, S. 2010. Grecia: Tre ipotesi per uscire dalla crisi, *Il Corriere della Sera* [25 March]. Available at: http://archiviostorico.corriere.it/2010/marzo/25/Grecia_tre_Ipotesi_per_uscire_co_9_100325003.shtml [accessed January 2011].

Romer, P. 2010. The EU can be a boon for Greece. *Financial Times* [2 September]. Available at: http://www.ft.com/intl/cms/s/0/de329284-b6c2-11df-b3dd-00144feabdc0.html#axzz1hjuykjIG [accessed December 2011].

Ronzheimer, P. 2011. Bringt er diesen Juden-Hasser an die Macht? *Bild* [7 November]. Available at: http://www.bild.de/politik/ausland/georgios-papandreou/juden-hasser-in-regierung-20857796.bild.html [accessed February 2012].

Ronzheimer, P. 2012. Die Drachme wäre eine Katastrophe für uns. *Bild* [22 August]. Available at: http://www.bild.de/politik/ausland/antonis-samaras/griechenlands-premier-ueber-schulden-sparen-und-euroausstieg-25779000.bild.html [accessed September 2012].

Ronzheimer, P. 2011.Das Kassieren die Pleite-Politker. *Bild* [5 May] Available: http://www.bild.de/politik/ausland/griechenland-krise/demonstrationen-in-athen-20316842.bild.html [November 2011].

Ronzheimer, P. 2011. Die Welt feiert Merkel nur die Griechen stänkern. *Bild* [27 November]. Available at: http://www.bild.de/geld/wirtschaft/euro-krise/griechenland-krise-euro-gipfel-bruessel-griechen-poebeln-gegen-kanzlerin-merkel-20679396.bild.html [accessed November 2011].

Ronzheimer, P. 2011. Griechen geben ihre Kinder im Heib ab. *Bild* [11 November 2011]. Available at: http://www.bild.de/politik/ausland/griechenland-krise/griechen-geben-ihre-kinder-im-heim-ab-20951494.bild.html [accessed November 2011].

Ronzheimer, P. 2011. Hier krammt eine Onassis-Erbin im Müll. *Bild* [20 October]. Available at: http://www.bild.de/politik/ausland/onassis-clan/hier-kramt-eine-erbin-im-muell-20543334.bild.html [accessed November 2011].

Ronzheimer, P. 2011. Hier plündern die Griechen ihre Konten. *Bild* [24 October]. Available at: http://www.bild.de/politik/ausland/griechenland-krise/angst-vor-schuldenschnitt-griechen-pluendern-ihre-konten-20624790.bild.html [accessed November 2011].

Ronzheimer, P. 2011. Horr-Woche für Griechenland. *Bild* [17 October]. Available at: http://www.bild.de/politik/ausland/griechenland-krise/griechenland-krise-streikt-sich-das-land-diese-woche-selbst-kaputt-20497260.bild.html [accessed November 2011].

Ronzheimer, P. 2010. Krise? Welche Krise? *Bild* [26 April] http://www.bild.de/politik/wirtschaft/pleite/machen-weiter-wie-bisher-von-krise-keine-spur-12327120.bild.html [accessed November 2010].

Ronzheimer, P. and Frenser, I. 2011. Papandreou weg – wer wird chef im Pleite-Land. *Bild* [6 November]. Available at: http://www.bild.de/politik/ausland/griechenland-krise/griechenland-papandreou-tritt-zurueck-uebergangsregierung-neuwahlen-20862260.bild.html [accessed December 2011].

Ronzheimer, P. and Schuler, R. 2011. Warum machen die Griechen uns zum Buhmann, *Bild* [21 June]. Available at: http://www.bild.de/politik/ausland/griechenland-krise/deutschland-zahlt-und-wird-dafuer-beschimpft-18452080.bild.html [accessed July 2011].

Roubini, N. 2010 Greece's best option is an orderly default. *Financial Times* [28 June]. Available at: http://www.ft.com/cms/s/0/a3874e80-82e8-11df-8b15-00144feabdc0.html#axzz1Dqko0ArR [accessed January 2011].

Roubini, N. 2011. Greece should default and abandon the euro. *Financial Times* [10 September]. Available at: http://blogs.ft.com/the-a-list/2011/09/19/greece-should-default-and-abandon-the-euro/#axzz1pb11j1Ef [accessed December 2011].

Rousselin, P. 2010. Grèce: Merkel et l'Effet Domino. *Le Figaro* [28 April]. Available at: http://www.lefigaro.fr/conjoncture/2010/04/28/04016-20100428ARTFIG00671-grece-merkel-et-l-effet-domino-.php [accessed November 2010].

Russo, P. 2011. Angelopoulos dirige Servillo: Come è grigia la mia Grecia. *La Repubblica* [15 October]. Available at: http://www.repubblica.it/spettacoli-e-cultura/2011/10/15/news/intervista_angheloupoulos_servillo-23190339/index.html?ref=search [accessed November 2011].

Salles, A. 2011 Des particuliers grecs retirent leurs dépôts des banques. *Le Monde* [3 June] Economie – Enterpises, 14.
Salles, A. 2011. En Grèce, la lutte contre les décharges s'organise à Kératéa. *Le Monde*, 12 April, 5.
Salles, A. 2011. L'odyssée de Papandréou. *Le Monde*, 16 September, 19.
Salles, A. 2012. Samaras: Si nous faisons notre travail, la Grèce peut être sauvée. *Le Monde* [23 August]. Available at: http://www.lemonde.fr/economie/article/2012/08/23/si-nous-faisons-notre-travail-la-grece-peut-etre-sauvee_1748749_3234.html [accessed September 2012].
Salles. A. 2011. Violences lors de la première grève générale de l'année en Grèce. *Le Monde*. [24 February].
Samuelson, R. 2010. Greece and the welfare state in ruins. *The Washington Post* [22 February]. Available at: http://www.washingtonpost.com/wp-dyn/content/article/2010/02/21/AR2010022102914.html [accessed December 2011].
Samuelson, R. 2010. We're all Greek now. *The Washington Post*, 22 February, A15.
Schäfer, U. 2010. Das Griechische Experiment. *Süddeutsche Zeitung* [1 February]. Available at: http://archiv.sueddeutsche.de/sueddz/index.php [accessed January 2011].
Schlötzer, C. 2011. Die Mauern der Bürokratie müssen fallen. *Süddeutsche Zeitung* [9 October]. Available at: http://www.sueddeutsche.de/politik/folgen-der-finanzkrise-fuer-griechenland-die-mauern-der-buerokratie-muessen-fallen-1.1157677 [accessed January 2012].
Schlötzer, Ch. 2010. Ich Kaufe eine Insel. *Süddeutsche* Zeitung [5 March]. Available at: http://www.sueddeutsche.de/geld/griechenland-in-not-ich-kaufe-eine-insel-1.1324 [accessed April 2011].
Schneider, F. 2011. Size and development of the shadow economy of 31 European and 5 other OECD countries from 2003 until 2011 [September]. Available: http://www.econ.jku.at/members/Schneider/files/publications/2011/ShadEcon31.pdf [accessed November 2011].
Schneider, H. and Birnbaum, M. 2011. Greek referendum calls upends euro-plans. [2 November]. Available at: http://www.washingtonpost.com/business/economy/greek-referendum-call-upends-euro-plans/2011/11/01/gIQAxQGZdM_story.html [accessed January 2012].
Schudson, M. 1999 Discovering the news: a social history of American newspapers in, *News: A Reader*, edited by T. Howard: Oxford, New York: Oxford University Press.
Schulz, B. 2010. Griechenland kämpft um Vertrauen. *Frankfurter Allgemeine Zeitung* [31 January]. Available at: http://www.faz.net/aktuell/wirtschaft/internationaler-finanzmarkt-griechenland-kaempft-um-vertrauen-1907934.html [accessed January 2011].
Schwartz. 2012. US companies brace for an exit from the euro by Greece. *The New York Times* [2 September]. Available at: http://www.nytimes.com/2012/09/03/business/economy/us-companies-prepare-in-case-greece-exits-euro.html?_r=2&hp [accessed September 2012].

Schwarz, N. and Dash, E. Banks bet Greece defaults on debt they helped hide. 2010. *The New York Times* [24 February]. Available at: http://www.nytimes.com/2010/02/25/business/global/25swaps.html?ref=global-business [accessed April 2011].

Siedenbiedel, C. 2010. Warum Darf Griechenland nicht Pleitegehen. *Frankfurter Allgemeine Zeitung* [28 April]. Available at: http://www.faz.net/s/Rub3ADB8A210E754E748F42960CC7349BDF/Doc~ECB2665B27C654CD5AE7456EB8AC181FE~ATpl~Ecommon~Scontent.html [accessed April 2011].

Simitis, C. personal website. 2011. Interview with *Vima tis Kyriakis* [17 April]. Available at: http://www.costas-simitis.gr/content/174 [accessed February 2012].

Simitis, C. personal website. 2011. Self-delusion syndrome [2 October]. Available at: http://www.costas-simitis.gr/content/177 [accessed January 2012].

Smith, H. 2011. Greece's euro future: the speculation goes on. *The Guardian* [11 December]. Available at: http://www.guardian.co.uk/business/2011/dec/11/greece-euro-future-speculation [accessed February 2012].

Smith, H. 2010. Greek protesters storm the Acropolis. *The Guardian* [4 May]. Available at: http://www.guardian.co.uk/business/2010/may/04/greek-protesters-storm-acropolis [accessed April 2011].

Smith, H. 2010. Greece: refusing to quit. *The Guardian* [2 September]. Available at: http://www.guardian.co.uk/commentisfree/2010/sep/02/greece-smoking-ban?INTCMP=SRCH [accessed December 2011].

Speech by Antonis Samaras on the national plan to overcome the crisis. 2012. [31 May]. Available at: http://www.nd.gr/web/12001/press/-/journal_content/56_INSTANCE_Rb5c/36615/998337 [accessed September 2012].

Speech by George Papandreou at BDI. 2011. Looking ahead: Europe's development and solidarity [27 September]. Available at: http://www.primeminister.gov.gr/english/2011/09/27/bdi-day-of-german-industry-looking-ahead-europes-development-and-solidarity-prime-ministers-speech-in-berlin/ [accessed September 2011].

Speech by George Papandreou at Newexchange 2010 Conference. 2010. [11 November]. Available at: http://www.primeminister.gov.gr/english/2010/11/11/newsxchange-2010-conference-prime-ministers-speech/ [accessed September 2011].

Speech by George Papandreou in the Hellenic Parliament. 2009 [17 June]. Available at: http://www.papandreou.gr/papandreou/content/Document.aspx?d=6&rd=7739474&f=1359&rf=1307755822&m=12343&rm=12724796&l=2 [accessed April 2011].

Speech by George Papandreou on a national social agreement. 2009. [14 December]. Available at: http://www.primeminister.gov.gr/2009/12/14/440 [accessed August 2010].

Speech by Prime Minister of Greece, Lucas Papademos, in the Hellenic Parliament. 2012. [13 January]. Available at: http://www.primeminister.gov.gr/2012/01/13/7352 [accessed September 2012].

Spiegel. 2010. It's a question of survival for Greece – *Spiegel* interview with Greek Prime Minister Papandreou' [22 February]. Available at: http://www.spiegel.de/international/europe/0,1518,679415,00.html [accessed April 2011].

Statement by Eurogroup on the support to Greece by euro area member states. 2010. [11 April]. Available at: http://www.consilium.europa.eu/uedocs/cms_data/docs/pressdata/en/ec/113686.pdf [accessed August 2011].

Statement by the Heads of State and Government of the euroarea. 2010. [25 March]. Available at: http://www.consilium.europa.eu/uedocs/cms_data/docs/pressdata/en/ec/113563.pdf, [accessed August 2011].

Statement by the Heads of State or Government of the euro area and EU institutions. 2011. [21 July]. Available at: http://www.consilium.europa.eu/uedocs/cms_data/docs/pressdata/en/ec/123978.pdf, [accessed July 2011].

Statement of the President of the Hellenic Republic Mr. Karolos Papoulias. 2012. [15 February]. Available at: http://www.presidency.gr/?p=2369 [accessed March 2012].

Statement by the Prime Minister, George A. Papandreou. 2010. [23 April]. Available at: http://www.papandreou.gr/papandreou/content/Document.aspx?d=6&rd=7739474&f=-1&rf=-1&m=12893&rm=20504593&l=1 [accessed September 2011].

Stefanidis, A. Highway to Hellas. 2010. *Süddeutsche Zeitung* [May edition of the magazine]. Available at: http://sz-magazin.sueddeutsche.de/texte/anzeigen/32559/ [accessed April 2011].

Steinbrück, P. 2010. *Unter dem Strich*. Hamburg: Hoffman und Kampe.

Stelzer, I. 2010. A successful restructuring in Greece may leave a weaker Europe economy. *The Wall Street Journal* [26 April]. Available at: http://online.wsj.com/article/SB10001424052748704627704575203940253330902.html [accessed April 2011].

Steltzner, H. 2010. Ein Griechischer Albtraum. *Frankfurter Allgemeine Zeitung* [24 April]. Available at: http://www.faz.net/aktuell/wirtschaft/europas-schuldenkrise/finanzhilfen-der-eu-ein-griechischer-albtraum-1574875.html [accessed January 2011].

Steltzner, H. 2010. Griechen oder Mark. *Frankfurter Allgemeine Zeitung* [6 March]. Available at: http://www.faz.net/s/Rub3ADB8A210E754E748F42960CC7349BDF/Doc~E3E65E7BC0DE541D9969AD355852177BA~ATpl~Ecommon~Scontent.html [accessed January 2011].

Stephens, P. 2012. Europe says goobye to solidarity. *Financial Times* [23 February]. Available at: http://www.ft.com/intl/cms/s/0/4085f508-5d56-11e1-869d-00144feabdc0.html [accessed February 2012].

Stern website. 2010. Wir erwarten nicht, dass die Deutsche uns retten. 2010 [3 March]. Available at: http://www.stern.de/politik/ausland/griechenlands-parlamentspraesident-wir-erwarten-nicht-dass-die-deutschen-uns-retten-1547803.html [accessed September 2011].

Strittmatter, K. 2009. Griechenland am Abgrund. *Süddeutsche Zeitung*. [5 October]. Available at: http://www.sueddeutsche.de/politik/parlamentswahlen-griechenland-am-abgrund-1.25816 [accessed September 2010].

Strittmatter, K. 2011. Profiteur des Untergangs. *Süddeutsche Zeitung* [21 June]. Available at: http://www.sueddeutsche.de/politik/griechenlands-oppositionsfuehrer-samaras-profiteur-des-untergangs-1.1110743.

Strittmatter, K. 2011. Pure Lust an der Gewalt. *Süddeutsche Zeitung* [3 November] http://www.sueddeutsche.de/politik/terror-in-griechenland-pure-lust-an-der-gewalt-1.1018986 [accessed April 2011].

Strupczewski, J. 2012. Spain discusses state bailout; ECB seen writing off Greek debt. *Reuters* website [27 July]. Available at: http://www.reuters.com/article/2012/07/27/us-eurozone-spain-idUSBRE86Q0JS20120727accessed August 2012].

Süddeutsche Zeitung. 2010. Dem Euro Retten, Europa Retten, 30 April.

Süddeutsche Zeitung. 2011. Europas Jugend ohne Arbeit. [11 August] http://www.sueddeutsche.de/wirtschaft/jobmangel-in-der-eu-europas-jugend-ohne-arbeit-1.1130405 [accessed November 2011].

Süddeutsche Zeitung. 2010. Gepfefferte Ratschläge aus Deutschland. [4 March]. Available at: http://www.sueddeutsche.de/geld/griechenland-in-der-krise-gepfefferte-ratschlaege-aus-deutschland-1.19557 [accessed April 2011].

Süddeutsche Zeitung. 2010. Nicht Hinnehmbar, 12 April.

Süddeutsche Zeitung. 2010. Vorwürfe gegen Ex-Besatzer Deutschland. [24 February]. Available at: http://www.sueddeutsche.de/wirtschaft/griechenland-der-ton-wird-rauer-vorwuerfe-gegen-ex-besatzer-deutschland-1.2839 [accessed April 2011].

Süddeutsche Zeitung. 2010. Weihnachtskarte, die geschrieben werden müssten: Ein satirischer Rundumschlag zum Jahr der Krisen. [24 December]. Available at: http://archiv.sueddeutsche.de/sueddz/index.php?id=A48594658_EGTPOGWPOPOWWRGRHSTRASH [accessed April 2011].

Swann, C. and Paisner, N. 2010. History is hardly on Greece's side. *The New York Times*, 13 April, Business and Financial Desk. 2.

Tables of Results – Public opinion in the European Union. 2012. Standard eurobarometer 77. Available at: http://ec.europa.eu/public_opinion/archives/eb/eb77/eb77_anx_en.pdf [accessed September 2012].

Tett, G. 2010. Bonds, Beijing and risk. *Financial Times* [10 February]. Available at: http://www.ft.com/intl/cms/s/0/f22721ea-1511-11df-ad58-00144feab49a.html#axzz1oEERGUZP [accessed November 2010].

Tett, G. 2010. Greek bondholders jittery over haircuts. *Financial Times* [27 May] http://www.ft.com/cms/s/0/3e2c01ec-69a8-11df-8432-00144feab49a.html#axzz1Dqko0ArR [accessed January 2011].

The European Stability Mechanism. 2011. *ECB Monthly Bulletin*, July, pp. 71–84. Available at: http://www.ecb.int/pub/pdf/other/art2_mb201107en_pp71-84en.pdf [accessed September 2012].

The Sun. 2010. Another week. And another financial problem for Greece, 24 April, p. 13.

The Sun. 2011. Avoiding a Greek Tragedy, 30 July, p. 60.
The Sun. Eur a Joke. 2011, 29 September, p. 8.
The Times. 2010. Greece is the word; A debt crisis in Southern Europe threatens to spread financial contagion, 29 April, p. 2.
The Wall Street Journal. 2010. Greece and the IMF. [22 March] http://online.wsj.com/article/SB10001424052748703775504575135793701057172.html [accessed February 2011].
The Wall Street Journal. 2012. Greek poll shows fragmented political landscape. [4 March]. Available at: http://online.wsj.com/article/BT-CO-20120304-701023.html [accessed March 2012].
The Wall Street Journal. 2010. The Greek Economy Explained. [7 May]. Available at: http://online.wsj.com/article/SB10001424052748703961104575226651125226596.html [accessed April 2011].
Thomas, L. and Kitsantonis, N. 2011. Pondering a dire day: leaving the Euro. *The New York Times*, 13 December, Business Desk, p. 1.
Tilford, S. 2010. Europe cannot afford to let Greece default. *Financial Times* [15 January]. Available at: http://www.ft.com/intl/cms/s/0/c5b67472-0174-11df-8c54-00144feabdc0.html#axzz1kH8dnNP2 [accessed January 2011].
Timeline: Greece's economic crisis. 2010. [11 March]. Available at: http://www.reuters.com/article/2010/03/11/us-eurozone-greece-economy-timeline-idUSTRE62A1KY20100311 [accessed August 2011].
Tortora, F. 2010. Crisi economica: La Grecia mette in vendita le sue isole. *Il Corriere della Sera* [25 June]. Available at: http://www.corriere.it/economia/10_giugno_25/grecia-vendita-itol_7676922a-805e-11df-85d3-00144f02aabe.shtml [accessed April 2011].
Traynor, I. 2011. Europe in turmoil: debt summit: European policymakers struggle for united front to save Greece. *The Guardian* [19 July] Financial Pages, p. 22.
Treanor, J. 2010 Eurozone turmoil: British banks sitting on £100bn exposure to toxic euro debt. *The Guardian*, 29 April, Financial pages, p. 28.
Treanor, J. 2011. Front. Eurozone crisis: exit strategy: how could Greece leave the euro. *The Guardian*, 22 June, p. 14.
To Vima. 2010, 30 May.
To Vima tis Kyriakis. 2011, 5 June.
Tsoukalis, L. 2012. Greece in the Euro area: odd man out, or precursor of things to come? in *Resolving the European Debt Crisis*, edited by W. Cline and G. Wolff. Peterson Institute for International Economics, Special Report (21, pp. 19–35).
Tsoukalis, L. 2011. The JCMS annual review lecture: the shattering of illusions – and what next, *Journal of Common Market Studies*, 49, Annual Review, pp. 19–44.
Tsoukalis, L. 2011. The delphic oracle on Europe. *The Delphic Oracle on Europe: Is There a Future for the European Union*, edited by L. Tsoukalis and Y.A. Emmanouilidis. Oxford and New York: Oxford University Press.
Tsoukalis. L. 2005. *What Kind of Europe?* Oxford and New York. Oxford University Press.

Typos tis Kyriakis. 2012, 16 February.
Tzogopoulos, G. interview for *Associated Press*. 2011. [1 November]. Available at: http://www.aparchive.com/OneUpPrint.aspx?xslt=1p&showact=results&sort=relevance&page=1&sh=1180&kwstyle=and&adte=1320376045&rids=67d537728f568c3757336669bdb239ed&dah=-1&pagez=20&cfasstyle=AND& [accessed January 2012].
Tzogopoulos, G. interview for *Associated Press* [3 November]. Available at: http://www.aparchive.com/OneUpPrint.aspx?xslt=1p&showact=results&sort=relevance&page=1&sh=1180&kwstyle=and&adte=1323256334&rids=851468e0f1e7dbb1a30e996a0fca31fc&dah=-1&pagez=20&cfasstyle=AND& [accessed February 2012].
Tzogopoulos, G. interview for *Bloomberg*. 2012. [6 December]. Available at: http://www.bloomberg.com/news/2012-12-06/depression-deepens-greek-middle-class-despair-with-crime-rising.html [accessed January 2013]
Tzogopoulos, G. interview with Ms. Filio Lanara, Head of the Press Office at the Ministry of Finance under Minister George Papaconstantinou. 2011, 17 January.
Tzogopoulos, G. interview with Professor Gikas Hardouvelis. 2009. *Apogevmatini*, 6 December.
Tzogopoulos, G. 2012. It's Germany stupid! The Greek German misunderstanding. EPIN Paper, No. 33, June. Available at: http://www.ceps.be/book/germany-viewed-other-eu-member-states [accessed September 2012], pp. 6–9.
Tzogopoulos, G. 2009, To Elleimma: Poion na pistepsoume (The Greek deficit: Whom can we trust?), *Apogevmatini ths Kyriakhs*, 25 October.
Uhlig, H. 2010. Eine Griechische Tragödie. *Handelsblatt* [12 February] http://blog.handelsblatt.com/oekonomie/2010/02/12/eine-griechische-tragodie/ [accessed January 2011].
Van de Velde, F. 2010. Quelle Dette Grecque. *Le Monde* [6 May] Available at: http://www.lemonde.fr/idees/article/2010/05/06/quelle-dette-grecque-par-franck-van-de-velde_1347660_3232.html [accessed April 2011].
Véron, A. 2010. 'Grèce: aide-toi, l'Europe t'aidera', *Le Monde* [6 Mach]. Available at: http://www.lemonde.fr/idees/article/2010/03/05/grece-aide-toi-l-europe-t-aidera-par-aurelien-veron_1314802_3232.html [accessed March 2011].
Von Petersdorff, W. 2010. Wer kauft eine Griechische Insel? *Frankfurter Allgemeine Zeitung* [25 April]. Available at: http://www.faz.net/aktuell/wirtschaft/europas-schuldenkrise/staatsbankrott-wer-kauft-eine-griechische-insel-1969140.html [accessed April 2011].
VPRC Poll. 2011. [8 April] Available at: http://www.vprc.gr/uplds/File/teleytaia%20nea/Epikaira/Political%20climate%20and%20governance_VPRC_April2011.pdf, [accessed August 2010].
VPRC Poll. 2012. Greek angry with Germany. [24 February]. Available at: www.epikaira.gr/epikairo.php?id=39059 [accessed March 2012].

Walker, M. 2011. Greek crisis exacts the cruelest toll. *The Wall Street Journal* [20 September]. Available at: http://online.wsj.com/article/SB10001424053111904199404576538261061694524.html [accessed November 2011].

Walker, M. 2010. Tragic flaw: Graft feeds Greek crisis. *The Wall Street Journal* [15 April]. Available at: http://online.wsj.com/article_email/SB10001424052702303828304575179921909783864-lMyQjAxMTAwMDEwNjExNDYyWj.html [accessed December 2011].

Weinberg, C. 2010. Only debt restructuring can save Greece. *The Wall Street Journal* [14 April]. Available at: http://online.wsj.com/article/SB10001424052702303695604575181421506589114.html [accessed January 2011].

Weisbrot, M. 2010. Why Greece should reject the euro. *The New York Times* [9 May]. Available at: http://www.nytimes.com/2011/05/10/opinion/10weisbrot.html?_r=1&hp [accessed November 2011].

Wergin, C. 2011. Why should tax-paying Germans bail-out tax-dodging Greeks? *The Times* [16 September]. Available at: http://www.thetimes.co.uk/tto/opinion/thunderer/article3165811.ece [accessed January 2011].

Wikileaks letter from the US Embassy of Athens. 2006. [13 July] ID: 71198. 4.

Will, G. 2010. European Union: a coalition of irresponsibility. *The Washington Post* [16 May]. Available at: http://www.washingtonpost.com/wp-dyn/content/article/2010/05/14/AR2010051404279.html [accessed January 2012].

Williams, P. 2012. Greeks punish government over crisis. Available at: *ABC* website [7 May]. Available at: http://www.abc.net.au/lateline/content/2012/s3497518.htm [accessed September 2012].

Wohlgemuth, M. 2010. Denn sie werden es wieder tun. *Frankfurter Allgemeine Zeitung* [26 April]. Available at: http://www.faz.net/aktuell/feuilleton/buecher/rezensionen/2.1716/denn-sie-werden-es-wieder-tun-1971814.html [accessed January 2011].

World Bank Data on military expenditure. 2012. Available at: http://data.worldbank.org/indicator/MS.MIL.XPND.GD.ZS [accessed September 2012].

Zakaria, F. 2010. America is no Greece – for now. *The Washington Post* [24 May]. Available at: http://www.washingtonpost.com/wp-dyn/content/article/2010/05/23/AR2010052303824.html [accessed January 2012].

Index

ADEDY 55–56
Agenda-setting 10
Al Jazeera 148
Almunia, Joachín 39
American Enterprise Institute (AEI) 93
Angelopoulos, Theodoros 117
Argentina 101
Associated Press 51, 160
Athens Public Transportation Company 30
Austerity xiii, 2, 12, 16, 23–24, 28, 37, 40–41, 47–49, 52, 53, 57, 63, 67–69, 73, 87, 90–91, 98, 116–117, 118, 121, 124, 131, 133, 135, 138, 155, 158, 162, 165
Australia 120
Austria 38

Bailout 2–3, 12, 37–38, 40–42, 46–47, 49, 51–54, 57, 59–60, 70, 79–80, 87–91, 93, 97, 102, 107, 114, 131, 135, 137, 158, 160, 163
Bakoyannis, Dora 49
Bank of Greece 7, 20, 24–25, 30, 34–35, 45, 81, 91, 121, 158
Barnier, Michel 137
Barroso, Manuel 50, 132, 136
BBC 20
    Brabant, Malcolm 148
    Gowing Nik 160
Belgium 38, 155
Berlusconi, Silvio 71, 138
Bild 9, 65, 67, 80, 82, 88, 90, 99, 101–103, 110, 114–117, 121, 123, 132, 147, 159–161
    Ronzheimer, Paul 67, 80, 101, 117, 121–123, 159, 161
Bloomberg 44, 132
BNP Paribas 79
Britain 9, 32, 60–61, 99, 100, 109, 120, 133, 138, 153

Brown, Gordon 58
Bruegel 91

Canada 3
Centre for Economic Studies 132
Centre for European Policy Reform 88
Chinon of Sparta 62
China 4, 84
Christian Democratic Union 60
Christian Social Union 60
Citigroup 164
CNN effect 155
Corruption xiv, 2, 12, 16–17, 26–28, 33, 61, 107–11, 116, 129, 133, 138, 142–146, 153, 157, 163–164
Cramme, Olaf 58
Crédit Agricole 79
Credit Default Swaps (CDS) 13, 150–151, 153, 157

Cyprus 57, 61, 162
    Cyprus Question 33

Damanakis, Maria 143
Daimler 109
Debt 3, 11, 17, 19, 28, 33, 37–39, 48–49, 61, 76–79, 83, 88, 93, 96–98, 102–104, 107, 114, 125, 127, 131, 133, 135, 137, 151, 157, 159, 164
    Debt burden/crisis/problem 2–3, 12, 15, 28, 58, 66, 72–73, 76, 78, 84, 86, 111, 133, 135, 151–152, 162
    Debt-restructuring 3, 38, 49, 69, 93–97, 99, 107, 136, 143, 153, 163
Default 3–4, 8, 12, 15, 18, 20, 29, 37, 44–49, 58, 65, 78, 83, 85, 88, 92–101, 104, 120, 127, 137, 146, 150–152, 157, 159, 162
Der Spiegel 142
Die Welt 80

Depository Trust & Clearing Corporation (DTCC) 151
Dizard, John 94
Draghi, Mario 164
Duffie, Darrell 150

Euro 5, 18–20, 33, 37, 54, 60, 81, 83, 86, 99–101, 113, 131, 133, 152, 160
European Banking Authority 39
Eurobarometer 134
Eurobonds 60
Eurohypo 79
Euronews 142
European Central Bank (ECB) 3, 38, 43–44, 56, 81, 164
European Commission (EC) 37, 41, 47, 50, 91, 101, 132, 143, 150–151
European Union (EU) xiv, 2–4, 11–12, 18, 23, 27, 28–29, 31, 35, 37, 39, 41–49, 57–61, 63, 68–69, 76, 88–93, 103–104, 107, 113, 115, 134, 137–138, 149, 153, 155, 157–158, 162
    Fiscal union 38, 60
    Political union xiv, 38, 164
Eurozone xiii, 2–4, 6–8, 11–12, 18–20, 28, 37–39, 42–43, 47, 57–66, 70–73, 77, 79, 81, 83, 86, 88–94, 97–101, 103–104, 107, 127, 132, 134, 135, 138, 142–144, 146, 152–158, 160–164
    European Financial Stability Facility (EFSF) 2–3, 47
    European Monetary Union (EMU) 19, 114–115
    European Stability Mechanism (ESM) 3, 60

Feldstein, Martin 38, 94
Ferrostaal 109
Financial Times 9, 39, 59, 61, 65, 67, 70, 72, 75, 77–78, 81, 84, 88, 90–92, 95–96, 99–101, 113, 120, 126, 128, 132, 138, 151, 161
    Barber, Tony 39
    Hope, Kerin 67, 120
    Münchau, Wolfgang 93
    Stephens, Philip 138

Tett, Gillian 94
Fitch 28, 45, 47, 76, 152
Flossbach, Bert 94–95
Focus 146–147
Framing 9
Frankfurter Allgemeine Zeitung 9, 11, 66–67, 76, 79–81, 85, 88–91, 95, 100–102, 110, 114, 117–120, 124, 126
    Martens, Michael 114
France 3, 9, 32, 38–39, 59–61, 77–78, 87, 89–90, 104, 109, 133, 137, 155, 158
Free Democratic Party 60
Fuest, Clemens 93

Germany xiv, 9, 32, 38–39, 58–61, 66–67, 77, 80, 89–90, 90, 92, 94, 98–99, 114–115, 119–120, 122, 133–134, 147
    Constitutional Court 89
Golden Dawn 52, 159
Goldman Sachs 152
Greece/Hellenic Republic xiii–xiv, 1–13, 15–35, 37–62, 63–105, 108–129, 131–156, 157–166
    Angry people movement 54, 121
    Budget/Fiscal deficit 19–20, 24–26, 28–29, 39–41, 44, 46, 83, 68, 78, 103, 151, 164
    Civil War 15
    Closed Professions 2, 44, 57
    Communist party 49
    Credibility Deficit 54, 85, 134, 137, 142–143, 148
    Current account deficit 34, 38, 76
    Democracy 15, 76, 86, 138–139
    Demonstrations 1, 9, 12, 37, 55, 57, 122–125, 133–134, 141, 153
    Fire Nuclei group 126–127
    Government / sovereign bonds 3, 21, 28–29, 38, 42, 45, 47, 49, 52, 61, 79, 81, 92, 94, 97, 136, 151–153, 158–159, 166
    Olympic Games 1–2, 17, 82–83
    Political parties 61, 85, 137–140
    Privatisation(s) 46, 55, 87, 91, 155, 163
    Public sector 16–17, 29–33, 40, 44, 48, 55, 76, 82, 103, 112, 41, 145, 154, 159

Reforms xiv, 2–3, 17, 21, 25, 41, 43–44,
    46, 51, 55, 68–69, 84–85, 87, 96–97,
    104, 108, 124, 131, 155–156, 163
Sect of Revolutionaries 126
Statistics 11, 19–20, 24–26, 81, 84,
    104, 107, 114–115, 119, 151
Strikes 9, 12, 37, 55–56, 68, 122–123,
    132–133, 153
Greek effect 154–155, 162
Grexit 69, 161, 164
Growth 4, 24, 38–39, 43, 46, 78, 92,
    97–98, 101, 104, 164–165
GSEE 55

Haircut 3, 38, 47–51, 61, 69, 79, 81, 94,
    97, 125, 151, 153, 159
Handelsblatt 9, 67, 72, 75, 77, 83, 86, 88–
    90, 93, 95, 98, 100, 111, 119–120,
    123, 126, 132, 161
Höhler, Gerd 67–68
Hatzidakis, Costis 124–125, 140
Hollande, François 5
Hypo Real Estate 79

Il Corriere della Sera 9, 11, 67, 78, 86, 89,
    92, 103, 111–112, 118, 124–126, 159
    Argentieri, Benedetta 67
    Giavazzi, Francesco 89
Institute of International Finance (IIF) 47,
    159
International Monetary Fund (IMF) 2–4,
    12, 37, 41–49, 56, 68, 76, 90–93,
    104, 135, 157, 159, 161, 163
International Swaps and Derivatives
    Association (ISDA) 92, 136
Ireland xiii, 2, 7, 11–12, 18, 26–33, 38, 57,
    61, 63, 70–72, 75, 78, 80, 96, 131,
    133–134, 138, 150, 162
Issing, Otmar 91
Italy xiii, 7, 9, 11–12, 27–28, 31–33, 38,
    57, 59–61, 71–73, 76, 78–79, 104,
    109, 112, 132–133, 134, 138, 150,
    153, 158, 162

Japan 31
Juncker, Jean Claude 57, 149

Kaplan, Robert 139

Karamanlis, Costas 16, 20–24, 139
Karamanlis, Constantinos 15–16, 139
Karatzaferis, George 137, 159.
Krugman, Paul 97, 101

Lachman, Desmond 93, 100–101
Labour market 30, 55, 158
La Repubblica 9, 64, 67, 76, 78, 85,
    97–98, 108–109, 117, 122, 124,
    129, 158
LAOS 15, 49, 52, 137, 158–159
Le Figaro 9, 11, 64, 67, 77–86, 89, 92, 96,
    98, 103, 107–108, 110, 120, 122,
    125–127, 158–159
    Kefalas, Alexia 67, 84
Lehman Brothers 21
Le Monde 9, 11, 65, 67, 76–77, 79–80, 86,
    89, 92, 95–99, 104, 108–109, 113,
    119–120, 122, 124–126, 161
    Salles, Allain 67

Man 109
Marshall Plan 15
McKinsey & Company 164–165
Medium Term Fiscal Strategy Plan
    (MTFSP) 38, 46, 50
Memorandum of Understanding xiii, 37,
    39, 43–44, 48, 50, 53–54, 58,
    68–69, 136–138, 147, 160
Merkel, Angela 4, 41, 58–60, 87, 92, 98–
    99, 114, 122, 132, 147, 149–150
Mitsotakis Constantinos 16, 139–140
Monti, Mario 138
Moody's 28, 76, 152

National Confederation of Hellenic
    Commerce 157
Nepotism 83–84, 139, 142
New Democracy (ND) 2, 16, 21–24,
    49–50, 52, 124, 137, 139–140, 165
Nye, Joseph 60

Obama, Barack 4
Orthodox Church 117
Outright Monetary Transactions (OMT)
    164

Pangalos, Theodoros 7, 140

Papaconstantinou, George 5, 10, 24–25, 40, 48, 50, 142–143, 148
Papademos, Lucas 1, 20, 29, 51–52, 137, 157–159
Papandreou, Andreas 16, 50, 52, 108
Papandreou, George 4, 6, 16, 21–28, 40–43, 51, 53, 57, 68–69, 83–87, 96, 99, 102, 107–108, 114–115, 124, 135–144, 148–150, 158
   Kastelorizo speech 43
   Referendum 51, 68–69, 85–87, 99, 108, 135, 137, 144, 158
Papandreou Vasso 50
Papoulias, Karolos 22, 134
PASOK 2, 16, 19, 21–23, 29, 40, 49–53, 55, 57, 84, 137, 139–140, 158, 161
Petsalnikos, Philippos 7, 137
Pisany-Ferry, Jean 91
Polydoras, Byron 141
Portugal xiii, 2, 7, 11–12, 18, 21, 26–33, 38, 57, 61, 64, 70–72, 75, 77, 96, 131, 133–134, 138, 150, 162
Postbank 79
Poverty 2, 16, 55, 117, 133, 157, 159, 162
Private Sector Involvement (PSI) 52, 151, 158–159
Prodi, Romano 101
Provopoulos, Georgios 24–25, 91

Rajoy, Mariano 138
Rakintzis, Leandros 33
Recession 2–3, 24, 34, 37, 40, 46, 49, 53–54, 76, 97–98, 103, 119, 134, 156–157, 163–164
Red Cross 117
Rehn, Olii 137
Rogoff, Kenneth 15, 134
Rogue-trading 8, 149, 152
Van Rompuy, Herman 132
Roubini, Nouriel 94–95, 100–101
Rapanos, Vassilios 30
Retirement 30, 41, 43, 52, 97, 116
Rössler, Philip 60

Samaras, Antonis 2, 5, 24, 50, 52, 85, 137, 139, 144, 157, 161, 164–165
Sarkozy, Nicolas 4–5, 41, 87, 122, 132, 149, 150

SAV Capital Advisors 152
Schäuble, Wolfgang 4, 58, 134, 147
Schioppa, Tommaso 88
Schultheiss, Wolfgang 7
Shadow / underground economy 31–32, 110
Siemens 109, 153
Simitis, Costas 16, 18, 20, 143
Social security 26, 31, 40
Societé Général 79
Söder Markus 60
Soros Fund Management 152
Spain xiii, 3, 7, 11–12, 18, 26–29, 32–33, 38, 57, 59–61, 71–73, 75, 77, 79, 132–133, 134, 138, 150, 153, 162
Spiliotopoulos, Aris 145
Stability and Growth Pact 115
Staikouras, Christos 151–152
Standard & Poor's 28, 69, 152
Starbatty, Joachim 89
Stelzer, Irwing 93
Strauss-Kahn, Dominique 43
Stournaras, Yannis xiv
Süddeutsche Zeitung 9, 64, 66–67, 80, 83, 85, 88–91, 100, 102, 108–109, 110, 113–116, 119, 122, 126–127, 161
   Schlötzer, Christiane 67, 112
   Strittmatter, Kai 67
SYRIZA 49–50, 52, 54, 69, 144, 160

Tax evasion xiv, 31, 43, 87, 110–112, 116, 138, 144, 146, 155, 157, 163–164
The Guardian / The Observer 9, 67, 70, 79–80, 95, 97, 102–103, 109, 118, 122–123, 126, 148, 152
   Beaumont, Peter 118
   Smith, Helena 67, 126
The Netherlands 38
The New York Times 9, 65, 67, 76, 79, 81–83, 90, 95, 97, 101, 110–111, 113, 118, 125, 127, 151, 159, 162
   Kitsantonis, Niki 67
   Landon, Thomas 84
The Sun 9, 70–71, 76, 86, 95, 100, 103, 111, 123, 132
The Times / Sunday Times 9, 67, 70, 76, 80, 82, 86, 88, 100, 116–117, 119–121, 169

Campbell, Matthew 113
Philip, Pangalos 67
The Wall Street Journal 9, 65, 67, 72, 75–80, 87, 90–95, 97, 99, 108, 112, 118, 127–128, 132, 152, 159
    Granitsas, Alman 112, 127
    Mattich, Allen 94, 127
The Washington Post 9, 67, 78, 83, 86–88, 95, 112, 114, 125
    Applebaum, Anne 112, 114
    Samuelson, Robert 88
ThyssenKrupp 109
Trichet, Jean Claude 96
Trikoupis, Harilaos 16
Troika 44, 46, 48, 51–54, 61, 64, 69, 108, 121, 137
Tsipras Alexis 52, 160
Tsochatzopoulos, Akis 33, 144
Tsoukalis, Loukas xiv, 16, 57

Truman Doctrine 15
Turkey 33, 82, 95

Uhlig, Harald 89
Unemployment 2, 16, 22, 35, 46, 55, 63, 116–117, 119, 129, 133, 141, 146, 158–159, 162
USA 3–4, 9, 16, 32, 39, 78, 80, 99, 133
    House of Representatives 150

Venizelos, Eleftherios 16
Venizelos, Evangelos 48, 50–51, 136,

WikiLeaks 148
World Bank 33
World War II 120
World War II reparations 7, 147

Zakaria, Fareed 78

In his book Tzogopoulos nicely explains why the international media focused more on Greece than on other problematic countries of the eurozone in the first years of the crisis. This rich and original work offers a fascinating analysis of the role of journalists from a theoretical and practical perspective and correctly employs the "Greek effect" as a new model in political communication.
   Paul Ronzheimer, Journalist, *Bild Newspaper*, Germany

Tzogopoulos' book offers us a profound and invaluable insight into the role the media have played during the crisis. It helps readers to get a more authentic picture of what is going on in Greece based on the author's thorough analysis and practical experience of being a regular contributor to international news agencies.
   Gong Ming, Correspondent, China Central TV (CCTV), Greece

George Tzogopoulos's book undoubtedly constitutes a valuable reference manual on the crisis prevailing in Greece. This talented analyst thoroughly explores the impact of austerity on Greek society and also gives an overall view through the eyes of a foreign correspondent. This book enables us to understand how Greece, a pocket-sized country but so rich in history, is the starting point, laboratory and mirror of a new Europe, which has changed very rapidly at the economic and political level, without necessarily leading to the shaping of a union of peoples, ideas and cultures, as envisioned by founder of the EU, Robert Schumann.
   Alexia Kefalas, Journalist, *Le Figaro*

When the crisis in Greece became acute in 2009, it took not only Greek society by surprise but also the foreign media that had neglected Greece in the years before. The coverage that followed was often perceived by Greek society and authorities as being inaccurate and biased. In his new book, George Tzogopoulos analyses the way the Greek crisis was presented in foreign media. A charismatic analyst with the prestigious Greek think tank ELIAMEP, he has been guiding foreign journalists - most of them not familiar with Greek society and language - through the crisis by providing them with much appreciated comments and insight about what is happening in Greece. Besides a profound comparison of how international and Greek media portrayed Greece, the book also includes a balanced summary and interpretation of how the PIIGS states are handling the crisis. Tzogopoulos provides a convincing explanation why the "Greek case" has drawn so much media attention. Thoroughly researched and written in an accessible style this piece is a good read that deserves a wide audience.
   Elena Panagiotidis, Journalist, *Neue Zürcher Zeitung*, Switzerland